River Road Recipes III

A Healthy Collection

Published by
The Junior
League of Baton
Rouge, Inc.

River Road Recipes III **Committee**

Shelly Alexander
Mary Aycock
Betty Backstrom
Sandy Bezet
Carol Anne Blitzer
Shelly Brunson
Mary Helen Borck
Julie McCarty
Chrissie Clark
Marilyn Davis
Rachel Ehricht
Machita Eyre
Leslie Gladney
Betsy Harper
Ann Hartman
Kay Hawthorne
Mary Karam
Sharon Lanius

Sugar McAdams
Julie McCarty
Elizabeth McKowen
Lauren Ragland
Emily Robinson
Donna Saurage
Jennifer Simmons
Mary Sue Slack
Debra Sledge
Annelie Smolinski
Ann Solanas
Toni Stodd
Lisa Town
Sari Turner
Ann Wallace
Betty Whitt
Carmen Williams
Helen Worthen

Copyright All Rights Reserved 1994
The Junior League of Baton Rouge, Inc.

20,000   First Printing   April 1994

Copies of the *River Road* series cookbooks
may be obtained by addressing
River Road Recipes, Inc.
The Junior League of Baton Rouge, Inc.
5280 Corporate Blvd.
Baton Rouge, LA 70808-2503

or by calling 504-924-0300
Fax 504-927-2547
Toll Free 800-204-1726

ISBN 0-9613026-4-X

River Road
Recipes III:
A Healthy
Collection *was*
named by
Chrissie Clark

Tradition is the cord that binds generation to generation. It is the element that lends spice, texture and a sense of belonging to life. When someone cares enough to pass on a tradition, a sense of well-being is shared by both the giver and receiver.

The tradition of the first two River Road cookbooks, *River Road Recipes* and *River Road Recipes II: A Second Helping* is now followed by *River Road Recipes III: A Healthy Collection*. The recipes in this book take the bounty of Louisiana cuisine, old favorites and new dishes…and modify it to fit today's healthier lifestyle.

The jambalayas, gumbos and other Creole and Cajun dishes loved by so many have been reduced in fat and calories to make cooking deliciously even more appealing. Fans of the first two cookbooks produced by The Junior League of Baton Rouge will be delighted to see some of their favorite recipes modified by a licensed dietitian to be healthier but just as delicious. And as an added bonus there are hundreds of brand new healthy recipes with the same fabulous taste that makes Louisiana cooking world famous.

A rich blending of different cultures has made Louisiana cooking internationally famous. Colonial settlers from France and Spain brought with them their unique cooking styles and adapted them to local ingredients, creating the well known "Creole cuisine." The Cajuns, who are descendants of the oppressed Acadians from Nova Scotia, added their own touches to Louisiana cooking, often using the abundance of seafood and game around them as the central ingredients of their dishes.

The love of food is deeply rooted in Louisiana tradition, as is the "passing on" of stories from generation to generation. Rarely is any gathering of friends and family held without healthy portions of both delicious food and southern memories being served. We're glad you've joined us for this gathering of some of the best recipes Louisiana's celebrated cooks have to offer, as well as their cherished traditions and memories.

Trade names of products are used only when necessary.

Over 700 recipes were collected from April 1992 to June 1993 from the League members, their families and friends, the community and regional chefs.

Each selected recipe was then submitted to an accredited dietitian for modification to reduce its fat and sodium content. The revised recipes were prepared by volunteers and taste-tested to ensure that they are as delicious as the original recipes.

3

The nutritional analysis for *River Road Recipes III: A Healthy Collection* was performed by a registered dietitian using computer analysis based on information primarily from the U. S. Department of Agriculture. The information is as accurate as possible and based on the following assumptions:
• The number of portions and/or serving size is stated. Nutritional information given is based on one serving (which is estimated and may vary). • All ingredients listed and quantified in the recipe ingredient list have been included in the analysis. • Ingredients listed as optional or as a serving suggestion within the text are not included in the analysis. • When more than one ingredient choice is given, the first ingredient listed is the one used in the analysis. • If a range of quantity is given, the lesser amount listed is used in the analysis (ex: 1/4 to 1/3 cup skim milk). • When a marinade is used, only the amount of the marinade used is calculated. Generally, 1/3 to 1/2 of the marinade ingredients are analyzed, while the remaining is discarded, thus not included in the analysis. • All meats are trimmed of fat and skin before they are cooked.

River Road Recipes III: A Healthy Collection was developed with both great taste and good health in mind. All of the original recipes (including the Chefs') were modified into lighter versions to help people lower their intake of calories, fat, saturated fat, cholesterol and sodium. This collection can help you adapt to and maintain a healthier approach to eating, while enjoying dishes ranging from "fast and easy" to more "gourmet."

Once the initial selection process was finished, the recipes were computer analyzed to determine nutritional content. Whenever the original recipe did not meet the lightened goals, I modified the recipe to reduce the fat, cholesterol and sodium. When necessary and possible, sugar and alcohol content were also reduced.

The adjusted recipes were taste-tested again to ensure that they were still packed with flavor. Our results were rewarding. Many were ranked as excellent, and as good or better than the original recipes.

These recipes were contributed by Junior League members, their friends and families, and area professional chefs, with selections ranging from Louisiana classics and ethnic favorites to southern traditionals.

Every recipe is accompanied by nutritional analysis information. The following "key" outlines which information is provided for each serving:

> Cal=calories
> Fat(g)=grams of total fat
> Sat Fat(g)=grams of saturated fat
> % Fat Cal=percent of total calories from fat
> Chol(mg)=milligrams of cholesterol
> Sod(mg)=milligrams of sodium

A detailed section on "how to lighten" when cooking at home is provided at the end of the book following the "Something Extra" section.

It is our hope that this collection of Louisiana favorites and the guide on light cooking will give you a delicious start to a new way of eating.

Linda P. Vannoy, M.S., L.D.N., R.D.

Contents

River Road Recipes *was first printed in 1959.* River Road Recipes II: A Second Helping *was produced in 1976. Over 1,000,000 copies have been sold. The proceeds of these sales have generated over $2,000,000 for League projects benefiting the Baton Rouge community. These noteworthy projects are listed throughout the book.*

The signature recipe from the original River Road Recipes, *Spinach Madeline from Madeline Noland Reymond, appears in modified form. Other recipes highlighted from the* River Road Recipes *cookbooks are: Sensation Salad, Crawfish Etouffée, Dutch Oven Doves, Garlic Cheese Grits, World's Fastest Strawberry Mousse, & Rabbit Hasenpfeffer.*

Linda Vannoy, M.S., L.D.N., R.D. has modified and provided the nutritional analysis for each recipe in this book to make it more healthful. Linda, a registered dietitian and nutritionist, has provided nutritional counseling to a diverse group of clients including nursing homes, hospitals, corporations and some of Louisiana's best known restaurants. She also shares with us tips on light cooking as a special feature in this book.

Thibodeaux2 Designs, a local design firm whose portfolio includes some of Baton Rouge and New Orleans' most recognized companies and corporations, provided graphic design and food styling for the book. Designers Kevin Thibodeaux and Jayne Hopkins Thibodeaux have amassed an impressive roster of local, regional, and national design awards. Thibodeaux2 was also recently designated one of the nation's top 60 design firms in a national competition.

During his 20-year career, photographer David Humphreys has acquired clients throughout Louisiana — as well as in Houston, Dallas and New York. His commercial work has won innumerable local, regional, and national awards. He brings that expertise to *River Road Recipes III* with the colorful cover and divider page photography and food styling.

Writer Dale Irvin is Creative Director for a prominent Baton Rouge advertising agency. His stories sprinkled throughout the book tell about local traditions and memories from Southern Louisiana. Writing is not only his vocation, but his avocation. In his spare time he writes poetry, publishes a travel newsletter, and is a contributing writer for a number of publications.

Franklin Press Inc. has produced over 1,000,000 copies of *River Road Recipes* and nearly 400,000 *River Road Recipes: Second Helping* for the Baton Rouge Junior League since 1959 and 1976, respectively. As one of the premier color printers in Louisiana, Franklin Press has established a reputation for quality printing and service to our community since 1922.

Appetizers

From its very beginning, the Junior League of Baton Rouge was committed to the community. From 1932, when 25 young women met to discuss how they could best serve their community and the Junior League was formed, continuing into 1994, when 1,385 women volunteer their time, talents and resources to contribute to projects as diverse as welfare, public service, history, arts and recreation, education, and voluntarism, the Junior League of Baton Rouge has played a vital role in the community.

Apple Wedge Dip
Yield: 2 cups, 48 servings

6 ounces light cream cheese
1/3 cup low fat ricotta cheese
1 cup chopped dates
1/3 cup toasted and chopped pecans
One 15-ounce can crushed pineapple, drained
4 apples, cut into wedges

In food processor, blend together cream cheese and ricotta cheese until very smooth. Stir in the remaining ingredients, except apple wedges. Refrigerate 24 hours.

Louella B. Romero

	Cal	Fat(g)	% Fat Cal	Sat Fat(g)	Chol(mg)	Sod(mg)
Per Serving	33	1.2	31	0.5	1	22

Gone in a Minute Bean Dip
Yield: 2 1/2 cups, 20 servings of 2 tablespoons each

One 15-ounce can pinto or great northern beans, no
    bacon
1-2 cloves garlic, pressed
1 tablespoon olive oil
1 1/2 tablespoons lemon juice
1/4 teaspoon ground cumin
1/2 cup picanté sauce
Chopped green onions to garnish

Drain and rinse beans well and blend in food processor along with the garlic, oil, juice and cumin. Transfer to medium-size bowl and stir in picanté sauce. Garnish with green onion tops. Serve with oven-baked chips, pita bread or raw vegetables. See Bagel Chips in "Something Extra" section.

Pati Ivey

	Cal	Fat(g)	% Fat Cal	Sat Fat(g)	Chol(mg)	Sod(mg)
Per Serving	26	0.9	30	0.1	0	108

Nutrition Nibble

Toasted Nuts

Spread nuts in single layer on a cookie sheet. Bake at 300 to 325 degrees for 5 to 10 minutes, until aromatic. Check and shake half way through; be sure not to burn. Cool and chop. This procedure enhances the flavor; less will taste like more.

One Step Further

Gone in a Minute Bean Dip

To reduce the sodium content, use freshly cooked beans or no-salt-added canned.

Boursin
Yield: 8 servings

6 ounces light cream cheese
4 ounces light sour cream substitute
1 tablespoon finely chopped parsley
1 tablespoon finely chopped green onions
2 cloves garlic, pressed
Parsley for garnish

Soften cream cheese at room temperature. Cream all ingredients in food processor. While soft, place in serving dish. Chill until firm. Decorate with parsley. Serve with crackers. Can be made in advance and stored in refrigerator for 1 to 2 weeks.

Sugar McAdams

	Cal	Fat(g)	% Fat Cal	Sat Fat(g)	Chol(mg)	Sod(mg)
Per Serving	67	5.5	69	3.4	13	126

On the Border Meatballs
Yield: 112 meatballs, 28 servings of 4 each

1 1/2 pounds round, well-trimmed and ground
1 1/2 cups bread crumbs
1/3 cup minced onion
1/3 cup skim/low fat milk
1/2 teaspoon garlic powder
3 tablespoons chopped parsley
1 teaspoon pepper
2 egg whites or 1/4 cup egg substitute
1 tablespoon corn oil
12 ounces light Velveeta cheese
One 4-ounce can green chilies, reserve liquid
One 1 1/2-ounce package taco seasoning mix
1 cup water

In a bowl, mix the ground meat, bread crumbs, onion, milk, garlic powder, parsley, pepper and egg. Shape into 1-inch meatballs and cook in a nonstick skillet in oil until browned. Set the meatballs aside to drain on paper towels. Spoon off the fat and wipe the skillet clean. In the same skillet, over

Nutrition Note

Boursin
This spread is still high in fat yet has less than 1/2 the calories and fat of the original version. Enjoy with low fat crackers, toasted french bread rounds or cucumber rounds.

On the Border Meatballs
This has less than 1/2 the fat and saturated fat found in the original. But this is still high in sodium due to the processed cheese and the taco seasoning.

One Step Further

On the Border Meatballs
If you want to trim off 95 mg of sodium each serving, omit taco mix and use the following spices:
1 tablespoon chili powder
1/2 tablespoon cocoa powder
1 tablespoon corn-starch
2 teaspoons sugar
1 teaspoon each onion powder, cumin, garlic powder and paprika
Stir seasonings together and then mix with 3 tablespoons of the water, forming a thin smooth paste. Stir into cheese mixture.

low heat, mix the cheese, green chilies with liquid, taco seasoning mix and 1 cup of water until cheese melts. Return the meatballs to the skillet. Cover and simmer until heated through. Serve hot with toothpicks. The sauce can be used as a dip when the meatballs are gone.

Lisa Town

	Cal	Fat(g)	% Fat(g) Cal	Sat Fat(g)	Chol(mg)	Sod(mg)
Per Serving	102	4.2	38	1.8	21	392

Hummus Be Tahini

Yield: 12 servings

5 cloves garlic, peeled
2 cups canned chickpeas, rinsed and drained
1/3 cup tahini
2/3-3/4 cup fresh lemon juice
1/2 teaspoon salt
1/2 teaspoon ground cumin
1/3 cup plain nonfat yogurt
6 pita bread, cut in triangles, toasted if you wish
1/3-1/2 cup defatted chicken broth, less salt
Paprika
Parsley

Chop the garlic in food processor. Add all the other ingredients except the chicken broth, paprika and parsley, and process until smooth. Correct seasonings. When it tastes "right," add chicken broth until it is a very smooth, creamy paste. Spread evenly on plate, sprinkle with paprika and garnish with parsley. Serve with pita triangles.

Linda Bowsher

	Cal	Fat(g)	% Fat Cal	Sat Fat(g)	Chol(mg)	Sod(mg)
Per Serving	129	4.2	28	0.6	trace	352

Tahini is a sesame seed paste found at Middle Eastern markets. Chickpeas are also called garbanzo beans.

Linda Bowsher

Cilantro Salsa
Yield: 1 1/2 cups, 12 servings

2 jalapeño chilies, seeded and minced
2 large ripe tomatoes, peeled, seeded and chopped
1/2 small white onion, minced
1 1/2 tablespoons white vinegar
1 clove garlic, minced
1/4 cup fresh minced cilantro
1/4 teaspoon salt, optional
Pepper to taste

Mix all ingredients. Chill. Serve with tortilla chips. Try no-fat-added chips or bake your own. Can make a day ahead.

Martha R. Singer

	Cal	Fat(g)	% Fat Cal	Sat Fat(g)	Chol(mg)	Sod(mg)
Per Serving	13	0.15	9	trace	0	74

Rosemary Olive Focaccio
Yield: 35 squares

One 10-ounce package refrigerated pizza crust
1 teaspoon olive oil
1/4 teaspoon freshly cracked black pepper
1 tablespoon minced fresh rosemary, OR 1 teaspoon dried and crumbled
1 egg white
1 tablespoon water
1/2 cup grated Romano cheese, divided
8 black olives, pitted and quartered
4 marinated sun dried tomatoes, drained, rinsed and cut into strips
2 large cloves garlic, thinly sliced

Preheat oven to 450 degrees. Place pizza crust in a bowl and add oil, black pepper and rosemary. Knead dough until combined. Press dough into 12x9-inch baking sheet. Using a pastry brush, brush with egg white and water mixed together. If needed, press out dough more at this

Nutrition Note

Cilantro Salsa

Before adding any salt, let ingredients chill for awhile. Then taste. You will probably find it is very tasty without the salt. If you choose to add salt, every 1/4 teaspoon will add over 44mg per serving in this dish.

point. Sprinkle with 1/4 cup Romano cheese, press into dough. Bake until bread is almost cooked through and cheese begins to brown. Arrange olives, tomatoes and garlic on top of bread. Sprinkle remaining 1/4 cup cheese and spray lightly with olive oil flavored vegetable oil spray. Continue baking until cheese melts and bread is cooked through, about 5 minutes. Cut into squares and serve.

Joan Chastain

	Cal	Fat(g)	% Fat Cal	Sat Fat(g)	Chol(mg)	Sod(mg)
Per Serving	36	1.3	33	0.4	2	72

South of the Border Torta
Yield: 20 servings

2 teaspoons chicken flavored bouillon
1/2 cup hot water
One 8-ounce package light cream cheese
16 ounces low fat ricotta cheese
1 tablespoon chili powder
1/2-1 teaspoon hot pepper sauce
1/2 cup egg substitute or 4 egg whites
1 cup finely chopped cooked skinless chicken
One 4-ounce can chopped green chilies, well drained
1 cup spicy salsa
1/2 cup grated reduced fat sharp cheddar cheese
Sliced green onions

Preheat oven to 325 degrees. Dissolve bouillon in water. Set aside. In large mixing bowl, beat cream cheese, ricotta cheese, chili powder, and hot pepper sauce until smooth. Add eggs and mix well. Add bouillon and beat until smooth. Stir in chicken and chilies. Pour in 9-inch spring form pan and bake until set, about 30 to 45 minutes. Cool for 15 minutes. Carefully run knife around edge of pan. Top with salsa, cheese, and green onions. Serve warm or chilled with tortilla chips.

Kate Brady

	Cal	Fat(g)	% Fat Cal	Sat Fat(g)	Chol(mg)	Sod(mg)
Per Serving	77	4.3	47	2.2	15	256

One Step Further

South of the Border Torta

To save sodium content, use reduced salt chicken bouillon, cutting out 60-100mg of sodium (depending on brand used) per serving.

Curried Meatballs *with Chutney*
Yield: 84 meatballs, 42 servings of 2 each

1 pound round, trimmed well and ground
One 8-ounce package herb stuffing mix
1 package beef flavored rice mix
1 cup defatted chicken or beef broth, less salt
2 egg whites or 1/4 cup egg substitute, well beaten
1 tablespoon curry powder
1/2 teaspoon white pepper

Combine all ingredients, shape into 1 1/4-inch balls and bake on foil covered cookie sheet at 300 degrees for 30 minutes. Serve with chutney.

Uli M. Goodwin

	Cal	Fat(g)	% Fat Cal	Sat Fat(g)	Chol(mg)	Sod(mg)
Per Serving	40	0.9	20	0.2	8	126

Mushroom Caps *with Creole Turkey Sausage*
Yield: 24 servings

3 pounds fresh mushrooms
3/4 pound light turkey breakfast sausage
1 pound skinless ground turkey
2 teaspoons minced garlic
4 tablespoons chopped parsley
3/4 cup shredded reduced fat cheddar cheese
1 cup shredded Mozzarella cheese
1/2 cup chopped onion
2 teaspoons light Creole seasoning, reduced salt
1/2 teaspoon white pepper
1/2 teaspoon sage
10 shakes Tabasco sauce
1/3 cup defatted chicken broth, less salt
1 egg white

Rinse mushrooms and pat dry. Remove and chop stems and combine with turkey sausage, turkey, garlic, parsley and onions. Cook until turkey and sausage is browned, stirring to crumble. Drain off pan drippings and pat meat with paper towels to further remove fat. Wipe skillet with paper towels. Return meat to skillet and stir in remaining seasonings and cheeses, mixing well till all cheese is melted. With a fork whip the chicken broth into the egg white, then toss with the turkey mixture. Spoon mixture into mushroom caps and place in an ungreased baking dish. Bake at 350 degrees for 20 minutes.

Celia Pope

	Cal	Fat(g)	% Fat Cal	Sat Fat(g)	Chol(mg)	Sod(mg)
Per Serving	86	4.4	46	1.7	21	188

Crawfish Quesadillas
Yield: 8 servings of 1/2 quesadilla each

One 8 count 10-inch package flour tortillas
1 pound peeled crawfish tails, lightly rinsed and drained
1 medium onion, chopped
1 tablespoon tub margarine or vegetable oil
1/2 cup chopped green onions
1 cup reduced fat grated Monterey Jack cheese OR 1/4
     cup regular Monterey Jack with 2/3 cup skim moz-
     zarella cheese

In a nonstick skillet, sauté onion in margarine on medium heat until tender. Add crawfish and green onions and sauté another 10 minutes. Just before serving, spray large skillet with vegetable oil cooking spray and place on medium heat. Put tortilla in skillet and spread with 1/2 cup crawfish mixture and cheese and top with another tortilla. Cook 1 minute on each side. Cut into 8 wedges. Serve 4 wedges for appetizer. Repeat and serve with hot sauce and light sour cream. Can also be used as a quick easy entree. **Variation:** Same as above but eliminate green onions and crawfish and add: 1 package frozen chopped spinach, thawed and squeezed dry. Use 1/4 cup spinach mixture and 1/4 cup Monterey Jack for each quesadilla. Serve as above.

Mary Karam
Joan W. Chastain

	Cal	Fat(g)	% Fat Cal	Sat Fat(g)	Chol(mg)	Sod(mg)
Per Serving	233	6.5	25	2.6	87	265

Nutrition Nibble

Crawfish fat is generally found in the crawfish heads and in bags of peeled crawfish tails. This yellowish fat is high in saturated fat and should be rinsed from the crawfish tails and heads before using.

Spinach Con Queso
Yield: 2 cups, 16 servings

One 10-ounce package frozen chopped spinach, thawed
8 ounces low fat ricotta cheese
3 tablespoons milk, divided
1/4 teaspoon paprika
1/2 pound light Velveeta, cubed
1 small onion, chopped
1/3 cup diced jalapeño peppers
1 medium tomato, peeled, seeded, and chopped

Place spinach in large strainer. With back of spoon, press out as much liquid as possible. Place ricotta cheese in a food processor, gradually add 2 tablespoons of milk blending until very smooth. Blend in paprika. Combine Velveeta, remaining milk, and onion. Heat until cheese is melted, stirring occasionally (can microwave this step). Add ricotta cheese mixture to the cheese and heat. Stir in spinach, jalapeño peppers and tomato. Serve warm with reduced fat tortilla chips or home toasted tortilla wedges (see Bagel Chips recipe in "Something Extra" section).

Martha R. Singer

	Cal	Fat(g)	% Fat Cal	Sat Fat(g)	Chol(mg)	Sod(mg)
Per Serving	**56**	**2.5**	**39**	**1.5**	**9**	**290**

Marinated Eggplant *with Red Pepper Flakes*
Yield: 6 servings

1 1/4-2 pound eggplant cut into 1/4-inch slices
1 teaspoon salt, divided
3 cloves sliced garlic
2 tablespoons chopped parsley
1 teaspoon red pepper flakes
1 tablespoon olive oil
2 tablespoons defatted chicken broth, less salt
2 tablespoons balsamic vinegar

Sprinkle eggplant slices with half the salt. Broil in oven. Turn over and salt, broil again. Place in flat bowl and layer eggplant, garlic slices, parsley, and red pepper flakes. Drizzle with oil, chicken broth and vinegar. Cover with

Nutrition Note

Marinated Eggplant

Still proportionally high in sodium, but only 1/3 the sodium content of the original. For persons who use very little salt, omitting the salt or at least cutting it further should still produce a very flavorful dish.

plastic wrap. Let sit for 1 hour. Serve with crackers. Will keep in refrigerator; however, garlic flavor becomes more intense.

Don Fourrier
Ann Felice Fourrier

	Cal	Fat(g)	% Fat Cal	Sat Fat(g)	Chol(mg)	Sod(mg)
Per Serving	46	2.5	45	0.4	trace	372

Caribbean Goulash
Yield: 20 servings

Marinade
3/4 cup reduced fat mayonnaise
1/2 cup nonfat plain yogurt
1/2 cup horseradish, well drained
1 1/2 teaspoons garlic powder
2 teaspoons dry mustard
1 tablespoon lemon juice
1/8 teaspoon salt
1/4 teaspoon onion powder
1/4 teaspoon ground celery seed

Mix marinade and add
10 ounces steamed scallops
1 head cauliflower, divided into buds
1 pound mushrooms, scrubbed with stems removed
1 1/2 pounds cooked shrimp
One 3.25-ounce can pitted ripe olives, lightly rinsed and
    drained
1 small box cherry tomatoes, washed and dried
One 8-ounce can sliced water chestnuts, lightly rinsed and
    drained
Parsley, chopped, for garnish

Marinate all items except water chestnuts and parsley for 5 to 6 hours. Add chestnuts at last minute, toss, and serve in a large bowl. Sprinkle with chopped fresh parsley, and use toothpicks for a "pickup" appetizer.

Sunny McCoy

	Cal	Fat(g)	% Fat Cal	Sat Fat(g)	Chol(mg)	Sod(mg)
Per Serving	107	3.7	30	0.8	74	315

Here in South Louisiana, you never go to somebody's house to play cards. Now you might play some cards before the evening's over . . . but you go there to eat. Here, you don't have people over to chat, or listen to music, or play games . . . you have them over to eat . . . and everything else is incidental . . . eating is the raison d'etre *for much of this part of the country. And once you've tasted the cooking, you get a pretty good idea why.*

Brochettes de Coquilles Saint Jacques
(Scallops and Shrimp on a Skewer)
Yield: 6 servings

12 bay or sea scallops (6 ounces)
18 large shrimp, peeled and deveined
Thyme, rosemary, savory and white pepper
3/4 cup seasoned flour
1 tablespoon olive oil
1 tablespoon tub margarine

Sauce
1/2 pound fresh tomatoes, diced
1 tablespoon diced onion
2 cloves garlic, minced
3 tablespoons defatted chicken or seafood broth, less salt
Rosemary

Soak scallops for 1 hour in water or 20 minutes in milk. Pat scallops dry. Position scallops and shrimp on wood skewers, add pepper and sprinkle with herbs. Roll skewer in flour and sauté in a nonstick skillet in oil and margarine mixture until brown on each side. Serve with a tomato sauce of fresh tomatoes, onion, and garlic sautéed in broth and rosemary.

Patty Young

	Cal	Fat(g)	% Fat Cal	Sat Fat(g)	Chol(mg)	Sod(mg)
Per Serving	147	4.5	28	0.8	50	140

Mango Quesadillas
Yield: 8 servings

1 bell pepper, julienned
1 onion, sliced in rings
Juice of 1 lime
Eight 10-inch flour tortillas
1 large mango, papaya, or 2 peaches, peeled and sliced
1 cup reduced fat Monterey Jack cheese (4 ounces),
    grated

Nutrition Nibble

1 tablespoon of oil = 13.5 grams of fat, 120 calories

1 tablespoon of defatted broth = trace of fat, 1.5 calories.

Coat skillet with vegetable oil cooking spray and sauté bell pepper and onion until soft. Squeeze lime over mixture and stir to blend. Place tortilla in a coated skillet. Layer 1/4 of vegetable mixture, fruit slices and grated cheese on tortilla and top with another tortilla. Cook 1 minute on each side. Cut into 8 wedges. Serve 4 wedges per serving. Top with mango chutney and light sour cream.

Joan W. Chastain

	Cal	Fat(g)	% Fat Cal	Sat Fat(g)	Chol(mg)	Sod(mg)
Per Serving	207	5.8	25	2.4	9	225

Shrimp and Crab Stuffed Mushrooms
Yield: 2 dozen

1/2 cup chopped onions
1 cup chopped celery
2/3 cup chopped red or yellow bell pepper
4 sprigs parsley, chopped
4 - 5 cloves garlic, chopped
1 can cream of mushroom soup, less salt and low fat
2 cups cooked rice
1 1/2-2 cups shrimp, cooked, peeled and coarsely
    chopped (8 ounces)
1 1/2-2 cups crabmeat (8 ounces)
2 tablespoons tub margarine
1/2 cup bread crumbs
2 dozen large mushrooms
1/2 teaspoon no-salt lemon-pepper seasoning
Black pepper to taste

Sauté onions, celery, bell pepper in margarine. Add garlic, parsley, 1/4 cup bread crumbs and stir. Add soup and stir. Fold in shrimp and crabmeat. Then fold in rice, lemon-pepper and pepper. Place mixture in mushroom caps. Place on cookie sheet and sprinkle with remaining bread crumbs. Bake 20 to 25 minutes at 375 degrees.

Chrissie Clark

	Cal	Fat(g)	% Fat Cal	Sat Fat(g)	Chol(mg)	Sod(mg)
Per Serving	143	3	19	0.8	56	272

Fresh Salsa

Yield: 6 cups, 24 servings

3/4 cup sliced jalapeño peppers, drained
One 15-ounce can artichoke hearts, drained and rinsed
One 2 1/4-ounce can chopped black olives, drained
2 pounds ripe tomatoes, chopped
4 tablespoons chopped green onions
1 1/2 teaspoons minced garlic
1 tablespoon red wine vinegar
1 tablespoon olive oil
1/4 teaspoon pepper
2 tablespoons cilantro or parsley
1/4 teaspoon salt, optional

Chop peppers and artichoke hearts. Mix with other ingredients except salt. Taste; only add salt if needed. Chill before serving. Serve with oven-baked tortilla chips or as side dish. This is spicy; may want to use less jalapeño.

Joanne Martin Roberts

	Cal	Fat(g)	% Fat Cal	Sat Fat(g)	Chol(mg)	Sod(mg)
Per Serving	27	1.7	49	0.2	0	151

Crawfish Mousseline

Yield: 60 servings of 2 tablespoons each

1/4 cup (1/2 stick) margarine
2 bunches green onion, chopped
1 bunch parsley, chopped
2 cloves garlic, chopped
2 pounds crawfish, chopped in food processor
Three 8-ounce packages light cream cheese
1/2 teaspoon salt
Black and red pepper to taste

Melt margarine. Sauté onion, parsley and garlic on medium heat. Add crawfish and cook for 10 minutes. Lower heat and add cream cheese. Cook until melted. Season with salt, pepper and red pepper.

Michele Bienvenu

	Cal	Fat(g)	% Fat Cal	Sat Fat(g)	Chol(mg)	Sod(mg)
Per Serving	45	4	56	1.4	25	99

Nutrition Note

Fresh Salsa
This recipe has less than 1/2 the calories and sodium and only 1/3 the fat of the original.

Crawfish Mousseline
This recipe is still high in fat but has 4gm less fat and 3gm less saturated fat for each serving than the original. A savings of more than 38 calories per serving.

Creole Chicken Mousse

Yield: 32 Servings

4 large skinless chicken breasts
1 can chicken stock
1 cup white wine
1/2 cup finely chopped red bell pepper
1/4 cup finely chopped green onions
1/2 cup finely chopped celery
8 ounces fat free cream cheese
1/2 cup light mayonnaise
1 cup light sour cream
1/4 cup chili sauce
1/2 tablespoon Worcestershire sauce
1/4 teaspoon each black and white pepper
3/4 teaspoon hot sauce
1 1/2 tablespoons unflavored gelatin
2 tablespoons lemon juice
1/8 cup cold water
1 pound each of snow peas and cherry tomatoes

Poach chicken in stock and wine. Drain, reserve broth for future stocks and cool chicken. Finely chop by hand to measure 3 full cups of chicken. Add vegetables. Mix the next 7 ingredients together in a separate bowl. Heat the gelatin, lemon juice and water to dissolve. Add to cream cheese mixture. Fold in chicken vegetable mixture. Pour into individual molds sprayed with vegetable oil cooking spray or one 3-quart mold. Refrigerate 3 to 4 hours. To remove mousse, set mold in hot water for 30 seconds. Pipe into steamed snow peas or cherry tomatoes.

Paula Sue Taylor

	Cal	Fat(g)	% Fat Cal	Sat Fat(g)	Chol(mg)	Sod(mg)
Per Serving	58	2.3	34	1.0	12	130

A good friend tells the story of the time he offered to have the well-worn cover of his Grandmother's copy of the River Road Recipes *cookbook replaced with a spotless new one. She thought about it awhile. "Would you be there while they did it?" she asked. "No," he replied. "I'd have to leave it overnight." After thinking it over a while longer she gently declined his offer. When he probed for the reason for her reluctance she revealed that she was afraid that someone might swap books on her if hers went unguarded. And she would lose years of margin notations that were to her . . . priceless. Certainly more valuable than a shiny new cover.*

Artichoke Cheese Bites *with Oregano*
Yield: 35 servings

1 cup chopped green onions
4 cloves minced garlic
1 tablespoon olive oil
1/4 cup white wine
Two 15-ounce cans water-packed artichoke hearts, drained and chopped
5 ounces reduced fat Swiss cheese, (1 1/4 cups grated)
5 ounces reduced fat sharp cheddar cheese (1 1/4 cups grated)
3/4 cup Italian bread crumbs
2 whole eggs and 3 egg whites, beaten together until foamy
1/2 cup chopped parsley
1/2 teaspoon oregano flakes
1 lemon, squeezed
1 teaspoon Tabasco sauce
1 teaspoon black pepper
1/4 teaspoon salt
1/2 pound crabmeat
1/4 cup grated Parmesan or Romano cheese

Sauté garlic and onion in olive oil in nonstick pan. Add wine and let bubble. Remove from fire and mix all ingredients except Parmesan. Pour into 9x13x2-inch glass baking dish sprayed with vegetable oil cooking spray and sprinkle with reserved cheese. Bake at 350 degrees until set and edges are lightly browned. Cut into squares. Serve hot or room temperature. Freezes well and can be heated in microwave. Garnish with lemon.

Judy Crochet

	Cal	Fat(g)	% Fat Cal	Sat Fat(g)	Chol(mg)	Sod(mg)
Per Serving	**56**	**2.5**	**40**	**1.2**	**24**	**135**

Nutrition Note

Artichoke Cheese Bites with Oregano

This has less than 1/2 the fat and saturated fat found in the original. If you cannot locate reduced fat Swiss, try 3 ounces (3/4 cup grated) regular Swiss and 1 ounce (1/4 cup grated) part skim mozzarella cheese.

One Step Further

Artichoke Cheese Bites with Oregano

Trim back on sodium by omitting the salt. Instead of commercial Italian bread crumbs use fresh bread crumbs from processed french bread or your favorite bread and 2 teaspoons Italian herb blend (a savings of 35 to 40mg sodium per serving).

Toasted Pecans
Yield: 24 servings of 1/8 cup each

4 cups pecan halves
1/3 cup salt
Enough warm tap water to cover pecans

Combine pecans, salt and water in bowl and stir. Make sure salt has dissolved. Soak pecans for 30 minutes. Pour off water. Drain pecans on paper towels for 2 hours. Spread pecans on cookie sheet. Bake at 250 degrees to desired doneness, about 1 hour. Stir every 15 minutes.

Nell W. McAnelly

	Cal	Fat(g)	% Fat Cal	Sat Fat(g)	Chol(mg)	Sod(mg)
Per Serving	120	12.2	89	1	0	825

Goat Cheese *with Sun Dried Tomatoes*
Yield: 12 servings

3 ounces soft goat's milk cheese
1/3 cup nonfat cottage cheese
1/2 ounce marinated sun dried tomatoes, no salt added
3-4 fresh basil leaves, chopped
2 tablespoons roasted pine nuts
8 ounces french bread sticks, sliced and lightly toasted

Pat oil from sun dried tomatoes with paper towels then coarsely chop. Drain off liquid from cottage cheese, then cream in a food processor until smooth. Mix all ingredients. Serve on bread slices. Can refrigerate, let come to room temperature, smooth out a little, then serve.

Sari L. Turner

	Cal	Fat(g)	% Fat(g) Cal	Sat Fat(g)	Chol(mg)	Sod(mg)
Per Serving	98	4.2	37	1.3	7	172

Nutrition Note

Toasted Pecans
This analysis is based on close to 1/2 the sodium drained off when the water and salt solution is drained off the pecans.

One Step Further

Toasted Pecans
This is one of the few recipes that does not add fat to pecans when toasting or roasting them. Pecans, as most nuts, are high in fat, but less than 10% of their calories come from the "bad" saturated fat. These are, of course, high in salt and sodium. Try just one teaspoon salt and 1/2 cup Worcestershire sauce, adding water needed to cover and continue with directions. This will contain less than 1/10 the sodium content.

Creamy Shrimp Cocktail
Yield: 30 servings of 3 tablespoons each

Two 8-ounce packages light cream cheese
One 8-ounce carton low fat sour cream
3 teaspoons Worcestershire sauce
1 clove garlic, pressed
3/4 cups cocktail sauce
1 pound peeled shrimp, boiled and diced
1/2 pound skim mozzarella cheese, shredded
6 green onions, chopped fine
1 small green pepper, chopped fine
1 tomato, peeled and chopped fine

Mix first 4 ingredients and place in serving dish. Add cocktail sauce and shrimp. Cover with shredded cheese. For top layer, add tomato, green onions and green peppers. Serve with crackers. Great color for the Christmas holidays!

Carolyn B. Landry
Denise Landry

	Cal	Fat(g)	% Fat Cal	Sat Fat(g)	Chol(mg)	Sod(mg)
Per Serving	80	4.9	54	3	36	214

Party Perfect Crabmeat
Yield: 4 cups, 32 servings of 2 tablespoons each

2 pounds lump crabmeat
1/2 cup finely chopped green onions
2 teaspoons margarine
2 tablespoons nonfat plain yogurt
2 tablespoons reduced fat mayonnaise
1/4 teaspoon salt
Pepper to taste (may use red, black and/or white)
2 teaspoons lemon juice

Lightly rinse and drain crabmeat. Check for shells. In a nonstick skillet, sauté green onions in margarine until slightly limp. Mix green onions, crabmeat, yogurt and mayonnaise together. Add salt and pepper and lemon juice; mix well. May want to add more yogurt. Spray vegetable oil

Nutrition Note

Creamy Shrimp Cocktail

This recipe is still fairly high in fat, but has only 1/2 the fat and saturated fat of the original version. Serve with very low fat crackers to complement. If you replace the light cream cheese with fat-free cream cheese or "yogurt cheese" (see "Something Extra" section), you can trim off another 2 1/2gm fat per serving.

Party Perfect Crabmeat

Most of the sodium content in this recipe comes from the crabmeat. Omitting the salt will save about 17mg per serving. I recommend crackers that have low fat and moderate-low sodium content. Also try on endive leaves, cucumber slices and cherry tomato halves.

cooking spray on a mold pan. Press crabmeat into mold. Refrigerate 3 hours. Serve with crackers.

Jane V. Smith

	Cal	Fat(g)	% Fat Cal	Sat Fat(g)	Chol(mg)	Sod(mg)
Per Serving	32	0.9	26	0.2	27	103

Spinach Basil Stuffed Mushrooms
Yield: 8 servings

3 tablespoons defatted chicken broth, less salt
1 cup finely chopped onion
2 ounces light cream cheese
One 10-ounce package frozen chopped spinach, thawed
    and squeezed dry
2 large cloves garlic, minced
5 tablespoons fresh chopped or 3 teaspoons dried basil
1/2 cup plain bread crumbs
1/4 cup lightly toasted chopped walnuts
1/2 cup grated low fat Swiss cheese
1/3 cup low fat ricotta, blended smooth
1/2 cup water chestnuts, rinsed lightly and diced
1/4 cup sherry
1/4 cup fresh parsley
1/4 teaspoon salt
1/4 teaspoon pepper
1 pound fresh mushrooms
1/4 to 1/2 cup dry white wine

Sauté onion in chicken broth until wilted. Break up cream cheese and stir into onion until melted, then remove from heat. Stir in spinach, garlic, basil, bread crumbs, walnuts, Swiss cheese, blended ricotta, water chestnuts, sherry and parsley. Season with salt and pepper. Clean mushrooms and remove steams. Stuff each mushroom, mounding stuffing on top. Place in single layer in a baking pan and pour just enough white wine in the pan to cover the bottom. Bake at 400 degrees for 10 minutes.

Michell Odom Nesbit

	Cal	Fat(g)	% Fat Cal	Sat Fat(g)	Chol(mg)	Sod(mg)
Per Serving	147	5.7	35	2	8	216

One Step Further

Spinach Basil Stuffed Mushrooms
Omit walnuts and save 2.2gm more fat per serving. Omit the salt for a savings of 65mg sodium per serving.

Spinach and Water Chestnuts *on Wheat*
Yield: 24 servings of 1/4 each

One 10-ounce package chopped spinach, defrosted
1/2 cup chopped water chestnuts
2 tablespoons reduced fat mayonnaise
1 tablespoon light sour cream
6 green onions, finely chopped
1/4 teaspoon salt
1/2 teaspoon pepper
1 teaspoon lemon juice
1/2 teaspoon paprika
Red pepper to taste
2 teaspoons Worcestershire sauce
3 tablespoons tub margarine
12 slices whole wheat bread

Squeeze water out of defrosted spinach. Mix all ingredients together except margarine and bread. Butter bread, then spread mixture onto slices. Cut in fours. Adds color and interest to a sandwich tray.

Margery Larguier Fabré

	Cal	Fat(g)	% Fat Cal	Sat Fat(g)	Chol(mg)	Sod(mg)
Per Serving	50	1.8	31	0.3	trace	145

Rosie's Crabmeat Dip
Yield: 15 servings

1 1/2 tablespoons tub margarine
2 tablespoons flour
1 cup evaporated skim milk
1/2 cup reduced fat Swiss cheese
1 cup chopped green onion
1/2 cup chopped parsley
1 pound lump or white crabmeat
1 tablespoon white wine
Dash of nutmeg
Pepper and Tabasco sauce to taste

Nutrition Note

Rosie's Crabmeat Dip

In this particular recipe, regular Swiss cheese would increase the per serving fat content by 1/2 to 1/3 of a gram.

Make white sauce by melting margarine in saucepan over low heat, blending in flour, and adding milk. Stir until thickened. Add cheese, stir to melt. Add chopped green onion, parsley, and crabmeat. Blend in wine and nutmeg. Season to taste with pepper and Tabasco sauce. Serve in chafing dish with crackers.

Melissa M. Fahrmann

	Cal	Fat(g)	% Fat Cal	Sat Fat(g)	Chol(mg)	Sod(mg)
Per Serving	73	2.2	27	0.7	33	129

Creole Marinated Crab Claws
Yield: 6 servings

1 pound crab claws, rinsed and drained

Marinade
1/3 cup extra virgin olive oil
1/2 cup defatted chicken broth, less salt
1/3 cup wine vinegar
1/3 cup lemon juice
1 cup chopped onions
2 green onions, chopped
2 tablespoons minced garlic
1 tablespoon black pepper
1 teaspoon celery seed or flakes
1/4 cup parsley flakes
1 teaspoon light Creole seasoning
Cherry tomatoes and black olives for garnish

Mix marinade and pour over crab claws in shallow dish. Refrigerate for at least 4 hours. Drain well and serve on a platter lined with lettuce leaves. Garnish with cherry tomatoes and black olives.

Cindy Stewart

	Cal	Fat(g)	% Fat Cal	Sat Fat(g)	Chol(mg)	Sod(mg)
Per Serving	101	6.6	57	0.9	24	136

Nutrition Note

Creole Marinated Crab Claws

This version has less than 1/2 the calories and almost 1/3 the fat and sodium of the original — yet all the flavor. Nutritional information is based on 1/2 the marinade drained off and discarded.

Marinated Shrimp and Onions
Yield: 8 servings

2 pounds shrimp, boiled and peeled
3-4 onions, sliced

Marinade
1/4 cup oil
1/3 cup defatted chicken broth, less salt, or reserved
    shrimp broth
1/4 cup vinegar
1/2 cup catsup
1 teaspoon sugar
1/2 teaspoon pepper
2 bay leaves

Alternate layers of shrimp and onions in a bowl or dish.
Pour marinade over top and cover and refrigerate for a
minimum of 24 hours. Remove bay leaves and drain. Is
good served with melba rounds (see Bagel Chips recipe in
"Something Extra" section).

Mrs. Mark McGlasson

	Cal	Fat(g)	% Fat Cal	Sat Fat(g)	Chol(mg)	Sod(mg)
Per Serving	119	4.5	34	0.7	113	238

Burgundy Mushrooms
Yield: 10 servings

3/4 stick margarine (6 tablespoons)
3 cups burgundy wine
1 1/2 tablespoons Worcestershire sauce
1 teaspoon dill seed
1 teaspoon black pepper
2 teaspoons minced garlic
3 beef bouillon cubes, reduced sodium
Two 14-ounce cans defatted chicken broth, less salt
4 pounds whole mushrooms

In a stockpot melt margarine, then add the remaining
ingredients, mushrooms last. Bring to a slow boil on medium heat. Reduce heat to medium low, cover and cook 3
hours. Remove cover and cook an additional 3 to 5 hours
on medium heat until the liquid is just covering the mush-

Nutrition Note

**Marinated Shrimp
and Onions**
Nutritional information
based on 1/2 the mari-
nade drained off and
discarded.

rooms. Let the mushrooms cool to room temperature. Skim off top liquid, especially any oily portion. Pour into container and refrigerate. Reheat to serve. These can be eaten as appetizer or with your favorite cooked meat. Can increase mushrooms to serve more.

Lisa Town

	Cal	Fat(g)	% Fat Cal	Sat Fat(g)	Chol(mg)	Sod(mg)
Per Serving	114	4.8	33	0.9	trace	359

Marinated Vegetables
Yield: 12 servings

Herb Marinade
One 8-ounce bottle reduced calorie Italian dressing
2 teaspoons dill weed
1/4 cup lemon juice

Vegetables
Small fresh button mushrooms
Large fresh mushrooms, sliced
Cauliflower
Green and red peppers
Carrots
Zucchini
Yellow squash
Snow peas
Broccoli

Combine marinade ingredients. Additional salt, pepper, or seasoned salt may be added to taste. Refrigerate. Wash and prepare about 2 pounds of raw vegetables. Layer in a shallow dish and pour marinade over them. Toss carefully to coat. Refrigerate overnight and baste with the marinade several times. Drain to serve and arrange on a platter as hors d'oeuvres.

Katheryn Darsey

	Cal	Fat(g)	% Fat Cal	Sat Fat(g)	Chol(mg)	Sod(mg)
Per Serving	36	1.2	26	0.2	trace	95

Nutrition Note

Marinated Vegetables

Nutritional information will vary depending on the particular reduced calorie Italian dressings you use. Some are higher or lower in sodium and fat content. Check labels and purchase according to your needs. I like the reduced fat dry mixes that call for mixing with some oil, but a lot less than bottled Italian dressings. Nutritional information is based on at least 1/2 of the marinade drained off and discarded.

Sweet Cream Cheese *with Peanuts*
Yield: 25 servings of 1 apple wedge and 1 tablespoon dip

8 ounces light cream cheese
3/4 cup brown sugar
2 teaspoons vanilla
1/3 cup chopped dry roasted peanuts
3 or more apples, cut into wedges

Combine first three ingredients and mix together well. Fold in peanuts. Refrigerate until ready to serve. Serve with slices of apples as a spread.

Joan M. Surso

	Cal	Fat(g)	% Fat Cal	Sat Fat(g)	Chol(mg)	Sod(mg)
Per Serving	65	2.6	34	1.1	3	68

Carrot Cheese Ball
Yield: 1 ball, 24 servings

2 cups shredded carrots
One 8-ounce package light cream cheese or Neufchatel cheese
1 cup shredded reduced fat sharp cheddar cheese
1 clove garlic, minced
1/4 cup Grape Nuts cereal
1 tablespoon chopped parsley

Shred carrots and press between paper towels to remove excess moisture; set aside. Combine cheeses in a medium bowl; stir well. Add carrots and garlic; stir well. Cover and chill 1 hour. Combine cereal and parsley. Shape cheese mixture into a ball, then roll in cereal and parsley. Wrap in waxed paper and chill at least 1 hour.

Celia Pope

	Cal	Fat(g)	% Fat Cal	Sat Fat(g)	Chol(mg)	Sod(mg)
Per Serving	42	2.5	52	1.5	7	100

One Step Further

Sweet Cream Cheese with Peanuts

Trim the fat content more by replacing 1/2 of the light cream cheese with low fat ricotta cheese or nonfat cottage cheese, blended smooth.

Carrot Cheese Ball

Replace light cream cheese with 8 ounces of low fat ricotta cheese, blend until smooth but still firm. This recipe is still proportionally high in fat (52% of the calories), yet is very low compared to traditional cheese balls.

Beverages

1930s

1932
➤ Baby Conference
➤ East Baton Rouge Parish Health Unit
➤ Milk Distribution
➤ Red Cross

1935
➤ Braille Books
➤ Girl Scouts

1937
➤ Crippled Children's Clinic

In the 30s, during the Great Depression, the League did its best to relieve the financial burdens of those in need. Donations collected from milk bottles helped buy milk for children. Members helped provide medical services, both financial and actual, to the East Baton Rouge Health Unit and local Red Cross. In some cases, babies and small children were treated by doctors only because of the assistance of the Junior League.

The Junior League concerned itself with the physically challenged children and adults of the community, donating machines which helped members transcribe books into braille, and volunteering at the Crippled Children's Clinic.

Driver's Punch

Yield: 20 servings of 4 ounces each

46 fluid ounces pineapple juice
33.8 fluid ounces sugar-free ginger ale
3-4 tablespoons lemon juice, fresh or concentrate
1 lemon and/or orange, sliced thinly

Pour pineapple juice and ginger ale over ice. Then add lemon juice. Garnish by adding lemon and/or orange slices.

Dorothy Floyd Reed

	Cal	Fat(g)	% Fat Cal	Sat Fat(g)	Chol(mg)	Sod(mg)
Per Serving	45	0.07	1	trace	0	9

Polynesian Crush

Yield: 6 servings of 6 ounces each

1/4 of a 3-ounce package of coconut instant pudding
     mix
3/4 cup skim milk
10 ounces frozen strawberries
1 ripe banana
1/4 cup grenadine or cherry juice
1 cup pineapple juice
1 cup crushed ice
1 teaspoon coconut extract/flavoring, optional

Blend pudding mix and milk together in blender. Gradually add the strawberries and banana and blend until smooth. Add remaining ingredients. This is a great drink for children and people of all ages.

Shelley Alexander

	Cal	Fat(g)	% Fat Cal	Sat Fat(g)	Chol(mg)	Sod(mg)
Per Serving	147	0.4	2	0.2	<1	71

Nutrition Note

Polynesian Crush
The original recipe contained cream of coconut, which is very high in saturated fat—the fat that tends to raise our blood levels of cholesterol. To trim off over 40 more calories per serving, use fresh or frozen unsweetened strawberries and sugar-free pudding mix.

Fruit Juice Punch

Yield: 2 gallons, 64 servings of 4 ounces each

Two 12-ounce cans frozen orange juice concentrate, thawed
Two 12-ounce cans frozen lemonade concentrate, thawed
One 46-ounce can pineapple juice
1/3 cup cherry syrup or grenadine syrup
3 1/2 quarts water
Two 28-ounce bottles of sugar-free ginger ale (sugar-free
    lemon-lime soda, club soda, sparkling water, or cham-
    pagne may be substituted)
White rum to taste, optional

Mix the first five ingredients. Freeze in 1-gallon containers. (Plastic ice cream containers are excellent for this.) Thaw to a slushy consistency. This takes about 4 hours. (If the metal handle is taken off the ice cream container, the punch can be quickly thawed in the microwave.) Once punch reaches the slush stage, add the ginger ale and add rum, if desired.

Mrs. Randall J. Lamont

	Cal	Fat(g)	% Fat Cal	Sat Fat(g)	Chol(mg)	Sod(mg)
Per Serving	40	0	0	0	0	4

With a sugar-free beverage

Bill's Fuzzy "Neighbors"

Yield: 8 servings of 6 to 7 ounces each

6 ounces orange juice concentrate
7 ounces peach schnapps
1 blender of crushed ice

Whirl all ingredients together in a blender and serve.

Maretta Creveling

	Cal	Fat(g)	% Fat Cal	Sat Fat(g)	Chol(mg)	Sod(mg)
Per Serving	113	trace	0	0	0	8

45% of calories from alcohol, 7.5gm per serving

Nutrition Note

Fruit Juice Punch

If punch is made with one bottle of champagne and one 28-oz. bottle of sugar-free soda, calories will increase by 9 per serving with 16% of calories from alcohol.

Bourbon Slush

Yield: 1 gallon, 14 servings of 8 ounces each

4 tea bags
2 cups boiling water
1/2-3/4 cups granulated sugar
7 cups water
One 12-ounce can frozen orange juice concentrate, thawed
One 6-ounce can frozen lemonade concentrate, thawed
1 cup bourbon

Steep tea bags in boiling water for 5 minutes. Remove and discard tea bags. Add sugar, stir until dissolved. Add all other ingredients. Stir. Pour into freezer containers. Freeze overnight. Remove from freezer 30 to 45 minutes before serving. Garnish with sprigs of mint. Keep it in the freezer all summer!

Mrs. Robert V. McAnelly

	Cal	Fat(g)	% Fat Cal	Sat Fat(g)	Chol(mg)	Sod(mg)
Per Serving	130	0	0	0	0	5

32% of calories from alcohol, 6gm per serving

Icy Spicy Coffee

Yield: 2 servings

1 1/2 cups hot brewed coffee
1 whole cinnamon stick
4 whole cloves
1/2 cup skim milk
Sweetener, optional
Nutmeg

Pour hot coffee into glass container. Add next two ingredients. Refrigerate until cool and ready to serve. Pour over ice in tall glasses until 3/4 full. Add skim milk to top of glasses. Add sweetener if desired. Dust with nutmeg. Stir and serve.

Donna M. Saurage

	Cal	Fat(g)	% Fat Cal	Sat Fat(g)	Chol(mg)	Sod(mg)
Per Serving	30	0.2	6	0.1	1	35

The most vivid memory of my great Uncle George centers around the coffee pot. This was not just any old pot, mind you. It was a small, old-fashioned drip pot that sat on the back of the stove, just waiting to be used in brewing the next heavenly, caffeine-filled pot of Uncle George's coffee. Likened to "T.N.T." by some, Uncle George always kept a well-used, battered pot filled with boiling water on the stove to "cut" the syrupy brew for the faint of heart.

Betty Backstrom

Pineapple-Orange Sparkler

Yield: 12 servings of 8 ounces each

One 12-ounce can frozen orange juice concentrate
36 ounces ginger ale
One 46-ounce can unsweetened pineapple juice

In a large pitcher, dissolve orange juice with 3 cans of ginger ale. Add the pineapple juice and stir well. Chill or serve over ice.

Elaine Dupuy

	Cal	Fat(g)	% Fat Cal	Sat Fat(g)	Chol(mg)	Sod(mg)
Per Serving	143	<1	0.1	trace	0	9

Panama Punch

Yield: 2 gallons, 32 servings of 8 ounces each

6 ripe bananas, mashed
3/4 cup granulated sugar
1/4 teaspoon salt
One 46-ounce can pineapple juice
1/2 cup lemon juice
One 20-ounce can pineapple tidbits packed in juice,
    undrained, coarsely chopped
One 11-ounce can mandarin oranges, undrained,
    coarsely chopped
One 16-ounce package unsweetened strawberries,
    coarsely chopped
One 16-ounce can frozen orange juice concentrate
Two 2-liter bottles sugar-free lemon-lime soda
1 cup light rum

Blend bananas, sugar, salt and half the can of pineapple juice in blender. It will require two batches. In an 8-quart bowl, add all ingredients, except the lemon-lime soda and rum, and mix well. Divide into four plastic containers (approximately 4-1/2 cups each) and freeze overnight. Remove container(s) from freezer 45 minutes prior to serving. Place in punch bowl and pour in the soda and rum. Each container of frozen fruit mixture takes 1 liter of soda and 1/4 cup rum to dilute. To prepare an individual serv-

Nutrition Nibble

The sugar content was generally reduced by at least 1/4 in most of these beverages. You may wish to cut this further or replace a portion or all with sugar substitute.

One Step Further

Pineapple-Orange Sparkler

Try club soda, sugar-free soda, or sparkling water in place of the ginger ale and save 8gm sugar and over 30 calories per serving.

ing, scoop out enough frozen fruit to fill a glass 3/4 full, and pour the soda over. This is a very filling punch. Delicious even without alcohol.

Sharon Randall Lanius

	Cal	Fat(g)	% Fat Cal	Sat Fat(g)	Chol(mg)	Sod(mg)
Per Serving	121	0.2	<1	trace	0	40

15% of the calories from alcohol, 2.6gm per serving

Peach Schnapps Slush
Yield: 22 servings of 3/4 cup each

1/4 cup sugar
2 cups water
One 12-ounce can frozen orange juice concentrate, thawed
One 12-ounce can frozen lemonade concentrate, thawed
3 cups water
2 1/2 cups peach schnapps
1/3 cup lemon juice
Two 20-ounce bottles ginger ale

In a saucepan, mix the sugar and 2 cups water. Bring to a boil and boil for 3 minutes. Let cool and mix with the next 5 ingredients. Put in a plastic container and freeze. Before serving, allow to sit at room temperature for 15 minutes. Add the ginger ale and serve.

Theresa Prendergast

	Cal	Fat(g)	% Fat Cal	Sat Fat(g)	Chol(mg)	Sod(mg)
Per Serving	165	trace	-	-	0	9

31% of the calories from alcohol, 7.5gm per serving

Nutrition Nibble

It is advised to limit alcohol intake due to its "empty" calories – it provides calories without significant nutrient content. One gram of alcohol has approximately 7 calories. The same quantity of carbohydrate or protein has only 4 calories, while 1 gram of fat has 9 calories. Many of the beverages in this section that contain alcohol were reduced to 1 ounce of alcohol or less per serving. You may wish to reduce further or omit. Look in the stores for alcohol-free liqueur substitutes. Try some of the extracts available in the spice sections. Orange liqueur can be replaced with equal quantity of orange juice plus a little orange rind. Kirsch or amaretto can be replaced by a little almond extract mixed with peach or apricot nectar. Experiment.

One Step Further

Peach Schnapps Slush

Try a sugar-free ginger ale or sparkling water to save close to 20 calories per serving.

Hot Cajun Coffee Mocha
Yield: 2 servings

3/4 cup brewed coffee
3/4 cup skim milk
1 teaspoon powdered unsweetened cocoa
1 teaspoon sugar or sweetener of choice
1/8 teaspoon cinnamon

Heat all ingredients in saucepan until hot, stirring frequently. Can also be microwaved by combining in heat-proof glass measuring cup. Stir. Heat in microwave until hot. Stir again and serve in mugs. Sprinkle with cinnamon if desired.

Donna M. Saurage

	Cal	Fat(g)	% Fat Cal	Sat Fat(g)	Chol(mg)	Sod(mg)
Per Serving	46	0.3	6	0.2	1.5	50

Cranberry Punch
Yield: 25 servings of 5 to 6 ounces each

One 12-ounce can frozen cranberry cocktail juice
    concentrate
One 10-ounce can frozen strawberry or raspberry
    daiquiri mix
One 12-ounce can frozen pink lemonade concentrate
One 2-liter bottle club soda
One 1-liter bottle ginger ale

Thaw frozen juices and mix together in a freezer-safe container. Freeze overnight. To serve, mix frozen juices with club soda and ginger ale in a large punch bowl.

Augusta Waggenspack

	Cal	Fat(g)	% Fat Cal	Sat Fat(g)	Chol(mg)	Sod(mg)
Per Serving	95	trace	0	0	0	20

Frozen Milk Punch
Yield: 26 servings of 6 ounces each

1/2 gallon skim milk
1/2 gallon diet vanilla ice cream alternative, fat-free
    and sugar-free
2 cups brandy
2 teaspoons pure vanilla extract
Ground nutmeg

Melt ice cream with milk in a large bowl. Add brandy (less may be used). Add vanilla and mix thoroughly, leaving no lumps. Freeze overnight in the milk and ice cream containers. Remove from freezer 1 hour before serving. If desired, sprinkle nutmeg on top of each drink.

Thomas H. Turner

	Cal	Fat(g)	% Fat Cal	Sat Fat(g)	Chol(mg)	Sod(mg)
Per Serving	122	0.1	<1	trace	1	79

37% of calories from alcohol, 6.5gm per serving.

Rosie's Eggnog
Yield: 6 servings

4 cups light frozen vanilla yogurt
2 cups light eggnog
1/4 cup dark rum
1/4 cup Kahlua
1 teaspoon nutmeg

Mix in blender and freeze.

Rosie K. Abide

	Cal	Fat(g)	% Fat Cal	Sat Fat(g)	Chol(mg)	Sod(mg)
Per Serving	282	1.5	5	1	50	114

13% of calories from alcohol, 5.6gm per serving

Good Coffee— The Right Way

• *Brew your coffee full strength by using 2 level tablespoons ground coffee for every 6 ounces of water. In "coffee lingo," a cup is actually 6 ounces.*
• *Add boiling water to the coffee in your cup if the brewed coffee is too strong for your taste. Never try to make "weaker" coffee by cutting down on the ground coffee during brewing.*
• *Keep brewed coffee on a warmer for no more than 15 minutes.*
You, too, can make a cup of delicious, satisfying coffee in true Louisiana fashion!

Donna M. Saurage

Nutrition Note

Rosie's Eggnog
Using the regular eggnog and ice cream would increase the total fat content by over 13gm (2 1/2 teaspoons of fat!) and calories by over 70 per serving.

From high octane Hurricanes, to soothing silky milk punches, to steaming mugs of chicory-laced dark roasted coffee . . . Louisianians are as adventurous and imaginative in what we drink, as we are what we eat!

Banana Slush

Yield: 26 servings of 8 ounces each

6 ripe bananas, mashed
One 6-ounce can frozen lemonade concentrate
One 12-ounce can orange juice concentrate
One 6-ounce can pineapple juice concentrate
1/2 cup granulated sugar
3/4 cup water
Two 64-ounce bottles sugar-free lemon-lime soda
1 pint fresh raspberries

Puree the bananas along with the lemonade, orange juice, and pineapple juice concentrates. Add to this mixture the sugar and water. Freeze. When ready to serve, allow mixture to thaw until mushy. Add the lemon-lime soda and raspberries.

Kathy Vinci

	Cal	Fat(g)	% Fat Cal	Sat Fat(g)	Chol(mg)	Sod(mg)
Per Serving	93	0.2	2	trace	0	26

Tallahassee Tea

Yield: 12 servings, 1 cup each

8 cups water
2-3 cinnamon sticks
1 1/2 teaspoons whole cloves
3 regular tea bags
3/4 cup sugar
2 cups orange juice
2 cups pineapple juice
1 1/2 cups freshly squeezed lemon juice

In large pot boil the 8 cups water, cinnamon sticks and cloves for 15 minutes. Then steep the tea bags for five minutes. Strain off cloves and cinnamon. Add to tea mixture the sugar, orange juice, pineapple juice and lemon juice. Stir well. Best when served next day.

Carol Winchester

	Cal	Fat(g)	% Fat Cal	Sat Fat(g)	Chol(mg)	Sod(mg)
Per Serving	99	0.1	<1	trace	0	7

Soups

1940s

1940
➤ Welfare

1941
➤ Defense Work

1943
➤ USO

1944
➤ Mobile Blood Bank

During the war years the Junior League volunteers did the work which needed to be done to help the defense effort—knitting, sewing, making bandages, selling defense bonds, and anything else that could be done. Entertaining the troops was a priority for everyone during that time, and the Junior League furnished a recreation room at Harding Field for the soldiers quartered there. In 1943, the Hostess Desk at the USO was manned by League volunteers 12 hours a day. The Mobile Blood Bank was staffed by members who served at the reception desk and helped with canteen units and the motor corps during the Blood Bank's visits to Baton Rouge.

Shrimp Gumbo

Yield: 12 servings

7 cups fish stock, OR reduced sodium fish bouillon
1/2 cup vegetable oil
3/4 cup flour
1 cup finely chopped onion
1 cup chopped celery
1 cup chopped bell pepper
3 cloves finely chopped garlic
1/4 cup chopped parsley
1/2 teaspoon thyme
1 teaspoon basil
1 teaspoon oregano
1 teaspoon black pepper
1 teaspoon Tabasco sauce
One 10-ounce package of frozen okra
1/2 pound reduced fat smoked turkey sausage, chopped
      in 1/2-inch chunks
1 pound medium shrimp
1 pound crabmeat
4 cups cooked rice

Dissolve fish bouillon in boiling water. Set aside. Make a roux by heating oil very hot, and slowly adding flour, whisking in an iron skillet and being careful not to let it burn. Keep whisking until the roux is the color of a candy bar. Next, stir in onion, celery, bell pepper, and garlic. Mix thoroughly with roux. Add to boiling fish stock a spoonful at a time, stirring constantly. Add all dry seasonings. Add Tabasco sauce, okra and sausage. Simmer covered for 45 minutes. Next add shrimp and simmer for 10 minutes. Remove from heat, add crabmeat and let sit for 15 minutes. Adjust seasonings. Serve with rice.

Mary Kay Gerace

	Cal	Fat(g)	% Fat Cal	Sat Fat(g)	Chol(mg)	Sod(mg)
Per Serving	**335**	**12.8**	**34**	**2.2**	**113**	**703**

For Turkey or Chicken Gumbo, use the same recipe but in place of the shrimp and crabmeat, use turkey or chicken. Replace the fish bouillon with chicken stock or bouillon. This recipe freezes well. It may be halved but does not double well. When chilled, skim off fat that rises to the top.

Mary Kay Gerace

One Step Further

Shrimp Gumbo
Omit oil and use fat-free roux instead, saving another 9gm fat and 80 calories per serving. Brown the flour in the oven or heavy skillet without oil, stirring frequently. Slowly stir fish stock into flour, making a smooth paste. Then slowly stir "paste" into simmering stock. Add raw vegetables (onion, celery and bell pepper) and simmer until vegetables soften and liquid thickens, stirring regularly. Continue with recipe. A homemade fish stock can help reduce sodium content further and contribute a richer flavor.

Perched on the levee that marks the edge of the Atchafalaya Basin, is the town of Henderson, known as the Crawfish Capital of the World. And it is there that we took a friend from the Midwest to sample this unique staple of Louisiana's diet. Our intense conversation over a bowl of Crawfish Bisque was interrupted by a loud crunching noise. We suddenly realized that we'd forgotten to explain to our friend that only the stuffing from the crawfish head floating atop the bisque was intended for consumption! All this noise didn't go unnoticed by the waiter. But he put our friend instantly at ease by telling the story of when he ate his first tamale. Corn husk and all.

Family Crawfish Bisque
Yield: 10 servings

Bisque
1 cup flour
1/2 cup vegetable oil
2 large onions, chopped
2-3 ribs celery, chopped
1 green pepper, chopped
One 6-ounce can tomato paste, no salt added
1 tablespoon chopped garlic
4 cups fish stock (2 bouillon cubes plus 4 cups water)
1 teaspoon lemon juice
1 teaspoon pepper
1/4 teaspoon cayenne pepper
3 cups chicken stock (3 bouillon cubes plus 3 cups water)
1 pound crawfish tails, lightly rinsed and drained
1 bunch green onions, tops and bottoms, chopped
1/2 cup fresh or 1/4 cup dried parsley

Dressing
1/4 cup defatted chicken broth, less salt
1 rib celery, chopped
1 1/2 onions, chopped
1/2 green pepper, chopped
1/4 cup fresh or 1/8 cup dried parsley
1/2 bunch green onions, chopped
1 pound crawfish tails, lightly rinsed, drained, and
     chopped
2 teaspoons Worcestershire sauce
2 tablespoons lemon juice
5 cups fresh bread crumbs
1/2 teaspoon salt
3/4 teaspoon pepper
1/4 teaspoon cayenne pepper

For the bisque: On high in microwave, make roux with flour and oil and cook 6 to 7 minutes, stirring frequently, until caramel colored. Add vegetables that have been chopped in processor and microwave 3 minutes. Remove to Dutch oven. Add next 3 ingredients, lemon juice and peppers. Simmer for 1 hour. Add remaining ingredients; simmer 15 to 20 minutes. **For the dressing:** In 4-quart glass measure, in microwave, wilt vegetables (except green onions) in chicken broth for 4 minutes, stirring once. Add green onions and tails, cook 2 more minutes. Add seasonings and remaining ingredients. Add additional bread curmbs if needed to make firm balls. Cool and refrigerate. Make boulettes (1" balls) or, if you're a purist, stuff cleaned crawfish "heads." Flour lightly. Bake on cookie sheet, uncovered, for 15 to 20 minutes at 400 degrees. To freeze, bake 10 minutes then quick freeze. To heat frozen balls or "heads," bake 20 minutes in 400 degree oven. Makes 45 balls. Freeze bisque and dressing separately. Serve bisque and balls or "heads" over rice.

Katherine A. Arbour

	Cal	Fat(g)	% Fat Cal	Sat Fat(g)	Chol(mg)	Sod(mg)
Per Serving	353	13.4	34	1.8	125	680

Mag's Potato Soup
Yield: 8 servings of 1 cup each

3 cups peeled red potatoes, sliced or cubed
1 cup chopped celery
1 cup chopped carrots
Two 14.5-ounce cans defatted chicken broth, less salt
4 ounces Velveeta cheese, reduced fat
2 cups evaporated skim milk
2 tablespoons white wine
1/2 teaspoon white pepper
1/2 teaspoon light Creole seasoning
1/2 cup chopped parsley
1/2 cup chopped green onions

In a large pot, cook the potatoes, celery, and carrots in the chicken broth until tender. Mash the vegetables coarsely with a potato masher or a fork. Add the processed cheese and stir over medium heat until melted. Add the milk and stir again. Do not let the mixture boil! Add the seasonings and adjust if necessary. Just before serving, garnish with the parsley and green onions.

Mag Wall

	Cal	Fat(g)	% Fat Cal	Sat Fat(g)	Chol(mg)	Sod(mg)
Per Serving	163	2.8	15	1.6	14	630

One Step Further

Family Crawfish Bisque
The sodium content of this recipe is less than 1/2 that of the original. Persons requiring further sodium reduction should use low sodium bouillon or homemade stocks or low sodium canned broths.

Mag's Potato Soup
This has only 1/4 the fat and 540mg less sodium per serving of the original. To reduce sodium by an additional 145mg, use only one can of broth and one can of water.

Fresh Peach Soup

Yield: 4 servings of 6 ounces each

5 pureed peaches
1/4 cup sugar
1 cup nonfat plain yogurt
1/4 cup fresh orange juice
2 tablespoons lemon concentrate
1/4 cup amaretto, sherry, or Grand Marnier

Mix all ingredients together and serve cold.

Kathleen Short

	Cal	Fat(g)	% Fat Cal	Sat Fat(g)	Chol(mg)	Sod(mg)
Per Serving	**179**	**0.1**	**less than 1**	**trace**	**1**	**41**

Real Estate Gumbo

Yield: 12 servings

2 whole skinless chicken breasts
One 3-pound freshly smoked chicken, skin removed
12 cups water
1/2 pound sliced beef sausage
2 cups chopped onion
1 bell pepper, chopped
1 stalk celery, chopped
4 cloves garlic, pressed
1/4 cup canola oil
1/2 cup flour
1 teaspoon black pepper
1 teaspoon salt
1/8 teaspoon thyme
1/4 teaspoon red pepper
1/4 cup dried parsley
4 cups cooked rice

One Step Further

Real Estate Gumbo
Use our fat-free roux recipe (see "Something Extra" section) and save another 4.5gm fat and 40 calories per serving. Omit the sausage and save 3.4gm fat and over 100mg sodium per serving.

Bring to boil the chicken breasts and the legs of smoked chicken in the 12 cups of water, then simmer on medium/low for 20 minutes. Remove the chicken and reserve the stock. Chill stock and skim off fat. In large heavy skillet, brown sausage. Drain off fat. Add vegetables (except parsley) and sauté until soft. Add a little water as needed. Drain on paper towels and set aside. Make a very

dark roux with the oil and flour (see "Something Extra" section). Add the reserved defatted stock and cook on low until thick. Add all chicken (deboned), sausage, vegetables and seasonings. Continue cooking for 45 minutes. Serve over rice. This recipe can be doubled and frozen.

Claire G. Gowdy

	Cal	Fat(g)	% Fat Cal	Sat Fat(g)	Chol(mg)	Sod(mg)
Per Serving	327	12	33	2.8	67	385

Mulled Spiced Fruit Soup

Yield: 6 servings of 6 ounces each

One 10-ounce package of any frozen unsweetened fruit, thawed
1 cup water
1/4 cup sugar
1/4 teaspoon cinnamon
1/4 teaspoon nutmeg
1/4 teaspoon cloves
1 tablespoon water
1 tablespoon cornstarch
2 tablespoons lemon juice
1/2 cup light sour cream
1/2 cup nonfat plain yogurt
1/2 cup skim milk or half-and-half
1/4 cup white wine

Drain and chop fruit, reserving the juice. In 1-1/2 quart saucepan combine reserved juice, 1 cup water, sugar and seasonings. Bring to boil; reduce heat and simmer for 5 minutes uncovered. Blend the 1 tablespoon water and cornstarch; stir into mixture. Cook and stir constantly until thickened and bubbly. Remove from heat. Add lemon juice. Cool to room temperature. Blend in sour cream, yogurt, fruit, milk and wine. Cover and chill. This is great for a summer brunch served in small pretty cups.

Mrs. Wray E. Robinson

	Cal	Fat(g)	% Fat Cal	Sat Fat(g)	Chol(mg)	Sod(mg)
Per Serving	105	2.5	21	1.5	9	35

Mama had at least a dozen wooden spoons in the kitchen drawer closest to her stove. But she always used the same one. She said she didn't know why. Maybe it was that comfortable coffee color it had become over the years, stirring countless pots of roux of about the same hue.

One Step Further

Mulled Spiced Fruit Soup

Omit sugar and use your favorite sugar substitute, adding once removed from heat and saving 30 calories per serving. Omit most of the fat content by replacing the light sour cream with nonfat yogurt.

Black Bean Soup

Yield: 6 servings

3 ounces Canadian bacon or lean ham, diced
1 large onion, chopped
1 clove garlic, minced
Two 15-ounce cans black beans, drained and rinsed lightly
One 10.5-ounce can beef broth, reduced salt
1 1/2 cups water
1 cup picante sauce
1/2 teaspoon oregano

Cook Canadian bacon and set aside. Coat nonstick skillet with vegetable oil cooking spray and sauté the onion and garlic. Add other ingredients, cover and simmer for 20 minutes. May serve with low fat sour cream or nonfat plain yogurt on top.

Genie Harrison

	Cal	Fat(g)	% Fat Cal	Sat Fat(g)	Chol(mg)	Sod(mg)
Per Serving	191	3	13	0.6	5	748

Picnic Basket Squash Soup

Yield: 6 servings

2 tablespoons tub margarine
1 cup chopped white onion
1 medium carrot, chopped
1 celery stalk, chopped
3 cups defatted chicken broth, less salt
2 cups beef broth
1 1/2 pounds yellow summer squash, diced
1 large (8 ounce) White Rose potato, peeled and diced
1/4 cup low fat sour cream
1/2 cup nonfat plain yogurt
2 tablespoons dijon mustard
1/2 teaspoon nutmeg
1/2 teaspoon white pepper
Grated carrot and fresh chives for garnish

Melt margarine in large saucepan or Dutch oven. Add onion, carrot and celery. Cook 10 minutes, stirring often, until onions are clear. Add broths, squash, potato and

Nutrition Nibble

Unless otherwise stated, the chicken broth used in these recipes and in their nutritional analysis is a canned condensed broth with 1/3 less sodium content (approximately 300mg per 1/2 cup). To cut the sodium further, use 1/2 broth concentrate and 1/2 water. Salt-free canned broths are also available. In addition, homemade broths can readily be made with little or no salt added.

One Step Further

Black Bean Soup

Use dry black beans, soaked and cooked, to reduce sodium content further.

bring to a boil. Reduce heat and simmer until vegetables are tender, about 30 minutes. Transfer to food processor in batches and puree until smooth. Pour into a bowl and chill. When cool, add sour cream, yogurt, mustard, nutmeg, and pepper. Garnish with carrots and chives before serving. This makes a great summer supper or picnic served with a green salad and cheese bread. It can be served hot but chilled is better. If serving hot, blend 1 1/2 teaspoons of flour into the yogurt before it is added to soup.

Shug Lockett (Mrs. Walker)

	Cal	Fat(g)	% Fat Cal	Sat Fat(g)	Chol(mg)	Sod(mg)
Per Serving	142	5.8	35	1.9	10	799

Brie Soup
Yield: 6 servings

1 bunch green onions, chopped (mostly white part)
4 tablespoons diced shallots, optional
1 1/2 cups sliced mushrooms
1 tablespoon tub margarine
6 tablespoons sherry, divided
3 cups defatted chicken broth, less salt
2 cups evaporated skim milk
4 ounce brie cheese, rind removed, cubed
2 tablespoons cornstarch
1/4 teaspoon pepper
1/8 teaspoon nutmeg
1/4 teaspoon salt

Sauté onions, shallots, and mushrooms in margarine for 5 minutes in a nonstick skillet. Add 3 tablespoons sherry and chicken stock and simmer for 10 minutes. Add milk and cheese and stir until cheese is melted and soup begins to thicken. Combine cornstarch and remaining 3 tablespoons of sherry and stir into soup. Continue cooking until soup is thickened. Season with pepper and nutmeg. Taste. Add salt if needed.

Chrissie Clark

	Cal	Fat(g)	% Fat Cal	Sat Fat(g)	Chol(mg)	Sod(mg)
Per Serving	202	7.5	33	3.9	28	651

One Step Further

Picnic Basket Squash Soup
To further reduce fat, replace the reduced fat sour cream with all nonfat yogurt. Vegetables can also be sautéed in some of the broth instead of margarine. To further reduce sodium, use reduced salt beef broth or bouillon.

Brie Soup
To reduce sodium further, use homemade chicken stock. Omitting the salt will save an additional 90mg sodium per serving. Use only 1 1/2 cups of less salt canned broth and 1 1/2 cups of water, trimming off 160mg more sodium.

Sunday Night Soup

Yield: 6 servings

1 pound extra lean ground meat
1 medium onion, chopped
One 6-ounce can tomato paste, no salt added
1 cup water
Two 16-ounce packages frozen mixed vegetables
1 1/2 teaspoons red hot sauce
2 beef bouillon cubes, reduced salt
One 11-ounce can zesty tomato soup

Brown the meat and onions; drain off any fat. Add rest of ingredients and simmer for at least 30 minutes.

Debbie Heroman

	Cal	Fat(g)	% Fat Cal	Sat Fat(g)	Chol(mg)	Sod(mg)
Per Serving	272	10.1	33	3.9	48	670

One Step Further

Sunday Night Soup

You can trim back more fat and calories by selecting a lean cut of meat (round or sirloin); have it trimmed well and then ground. Skinless ground turkey may also be used for a portion or all of the ground meat for fat savings. Further reduce sodium by using a reduced salt tomato soup and adding fresh seasonings.

Nutrition Note

After the Boil Soup

Nutritional information of sodium content is an estimate; sodium content will vary according to salt used at the crawfish boil. Can reduce sodium by using salt-free broth, canned or homemade.

After the Boil Soup

Yield: 8 servings

Two 14.5-ounce cans defatted chicken broth, less salt
2 cups seasoned potatoes (from crawfish boil), thinly sliced
    or chopped
1 cup chopped onion
1 cup seasoned corn, scraped and chopped from ear
    (from crawfish boil)
1 1/2 cups crawfish tails (from the boil)
1 teaspoon lemon juice
Pepper to taste

In one can of chicken broth, boil thinly sliced potatoes with freshly chopped onions until mushy. Blend in blender until smooth. Return to pot; add remaining chicken broth, corn and crawfish. If you want a thin soup, add more chicken broth, as it may turn out as a thick chowder. Add lemon juice. The "salty" and "peppery" hotness will increase by the next day.

Maretta Creveling

	Cal	Fat(g)	% Fat Cal	Sat Fat(g)	Chol(mg)	Sod(mg)
Per Serving	127	1.1	8	0.4	52	584

Shrimp and Corn Chowder

Yield: 10 servings

3 tablespoons vegetable oil
2 cups finely chopped onions
1 cup finely chopped celery
1/2 cup grated carrots
1/2 cup finely chopped bell pepper
1 bay leaf, crumbled
2 cups diced potatoes
1/4 cup water
2 tablespoons flour
1 teaspoon garlic granules or 1 clove garlic, minced
4 cups shrimp stock, reserved from boiling shrimp
One 16 1/2-ounce can cream-style corn
16 ounces frozen whole kernel corn
One 12-ounce can evaporated skim milk
1/4 cup parsley
1 teaspoon salt
1 teaspoon lemon juice
1/2 teaspoon cayenne pepper
1/2 teaspoon black pepper
Tabasco sauce to taste
2 pounds shrimp, cooked and peeled

In a 10-quart stockpot, sauté onions, celery, carrots and bell pepper in oil. Wipe pot with paper towel to remove oil left from sautéing. Add bay leaf, potatoes and water. Cook for 5 to 10 minutes. Sprinkle flour and garlic over mixture, stir well and add shrimp stock. Bring to a boil. Add corn, milk, parsley, salt, lemon juice, pepper and Tabasco sauce. Simmer over low heat for 30 minutes. Add the boiled shrimp 5 to 10 minutes before serving.

Margery Larguier Fabre

	Cal	Fat(g)	% Fat Cal	Sat Fat(g)	Chol(mg)	Sod(mg)
Per Serving	232	5.7	22	0.8	77	497

Nutrition Nibble

Using evaporated skim milk to replace creams saves fat and calories. An added benefit is that it can be kept "fresh" on the shelf and ready to use for months.

One Step Further

Shrimp and Corn Chowder

Omit the oil and sauté or wilt all the vegetables in a small amount of shrimp stock. This will save 4gm more fat and over 36 calories in each serving. Omit salt to save over 200mg more sodium per serving.

Zucchini and Carrot Bisque

Yield: 6 servings

1 large onion, chopped
1 teaspoon tub margarine
1 teaspoon olive oil
1 pound fresh carrots, peeled and cut in 2-inch pieces
2 medium zucchini, cut in 2-inch pieces
2 cups defatted chicken broth, less salt
1/4 teaspoon freshly ground black pepper
2 tablespoons half-and-half

Sauté onions in margarine and oil until soft. Add carrots, zucchini and chicken stock. Heat to boiling, reduce heat and simmer until vegetables are soft. Puree mixture in food processor and return to pot. Season with pepper. Add half-and-half and heat just to boiling.

Mary Karam

	Cal	Fat(g)	% Fat Cal	Sat Fat(g)	Chol(mg)	Sod(mg)
Per Serving	81	2.4	25	0.8	6	272

Creole Tomato Soup

Yield: 6 servings

3 tablespoons defatted chicken broth, less salt
1/2 cup chopped onion
2 tablespoons cornstarch
1 cup water
6 Creole tomatoes, peeled and coarsely chopped
1 tablespoon minced fresh dill
1 tablespoon sugar
1/2 teaspoon salt
1 tablespoon minced fresh parsley
1/4 teaspoon black pepper
Dash of hot sauce
1 bay leaf
Fresh dill sprigs, for garnish
Sour cream, for garnish, optional

In a large Dutch oven, heat the chicken broth. Add the onion and sauté over medium heat until tender, about 3 minutes. Reduce heat to low. Blend the cornstarch with 1/4

One Step Further

Zucchini and Carrot Bisque

To cut the saturated fat (bad fat) content by 1/2 and reduce the total fat per serving, omit half-and-half and use 2 tablespoons of nonfat yogurt or 1/4 cup evaporated skim milk reduced by 1/2.

Creole Tomato Soup

Save over 170mg of sodium per serving when salt is omitted. Try dash of lemon juice and/or your favorite salt-free seasoning blend. A fat-free roux (1/4 cup) may also be used in place of the cornstarch for similar results.

cup of water to make a smooth paste, then gradually blend in the remaining water. Add to the onions and broth mixture and cook over medium heat, stirring constantly until thickened and bubbly, about 5 minutes. Add the tomatoes and seasonings, and bring to a boil. Cover, reduce heat, and simmer for 30 minutes. Discard the bay leaf, then transfer 1/3 of the mixture to a food processor and process until smooth. Pour into a warmed serving tureen. Repeat with the remaining soup mixture. Serve garnished with fresh dill sprigs and light sour cream or nonfat plain yogurt, if desired.

Margo Bouanchaud, Unique Cuisine

	Cal	Fat(g)	% Fat Cal	Sat Fat(g)	Chol(mg)	Sod(mg)
Per Serving	57	0.6	8	trace	trace	207

Potage Verde
Yield: 8 Servings

1 medium onion, chopped
1 green pepper, chopped
1 tablespoon oil
1 pound smoked turkey sausage (or other reduced fat)
One 16-ounce can great northern beans (no meat added)
One 16-ounce can navy beans with jalapeño
Two 14 1/2-ounce cans defatted chicken broth, less salt
2 cans water (use chicken broth can)
One 10-ounce package chopped, frozen mustard greens
3 large red potatoes, peeled and diced

In a large pot, sauté onion and bell pepper in oil until clear. Slice or cube sausage. In a heavy skillet or nonstick pan lightly brown the sausage, stirring frequently. Drain on paper towel, blotting off fat. Lightly rinse and drain beans and add all ingredients to the onions and green pepper in the large pot and bring to a boil. Reduce heat and simmer for 2 hours. May be served over rice as a main dish with no additional meat needed at this meal.

Louella B. Romero

	Cal	Fat(g)	% Fat Cal	Sat Fat(g)	Chol(mg)	Sod(mg)
Per Serving	298	8.4	25	2.9	36	832

One Step Further

Potage Verde

Although this soup has less than 1/2 the sodium of the original, it is still moderately high in sodium. To cut sodium content, try dry beans that you pre-cook and add, or frozen beans. Sausage also is high in sodium; you can cut back more fat and sodium by omitting (saving over 350mg per serving) or at least reducing the amount of sausage.

Spicy Dicey Gazpacho
Yield: 12 servings

3 pounds ripe tomatoes, peeled and diced, reserving juice
2 medium cucumbers, peeled and diced
3 cups tomato juice
3 tablespoons red wine vinegar
2 tablespoons olive oil
One 16-ounce jar salsa, hot
1 cup defatted chicken stock, less salt
1 tablespoon sugar
1 tablespoon basil
3 tablespoons fresh parsley
1/4 teaspoon salt
Pepper to taste

Combine all ingredients in large container. Chill for 4 to 6 hours before serving.

Shug Lockett (Mrs. Walker)

	Cal	Fat(g)	% Fat Cal	Sat Fat(g)	Chol(mg)	Sod(mg)
Per Serving	79	3.7	36	0.4	trace	477

Summer/Winter Soup
Yield: 6 servings

One Step Further

Summer/Winter Soup

Further reduce the fat content by omitting the oil. Instead wilt the onions and garlic in some of the chicken broth, then add the potatoes and the rest of the broth. This will cut out more than 2gm fat and close to 20 calories from each serving. Try a fat-free sour cream alternative or nonfat plain yogurt to cut close to 2-1/2gm more fat from the "summer version." The salt addition will raise sodium content by 180mg per serving.

1 medium white onion, chopped
1 bunch green onions, chopped
1 small clove garlic, minced
1 tablespoon olive oil
One 14-ounce can low sodium chicken broth
2 cups peeled and cubed potatoes
One 12-ounce can evaporated skim milk
4 dashes pepper
1 dash nutmeg
1/2 teaspoon salt, optional
1/2 cup low fat sour cream - summer version
1/2 cup shredded low fat cheese - winter version

In a saucepan sauté onions, green onions and garlic in olive oil until soft. Add broth and potatoes. Cover and simmer until potatoes are soft, about 15 minutes. Puree in blender. Add milk and seasonings, only add salt if needed.

Chill for summer and garnish with sour cream. Heat for winter and garnish with the grated cheese. This soup is a pretty pale green.

Mrs. Frank Bacot, Jr.

Winter Version

	Cal	Fat(g)	% Fat Cal	Sat Fat(g)	Chol(mg)	Sod(mg)
Per Serving	169	4.5	24	1.6	13	343

Summer Version

	Cal	Fat(g)	% Fat Cal	Sat Fat(g)	Chol(mg)	Sod(mg)
Per Serving	169	5.3	28	2.1	14	281

Oyster Rockefeller Soup

Yield: 6 servings

5 tablespoons light margarine OR 2 1/2 tablespoons margarine or oil
5 tablespoons flour
2 cloves garlic, minced
1 bunch green onions (tops only)
Two 10-ounce containers oysters, drained and minced
One 14.5-ounce can reduced salt chicken broth
1 1/2 cups skim milk
One 12-ounce can evaporated skim milk
Two 10-ounce boxes frozen chopped spinach, cooked
1/8 teaspoon cayenne
1/8 teaspoon Tabasco sauce
Salt, optional

Melt margarine and stir in flour. Add garlic and onions; cook over medium high heat till onions are transparent. Add oysters and cook till firm. Add chicken broth, milk and evaporated milk; stir well to combine. Drain and add spinach and bring to a boil. Remove from heat and allow to cool slightly. Process in blender or food processor until well blended. Season with cayenne and Tabasco sauce. Taste. Salt only if needed. This is a wonderful soup for a holiday dinner or buffet.

Mrs. Donald W. Solanas, Jr.

	Cal	Fat(g)	% Fat Cal	Sat Fat(g)	Chol(mg)	Sod(mg)
Per Serving	221	8	32	2.6	50	587

For the purists, nothing more than a dab of Tabasco sauce, a dollop of horseradish, and and a cracker are allowed to come between their beloved raw oysters and their taste buds. On the other hand there are many who prefer these little delights decked out in something a bit more elegant. And so Oysters Rockefeller was born!

She Crab Soup
Yield: 6 servings

2 tablespoons tub margarine
3 tablespoons flour
One 12-ounce can evaporated skim milk
2 1/2 cups skim milk
2 cups defatted turkey or chicken stock, less salt
5 shallots, chopped
1 pound crabmeat
1/4 cup white wine

In double boiler, melt margarine. Stir in flour and slowly add milks. Cook until it thickens. Heat 1/2 cup chicken broth in a separate saucepan and sauté the shallots until soft. Add this mixture to the sauce and stir well. Then gradually stir in remaining stock. Add crabmeat and wine. Heat thoroughly and serve.

Nan D'Agostino

	Cal	Fat(g)	% Fat Cal	Sat Fat(g)	Chol(mg)	Sod(mg)
Per Serving	223	4.9	20	1.2	80	589

Cream of Garlic and Onion Soup
Yield: 6 servings

1 tablespoon tub margarine
1 tablespoon olive oil
1 pound onions, coarsely chopped
28 medium garlic cloves, peeled (about 2 heads)
3 cups defatted chicken broth, less salt
1 slice french bread, torn into pieces
1 bouquet garni (6 fresh parsley sprigs, 4 fresh thyme
        sprigs and 1 bay leaf tied in a cheesecloth square)
1 cup evaporated skim milk
1 tablespoon white wine
1/2 teaspoon white pepper
1/4 teaspoon salt

Melt margarine with oil in heavy large saucepan over low heat. Add onions and garlic and cook until tender and golden brown. This takes about 30 minutes. Add broth, bread and bouquet garni to onion-garlic mixture and bring

Nutrition Nibble

Defat fresh or canned broths by placing in the refrigerator for 20 to 30 minutes or freezer for 2 to 5 minutes. Remove hardened fat on top and discard.

One Step Further

She Crab Soup

This version saves over 300mg sodium and 14gm fat per serving. To cut the sodium content by an additional 100mg, use only 1/2 of the canned concentrate stock and the other 1/2 as water.

Cream of Garlic and Onion Soup

To cut sodium content further, use only 2 cups of canned broth and 1 cup of water and omit the salt, saving close to 200mg sodium per serving.

to a boil. Reduce heat and simmer for 15 minutes. Discard bouquet. Puree mixture in blender or food processor until smooth. Transfer back to saucepan and add milk, wine and pepper. Heat over low heat until heated through. Taste. Add salt only if needed.

Sandy Bezet

	Cal	Fat(g)	% Fat Cal	Sat Fat(g)	Chol(mg)	Sod(mg)
Per Serving	145	4.8	29	1	7	518

Seafood and Okra Gumbo
Yield: 12 servings

1/4 cup olive oil
1/3 cup flour
2 large onions, sliced
2 cloves garlic, chopped
One 16-ounce can tomatoes
7 cans water
1 bag crab boil
2 pounds fresh okra
1 pound lump crabmeat
2 boiled crabs, broken into quarters
2 pounds fresh peeled shrimp
1/4 teaspoon crushed red pepper
1 teaspoon salt
1 teaspoon black pepper

Make a roux of oil and flour, add onion and garlic and simmer for a few minutes until soft. Add tomatoes, water and crab boil bag and cook for 45 minutes. Meanwhile, cook okra in a little oil until slime disappears. This takes about 30 minutes on a medium fire, stirring frequently. Add this to gumbo mixture, remove crab boil and cook together another 30 minutes. Add crabmeat, crabs and shrimp and cook another 30 minutes. Season to taste. Serve over steamed rice. Makes 10 generous servings. Can be frozen for later use.

Katherine Melius

	Cal	Fat(g)	% Fat Cal	Sat Fat(g)	Chol(mg)	Sod(mg)
Per Serving	218	6.3	28	1.0	159	546

One Step Further

Seafood and Okra Gumbo

Omit the oil and instead use 1/3 cup fat-free roux (see "Something Extra" section). Slowly stir 1/2 to 1 cup of the water into the fat-free roux, making a smooth paste. Bring the rest of the water to a boil and slowly stir the water/roux mixture into the pot. Stir until blended well, then add onions, garlic, tomatoes and crab boil. This will cut 4.5gm more fat and 40 calories from each serving. Omit salt and save over 175mg sodium per serving.

Buck's Oyster Stew
Yield: 6 servings

2 stalks celery, chopped
1 large onion, chopped
1 tablespoon tub margarine
Two 10-ounce jars oysters, drained and liquid reserved
3 1/2 cups skim milk
1/2 teaspoon salt-free lemon-pepper
1/4 teaspoon pepper
1 teaspoon Accent
1/4 cup chopped green onion tops

Sauté celery and onion in margarine on medium heat until tender, about 5 minutes. Add the drained oysters and cook until the edges curl, between 5 to 10 minutes. Add oyster juice and cook 10 minutes. Add milk. Lower heat and simmer for 15 minutes. Add lemon-pepper, pepper and Accent. Garnish with green onion tops before serving.

S.W. "Buck" Gladden III

	Cal	Fat(g)	% Fat Cal	Sat Fat(g)	Chol(mg)	Sod(mg)
Per Serving	136	3.8	25	1	46	373

Crab Bisque
Yield: 10 servings

3/4 cup finely chopped celery
1 bunch shallots, finely chopped
3 tablespoons tub margarine
2 tablespoons flour
2 large cans evaporated skim milk
1 1/2 cups skim milk
One 10 3/4-ounce can each cream of mushroom and
    cream of chicken soup, low fat/less salt
1/2 cup white wine
1 pound lump crabmeat
Black pepper, red pepper and Tabasco sauce to taste
Salt, optional

Sauté celery and shallots in margarine. Stir in flour to thicken. Slowly stir in evaporated milk, skim milk and soups. Shortly before serving stir in wine. Add seasonings. Gently

Nutrition Note

Buck's Oyster Stew
Accent can be replaced with 1/4 teaspoon of salt for similar sodium composition. If you are used to seasoning without salt or Accent, omit and save 100mg sodium per serving. Taste and, if necessary, add salt-free lemon-pepper blend or your favorite salt-free seasoning blend.

fold in crabmeat. Heat to desired temperature but do not boil. Stir as little as possible. More milk may be added if bisque is too thick.

Nell W. McAnelly

	Cal	Fat(g)	% Fat Cal	Sat Fat(g)	Chol(mg)	Sod(mg)
Per Serving	198	5.3	23	1.5	42	541

Lentil Lemon Soup
Yield: 12 servings

2 tablespoons olive oil
2 onions, chopped
7 garlic cloves, minced
2 carrots, chopped
4 teaspoons ground cumin
Four 14.5-ounce cans defatted chicken stock, less salt
5 cups water
2 1/3 cups dried lentils, rinsed
2 teaspoons light Creole seasoning
2 bay leaves
1/2 teaspoon paprika
1/4 teaspoon red pepper
1/2 teaspoon pepper
1/3 cup chopped parsley
2 lemons, sliced

Heat oil, sauté onion, garlic, and carrots for 15 minutes or until onion is clear. Add cumin, chicken stock and water. Add lentils, Creole seasoning, bay leaves, paprika, peppers, parsley and lemons. Simmer for 30 minutes over a low heat. Stir, then cover and simmer for an additional 30 minutes.

Sugar McAdams

	Cal	Fat(g)	% Fat Cal	Sat Fat(g)	Chol(mg)	Sod(mg)
Per Serving	165	3.6	18	0.7	2	511

Nutrition Nibble

The oil or margarine was reduced in these soups. You can produce even lower fat results by omitting the oil or margarine all together and sauté in the broth or liquid the soup calls for. Many of these soups may also be lightened further by using our fat free roux found in the "Something Extra" section. Every tablespoon of oil or margarine saved will save an additional 15gm fat and 120 calories.

One Step Further

Lentil Lemon Soup
Use only 2 cans of the concentrated chicken broth and save over 180mg more sodium, adding 3 to 4 additional cups of water.

Tortilla Soup

Yield: 10 servings

1 small onion, chopped
1 small fresh jalapeño pepper, seeded and chopped
2 cloves garlic, minced
6 skinless, boneless chicken breast halves, sliced
1 tablespoon vegetable oil
One 16-ounce can stewed tomatoes, no salt added
One 10-ounce can tomatoes and green chilies
One 10 3/4-ounce can defatted beef bouillon, less salt
One 10 3/4-ounce can defatted chicken broth, less salt
One 10 3/4-ounce can tomato soup, less salt
1 1/2 cups water
2 teaspoons ground cumin
2 teaspoons chili powder
2 tablespoons fresh cilantro
2 carrots, sliced
2 zucchini, cubed
6 corn tortillas
1/2 cup grated reduced fat sharp cheddar cheese

Sauté onion, jalapeño, garlic, and chicken breast in oil in a nonstick skillet. If it begins to stick, add some of the broth to finish sautéing. Add tomatoes, soups, water, seasonings and vegetables. Bring to a boil. Lower heat. Simmer, covered, 1 hour. Cut tortillas into 1/2-inch strips; place on nonstick cookie sheet. Spray with vegetable oil cooking spray and bake in oven at 325 degrees for 8 to 12 minutes. Place tortilla strips in bottom of bowl. Cover with soup. Sprinkle with grated cheese. Avocado slices may be added for garnish. Serve with salad and bread. This recipe is spicy and is especially good on a cold, winter day. Easily doubled.

Carol Little

	Cal	Fat(g)	% Fat Cal	Sat Fat(g)	Chol(mg)	Sod(mg)
Per Serving	224	6.6	26	1.7	50	552

Nutrition Nibble

Freeze leftover canned or homemade broth in ice trays. Once frozen, place in freezer bags. These cubes are now ready to use as needed, in small or larger quantities.

Oyster and Artichoke Soup

Yield: 6 servings

4 ribs celery, chopped
1 medium onion, chopped
1/2 bell pepper, chopped
2 cloves garlic, minced
Three 10.5-ounce cans defatted chicken broth, less salt
Three 14-ounce cans artichoke hearts, drained and rinsed
One 12-ounce can evaporated skim milk
One 10 3/4-ounce can cream of asparagus soup
One 10 3/4-ounce can low fat, less salt cream of mushroom soup
1 quart oysters with water
2 cups mushrooms, chopped
2 bay leaves
1/4 cup freshly grated Parmesan cheese
1/8 teaspoon nutmeg
1/4 teaspoon white pepper
1 tablespoon Worcestershire sauce
1/2 teaspoon Tabasco sauce
1/2 teaspoon cayenne pepper

Simmer celery, onions, bell pepper and garlic in a little chicken broth until onions turn clear. Place 2 cans artichoke hearts in food processor, adding milk to puree. Add cream soups and artichoke mixture to pot with vegetables. Add chicken stock, oyster liquid, chopped mushrooms, bay leaves and last can of artichokes, cut in quarters. Add grated Parmesan cheese. Bring to a boil, lower heat and add oysters. Simmer 5 minutes. Add salt to taste, nutmeg, white pepper, Worcestershire sauce, Tabasco sauce and cayenne pepper. Turn off heat and set stand 1 hour before serving.

Alice Witcher

	Cal	Fat(g)	% Fat Cal	Sat Fat(g)	Chol(mg)	Sod(mg)
Per Serving	120	3.3	25	1.2	37	589

One Step Further

Oyster and Artichoke Soup

To reduce sodium further, omit the cream of asparagus soup and then double the evaporated skim milk content, add a small can of no-salt-added asparagus and 1 tablespoon of cornstarch saving roughly 100mg sodium per serving. Use salt-free broth for savings of 150mg per serving.

Curried Pumpkin Soup
Yield: 8 servings

1 large onion, chopped
1 clove garlic, minced
1 tablespoon tub margarine
One 16-ounce can solid pack pumpkin OR 2 cups
        pumpkin puree
1 1/2 tablespoons curry powder
1/4 teaspoon pepper
1/2 teaspoon lemon-pepper seasoning, salt-free
1 teaspoon sugar
1/4 teaspoon nutmeg
1 bay leaf
4 cups defatted chicken stock or broth, less salt
2 cups skim milk
1/4 cup toasted shredded coconut
1/2 cup or less toasted pumpkin seeds

In a nonstick skillet, sauté onion and garlic in margarine until very soft, about 5 minutes. Stir in pumpkin, curry, pepper, lemon-pepper, sugar, nutmeg, bay leaf and broth. Bring to a boil, reduce heat and simmer for 30 minutes. Remove from heat. Discard bay leaf. Stir in milk and reheat gently; do not boil. Serve garnished with toasted coconut and pumpkin seeds. If fresh pumpkin is available, use the inside for the pumpkin seeds and puree the meat. Then use the hollowed-out pumpkin for an attractive serving bowl. Freezes well.

Ashley Hamilton Higginbotham

	Cal	Fat(g)	% Fat Cal	Sat Fat(g)	Chol(mg)	Sod(mg)
Per Serving	108	3.9	31	1.7	7	392

Nutrition Nibble

1 cup evaporated skim milk = 0.5gm fat, 199 calories

1 cup half and half = 27.8gm fat, 315 calories

1 cup of heavy cream = 88gm fat, 820 calories

One Step Further

Curried Pumpkin Soup

To omit 1gm more fat per serving and cut more than 1/2 the saturated fat, omit the coconut.

Surprisingly Good Cheese Soup
Yield: 8 servings

1 tablespoon margarine
1 medium onion, chopped
2 carrots, chopped
2 stalks celery, chopped
1 tablespoon flour
1/2 teaspoon dry mustard
1/8 teaspoon black pepper
1/8 teaspoon white pepper
Dash of nutmeg
Dash of paprika
1 1/2 cups or one 12-ounce can evaporated skim milk
2 1/2 cups skim milk
2 beef bouillon cubes, reduced salt
5 ounces frozen green beans or chopped broccoli
2 cups water
6 ounces light Velveeta

In a nonstick skillet, sauté chopped vegetables in margarine for 5 minutes. Blend in flour, then seasonings, then evaporated milk and skim milk. Add cubes, beans and water. Simmer 30 minutes. Add cheese and stir until it melts. Do not boil.

Rosemary Gunning

A great meal for men "after the hunt or game," especially when served with mini loaves of bread and cold beer.

Rosemary Gunning

	Cal	Fat(g)	% Fat Cal	Sat Fat(g)	Chol(mg)	Sod(mg)
Per Serving	160	5.1	29	2.5	16	630

Crawfish and Broccoli Soup

Yield: 6 servings of 12 ounces each

1 tablespoon margarine
1 tablespoon oil
1 bunch green onions, chopped
1 bunch parsley, chopped
3 tablespoons flour
1 pint evaporated skim milk
1/2 teaspoon red pepper
1/2 teaspoon black pepper
1/2 teaspoon salt
1 pint 1% low fat milk
One 1-pound bag frozen broccoli cuts
1/2 cup water
1 pound crawfish tails, lightly rinsed and drained

In a nonstick skillet over medium heat, heat margarine and oil, then sauté onions and parsley until tender, about 15 minutes. Add flour and mix well. Slowly add the evaporated milk and seasonings and cook until it thickens; then add milk and cook 10 more minutes. Cook the broccoli cuts in water on high in the microwave for 10 minutes. When tender, drain and cut up any large pieces. Add crawfish and broccoli to the soup. Stir and cook on low 15 more minutes. Serve warm.

Mrs. Sherry H. Eubanks

	Cal	Fat(g)	% Fat Cal	Sat Fat(g)	Chol(mg)	Sod(mg)
Per Serving	255	7.6	27	2.3	113	456

Salads

1940s

1946
- ➤ Baton Rouge General Hospital
- ➤ Radio
- ➤ Recreation

1947
- ➤ East Baton Rouge Parish Library Story Hour

1948
- ➤ Children's Theater
- ➤ Christmas Bureau

Later, after the war, the Junior League moved away from the grim necessities of war volunteer work and helped the community recover its spirits by hiring a full-time recreational director for Victory Park. Children were entertained—and educated—by Story Hour at the local library, by Children's Theatre, and by a radio program bringing classic children's books to life. Already, though, a new era was beginning—television—which demonstrated in black-and-white the postwar prosperity the country was beginning to enjoy.

Mixed Greens with Warm Goat Cheese
Yield: 8 servings

Vinaigrette
2-3 green onions, minced
1/2 teaspoon garlic
1/3 cup sherry vinegar
1 tablespoon sugar
Few drops of lemon juice
1 tablespoon dijon mustard
3 tablespoons walnut or hazelnut oil
2/3 cup defatted chicken broth, less salt
2 tablespoons safflower oil
1/8 teaspoon salt
1/8 teaspoon pepper

Salad
2 large heads red tip lettuce
2 heads bibb or Boston lettuce
2-3 hearts of romaine lettuce
4-5 clumps maiche, arugula (seasonal) or watercress
1 head raddichio, cleaned (optional)
1 small bunch red seedless grapes, halved

Garnish
4 ounces mild but firm goat cheese (in a 1-inch diameter round)
Defatted chicken broth, less salt
2 tablespoons finely diced pecans
Minced fresh parsley
16 pecan halves

Whisk vinaigrette ingredients together in a blender and set aside. Prepare all lettuces and dry thoroughly. Toss lettuces, and grapes together. Slice goat cheese into rounds (1/4" thick, 1" diameter), then dip in chicken broth, minced pecans and parsley. Place on cookie sheet. Warm the goat cheese in a 325-degree oven. Toss salad with the dressing; arrange on plate. Sprinkle pecan halves with pepper, toast at 275 degrees for 3 to 6 minutes. Garnish with pecan halves and cheese rounds. Serve immediately with fresh cracked pepper.

Susan Saurage-Altenloh

	Cal	Fat(g)	% Fat Cal	Sat Fat(g)	Chol(mg)	Sod(mg)
Per Serving	219	17.5	67	3.4	14	254

This salad is easy in winter or summer and is a perfect accompaniment to chicken, pork, veal or beef. Substitute chunks of asiago cheese mixed into the salad for the warmed goat cheese. A nice winter switch: apple chunks instead of grape halves.

Susan Saurage-Altenloh

Nutrition Note

Mixed Greens with Warm Goat Cheese
This salad has 43gm less fat than the original, with close to only 1/2 the calories in saturated fat.

Curried Chicken Salad *With Mango Chutney*
Yield: 4 servings

1 pound skinless chicken, cooked, and cubed (2 1/4 cups)
2 cups seedless grapes or golden raisins
2-3 green onions, thinly sliced
1/4 cup lightly toasted chopped walnuts
1/4 cup low fat/low calorie mayonnaise
1/4 cup plain nonfat yogurt
1 teaspoon curry powder
Lettuce leaves
4 tablespoons mango chutney

In a bowl, combine first 7 ingredients. Chill for 2 to 3 hours. Serve on lettuce leaves with mango chutney on the side.

Shug Lockett (Mrs. Walker)

	Cal	Fat(g)	% Fat Cal	Sat Fat(g)	Chol(mg)	Sod(mg)
Per Serving	324	14.4	40	2.9	71	190

Avocado and Sunflower Seed *on Red Leaf*
Yield: 6 servings

1 head romaine or red leaf lettuce, torn into
    bite size pieces
1 avocado peeled, pitted and chopped (about 2/3 cup)
3 tablespoons lightly toasted sunflower seeds
1/4 cup minced onion
1/4 cup grated fresh Parmesan cheese
2 tablespoons white wine vinegar
1 1/2 tablespoons dijon mustard
1 tablespoon olive oil
1/4 cup defatted chicken broth, less salt
1/4 teaspoon fresh ground pepper
1/4 teaspoon salt

Place lettuce in large bowl. Add avocado and next four ingredients. Whisk vinegar and mustard in small bowl. Gradually whisk in oil and chicken broth. Season with salt

Nutrition Note

Avocado and Sunflower Seed

Although this recipe is still proportionally high in fat, it has close to only 1/3 of the fat of the original and less than 1/2 the calories. In this salad, fat is contributed by the avocado, sunflower seeds, cheese and oil. Omit salt for an additional savings per serving of 88mg sodium.

One Step Further

Curried Chicken Salad with Mango Chutney

To cut fat more, omit walnuts and add in 1/2 cup chopped water chestnuts. This will reduce over 4gm more fat per serving, bringing calories from fat to only 32%. Use a fat free mayonnaise and trim 4gm more fat per serving.

and pepper. Pour over salad and toss. This salad is very versatile. Change the type of nuts or cheeses for a different taste, e.g. walnuts and feta cheese.

Jean W. Comeaux

	Cal	Fat	% Fat Cal	Sat Fat	Chol	Sod
Per Serving	127	9.8	68	2	4	299

Confetti Fruit Aspic *with Avocado Dressing*
Yield: 8 servings

2 tablespoons gelatin
1 cup cold water
1 cup boiling water
3 tablespoons lemon juice
2/3 cup sugar
Two 16-ounce cans grapefruit sections, juice packed
One 15-ounce can pineapple chunks, juice packed
1 cup chopped celery
3 cups fresh apples, grapes, cherries, or other fruits
       (enough that you are just holding the fruit together
       with the gelatin)
1/2 cup lightly toasted slivered almonds

Dressing
1 avocado (2/3 cup)
3 tablespoons nonfat yogurt
1 dash Tabasco sauce
2 teaspoons lemon juice
1/4 cup low fat sour cream

Soften gelatin in 1 cup cold water. Dissolve in 1 cup boiling water, add lemon juice and sugar. Chill until almost set. Add fruit, celery and almonds. Chill. For dressing combine avocado and other ingredients in food processor. Serve dressing on the side. You may use any fruit in season. Keeps several days.

Mrs. C. Lenton Sartain
Mrs. Bill Bizzell

	Cal	Fat(g)	% Fat Cal	Sat Fat(g)	Chol(mg)	Sod(mg)
Per Serving	256	8	28	1.5	3	36

One Step Further

Confetti Fruit Aspic with Avocado Dressing
To cut fat further, omit almonds and save another 4gm fat per serving. Omit dressing and save more than 3.5gm fat.

🍄 69

Indian Spinach *with Apples, Raisins, and Peanuts*
Yield: 4 servings

1 package fresh spinach
1 1/2 cups chopped apples
1/2 cup golden raisins
1/4 cup unsalted roasted peanuts
2 tablespoons chopped green onions

Dressing
3 tablespoons white wine vinegar
1 1/2 tablespoons salad oil
2 tablespoons chutney
1 teaspoon sugar
1/4 teaspoon salt
3/4 teaspoon curry
1 teaspoon dry mustard
2 tablespoons defatted chicken broth, less salt

Mix dressing by combining all ingredients; shake well and chill. Wash and tear spinach. Sprinkle apples, raisins, peanuts, and green onions over spinach. Toss with dressing.

Debbie Heroman (Mrs. Richard)

	Cal	Fat(g)	% Fat Cal	Sat Fat(g)	Chol(mg)	Sod(mg)
Per Serving	230	10.4	40	1.4	trace	213

Autumn Salad *with Bleu Cheese*
Yield: 6 servings

1/4 cup orange juice
1/4 cup Canola oil
3 tablespoons apple cider vinegar
2-3 packets sugar substitute
1/4 teaspoon salt
1/8 teaspoon pepper
8 cups torn chilled salad greens
1 cup diced red apples
1/4 cup crumbled bleu cheese
1/4 cup chopped toasted pecans

Combine the first 6 ingredients in a jar. Cover and shake vigorously. Chill to blend flavors. Before preparing salad,

Nutrition Nibble

Nuts are high in fat and should be used in small amounts. Toasting nuts will enhance the flavor and allow you to use smaller quantities with better results.

Nutrition Note

Autumn Salad

This recipe has 13gm less fat per serving than the original, but is still high in total fat. Serve with a very low fat meal or omit the above oil, vinegar, sugar substitute, and salt and instead use a fat free/low calorie Italian dressing (3/4 cup) for an additional savings of 8.5gm fat and over 75 calories per serving.

chop the apples and put a little of the dressing on the apples to prevent them from browning. Shake dressing again and toss with salad greens, drained apples, and blue cheese. Garnish with toasted pecans.

Mrs. Robert W. Scheffy

	Cal	Fat(g)	% Fat Cal	Sat Fat(g)	Chol(mg)	Sod(mg)
Per Serving	168	14	75	2	4	177

Marinated Tomatoes
Yield: 8 servings

6 tomatoes, peeled and sliced
2 tablespoons salad oil
1/4 cup defatted chicken broth, less salt
1 tablespoon sugar or honey
1/4 cup chopped fresh parsley
1/4 cup chopped green onions
1/4 teaspoon pepper
1 clove garlic, minced
1/4 cup red wine vinegar
1/2 teaspoon salt
1/2 teaspoon thyme
1/2 teaspoon marjoram

Place tomatoes in shallow dish. Mix the remaining ingredients together in a bowl and pour over the tomatoes. Cover and marinate in refrigerator for 24 hours. Drain and serve on lettuce leaves. This is especially good when home grown tomatoes are available.

Glenda McCarty

	Cal	Fat(g)	% Fat Cal	Sat Fat(g)	Chol(mg)	Sod(mg)
Per Serving	47	2.4	44	0.3	trace	123

One summer we had an "automatic" garden. It was a tiny patch behind the garage that we planted with a few basic vegetables. It became "automatic" when our elderly but remarkably spry neighbor spotted our efforts. From that day forward the garden never had a weed. And when a tomato reached its peak ripeness, it would magically appear on our front porch when we came home from work that day.

Nutrition Note

Marinated Tomatoes
Nutrition information is based on at least 1/2 of the marinade drained off and discarded.

One Step Further

Marinated Tomatoes
Omit the salt and save over 100mg more sodium per serving— most of us will not miss it with all the other wonderful flavors!

71

Southwestern Fruit Salad
Yield: 8 servings

1 cup seedless grapes
1 cup diced mangoes or papayas
2 oranges, peeled and sliced
1 cup peeled, sliced kiwis
1 cup berries (strawberries, raspberries, or blueberries)
5 tablespoons confectioners sugar
3 tablespoons Triple Sec
3 tablespoons tequila
1 1/2 tablespoons lime juice

Combine all of the fruits in a large bowl. Combine the sugar, Triple Sec, tequila and lime juice in a jar and shake to thoroughly combine. Pour over fruit and gently stir to coat fruit. Good as a dessert or salad. Serve alone or with orange sorbet. Try with less sugar and/or less liquor.

Joan W. Chastain

	Cal	Fat(g)	% Fat Cal	Sat Fat(g)	Chol(mg)	Sod(mg)
Per Serving	106	0.4	3%	trace	0	2

21% of calories from alcohol, 3.3gm per serving

Oriental Cabbage *with Sesame Seeds & Almonds*
Yield: 4 servings

1 tablespoon olive oil
3 tablespoons sugar
1/3 cup defatted chicken broth, less salt
4 tablespoons raspberry vinegar
Flavor packet from chicken flavored Oriental soup mix
1/4 cup slivered almonds
1 tablespoon sesame seeds
Noodles from chicken flavored Oriental soup mix
3 cups shredded cabbage
6 green onions, chopped

Make dressing by mixing first 5 ingredients well. Brown almonds and sesame seeds in 275 degree oven for 3 to 6 minutes, stirring often. Break up noodles in small pieces and mix with cabbage, onions, almonds, and sesame

Nutrition Note

Oriental Cabbage

This recipe is almost free of cholesterol, low in saturated fat and has less than 1/3 the fat and 1/2 the calories of the original version. To cut the sodium/salt content try using just 1/2 of the Oriental soup mix flavor package.

seeds. Right before serving toss salad with dressing and serve immediately.

Barbara Hornbeck (Mrs. Donald)
Lisa Town

	Cal	Fat(g)	% Fat Cal	Sat Fat(g)	Chol(mg)	Sod(mg)
Per Serving	236	12.5	46	2.6	trace	530

Spicy Tomato Aspic *with Artichoke Hearts or Seafood*
Yield: 16 servings

4 envelopes plain gelatin
One 48-ounce can vegetable juice, low sodium
1 cup whole parsley
3 pods garlic
2 cups finely chopped celery
1 cup finely chopped green pepper
1/2 cup chopped green onion
3 tablespoons fresh lemon juice
1 tablespoon Louisiana hot sauce
3 tablespoons Worcestershire sauce
1/2 teaspoon salt
2 teaspoons ground celery seed
Two 8 1/2-ounce cans artichoke hearts, drained OR
    1-2 cups chopped cooked shrimp OR
    1-2 cups crabmeat

Dissolve gelatin in 4 ounces of vegetable juice. Simmer parsley and garlic in the rest of the juice for 10 minutes. Strain and pour into gelatin. Cool. Add all other ingredients except artichoke hearts or seafood. Grease individual molds with nonstick spray. Pour into molds. Add artichoke hearts or seafood to molds. (Artichoke hearts should be put into middle; shrimp or crab is scattered about.) Chill and serve on lettuce or alone with dollop of homemade mayonnaise. Better yet, try reduced calorie mayonnaise or nonfat yogurt with a touch of dijon mustard blended in.

Mary Terrell Joseph

	Cal	Fat	% Fat Cal	Sat Fat	Chol	Sod
Per Serving	40	0.1	2	trace	0	167

Nutrition Note

Spicy Tomato Aspic
If you replace artichokes with shrimp, fat per serving slightly increases to 0.3gm and cholesterol to 31mg, with only 5% of the calories from fat.

Raspberry and Applesauce Mold

Yield: 6 servings

One 0.33-ounce package sugar-free raspberry gelatin
  dessert
1/2 cup water
One 12-ounce bag of frozen raspberries, thawed
1 cup applesauce, no sugar added
2 teaspoons lemon juice, divided
Lettuce leaves
1/4 cup nonfat plain yogurt
1/4 cup light sour cream
1/4 cup toasted chopped pecans or walnuts

Dissolve gelatin in boiling water. Add raspberries, applesauce, and 1 teaspoon lemon juice. Pour into 8-inch
square glass container and refrigerate until congealed. Cut
into squares, serve on a lettuce leaf. Top with mixture of
yogurt, sour cream, and remaining lemon juice. Sprinkle
with nuts.

Shug Lockett (Mrs. Walker)

	Cal	Fat(g)	% Fat Cal	Sat Fat(g)	Chol(mg)	Sod(mg)
Per Serving	133	4.4	29	1	4	53

Romaine *with Mandarin Oranges & Raspberry Vinaigrette*

Yield: 4 servings

1/4 head iceberg lettuce
1/4 bunch romaine lettuce
1 ounce Canadian bacon, cut in thin short strips and
  browned
One 11-ounce can mandarin oranges drained, reserve 3
  tablespoons liquid
2 tablespoons sugar
2 tablespoons raspberry vinegar
1 tablespoon olive oil
1/2 teaspoon pepper
1/4 cup sliced toasted almonds

Tear lettuce into bite-size pieces. Add bacon and mandarin oranges. Mix reserved mandarin orange liquid,

Nutrition Note

Raspberry and Applesauce Mold

Omitting the topping and nuts can save most of the fat content. Nonfat yogurt alone can be used – plain or lightly sweetened with lemon added – or use nonfat vanilla yogurt.

sugar, vinegar and olive oil. Pour dressing over lettuce, bacon and oranges; toss well. Serve with pepper and almonds on top. See "Something Extra" section for raspberry vinegar recipe.

Joan M. Surso

	Cal	Fat(g)	% Fat Cal	Sat Fat(g)	Chol(mg)	Sod(mg)
Per Serving	145	6.8	42	0.9	3	76

Cranberry/Pineapple Mold *with Pecans*
Yield: 8 servings

One 3-ounce package sugar-free cherry-flavored gelatin
1 cup hot water
1 envelope plain gelatin
1/4 cup cold water
1 tablespoon lemon juice
1/2 cup sugar
1 cup pineapple juice
1 cup crushed pineapple, juice packed
1 cup ground raw cranberries
1 cup finely chopped celery
1/2 cup finely chopped nuts (pecans or walnuts)

Dissolve cherry gelatin in hot water. Let cool. Dissolve plain gelatin in cold water. Combine both gelatins with rest of ingredients and refrigerate in a 2-quart mold until set.

Mignonne Y. White
from my mother-in-law, Edith White

	Cal	Fat(g)	% Fat Cal	Sat Fat(g)	Chol(mg)	Sod(mg)
Per Serving	132	3	19	0.2	0	54

Nutrition Note

Cranberry/ Pineapple Mold with Pecans
This recipe has less than 1/2 the calories and fat of the original.

Fruit Compote
Yield: 6 Servings

2 cups diced watermelon (or use melon scoop to make
    balls)
1 cup diced cantaloupe (or use melon scoop to make balls)
1 cup red or green seedless grapes
1 cup blueberries (Can also use any fresh fruit available
    such as strawberries, peaches, kiwis, honeydew, etc.)
1 tablespoon shredded orange peel
3/4 cup orange juice
2 tablespoons Kirsch or orange flavored liqueur (optional)
2 tablespoons sugar

Layer fruit in a pretty crystal serving bowl or 6 8-ounce
glasses. Stir remaining ingredients together until sugar is
dissolved. Pour over fruit. Chill at least 1 hour.

Mrs. Wray E. Robinson

	Cal	Fat(g)	% Fat Cal	Sat Fat(g)	Chol(mg)	Sod(mg)
Per Serving	72	<1	4	trace	0	4

Broccoli Salad *(to President's taste)*
Yield: 8 servings

2 bunches fresh broccoli
2 small white onions sliced in rings
2/3 cup chopped parsley
2 cloves garlic, minced
1/4 teaspoon salt
1/2 teaspoon pepper
2 tablespoons olive oil
1/4 cup tarragon vinegar
1/4 cup orange juice
1 tablespoon honey
1/4 cup nonfat plain yogurt
2 tablespoons dijon mustard
3 slices turkey bacon, cooked and crumbled

One Step Further

Broccoli Salad
To reduce sodium further, omit salt for a savings of over 65mg sodium per serving.

Split broccoli stems and flowers (discard at least 1/2 of the
stems). Slice and wash in warm water. Drain well and put
in plastic zipper bag. Mix onion rings, parsley, garlic, salt
and pepper. Add to broccoli. Beat oil, vinegar, orange

juice, honey, yogurt and mustard until creamy. Pour over salad. Let sit a day in refrigerator if possible. Toss with bacon when ready to serve.

Katherine B. Melius

	Cal	Fat(g)	% Fat Cal	Sat Fat(g)	Chol(mg)	Sod(mg)
Per Serving	108	5.2	43	0.9	4	272

Marinated Yellow Squash
Yield: 10 servings

5 medium yellow squash (1 1/2 pounds)
1/2 cup thinly sliced green onion
1/2 cup julienned green pepper
1/2 cup diagonally sliced celery
2 tablespoons wine vinegar
1/2 cup sugar
1/2 teaspoon salt
1/2 teaspoon pepper
3 tablespoons canola salad oil
1/2 cup cider vinegar
1 clove garlic, crushed
1/4 cup freshly chopped parsley

Slice squash, place in colander and blanch by lowering into boiling water for 15-30 seconds. Immediately lower colander into ice cold water, remove and drain well. Combine squash, onion, green pepper, and celery in large bowl. Toss lightly. Combine wine vinegar, sugar, salt, pepper, salad oil, cider vinegar, garlic, and parsley. Stir well and spoon over vegetables. Chill at least 12 hours, stirring occasionally. Drain and serve.

Miriam Y. Byars

	Cal	Fat(g)	% Fat Cal	Sat Fat(g)	Chol(mg)	Sod(mg)
Per Serving	65	2.9	38	0.2	0	89

Nutrition Note

Marinated Yellow Squash
Nutritional information based on at least 1/3 of the marinade drained off, about 4 tablespoons.

Marinated Shoe Peg Corn *with Pimento*
Yield: 10 servings

Four 11-ounce cans white shoe peg corn, rinsed and
    drained
One 2-ounce jar chopped pimento
1/2 cup chopped green onions
1/2 cup chopped green pepper
2 stalks celery, chopped
1/4 cup sugar
1/4 cup vegetable oil
1/2 cup vinegar
1/4 teaspoon salt
1 teaspoon pepper
1/4 cup defatted chicken broth, less salt

Combine vegetables and toss. Mix remaining ingredients
until dissolved. (You may heat to speed up this process. If
so, cool well before combining with vegetables.) Toss with
vegetables. Cover and chill several hours, overnight is better. Drain well before serving or ladle with slotted spoon.
Serve on lettuce leaf or plain as an accompaniment. Keeps
well.

Marie L. Gastinel

	Cal	Fat	% Fat Cal	Sat Fat	Chol	Sod
Per Serving	111	3	24	0.4	trace	305

Chilled Black Beans and Rice *on Iceberg*
Yield: 6 servings

1 cup raw rice
One 14- or 15-ounce can black beans, rinsed and drained
1/2 cup low fat Italian salad dressing, divided
1 head iceberg lettuce, shredded
1/2 cup chopped black olives
2-3 green onions, chopped
1 large tomato, chopped
1/2 cup shredded reduced fat sharp cheddar cheese

Cook rice according to directions but do not add salt.
Marinate rice in 1/4 cup of salad dressing for 3 to 4
hours. Marinate beans in 1/4 cup of salad dressing for

One Step Further

**Marinated Shoe
Peg Corn with
Pimento**
Omit salt and use
frozen corn or low sodi-
um canned corn and
save at least 250mg
more sodium.

Nutrition Note

**Marinated Shoe
Peg Corn with
Pimento**
Nutrition information is
based on at least 1/2
of the marinade
drained off.

**Chilled Black Beans
and Rice**
Use a mixture of let-
tuces such as red-tip,
romaine, spinach, leaf
lettuces, etc., added to
the iceberg for
increased color, interest
and nutrients. To
reduce the sodium con-
tent, omit the olives and
you'll save approxi-
mately 175mg sodium
per serving and about
2gm fat!

78

same length of time. When ready to serve, layer salad on large platter as follows: lettuce, marinated rice, marinated beans, olives, onions, tomatoes, and cheese. May also top with nonfat plain yogurt or reduced fat sour cream.

Shug Lockett (Mrs. Walker)

	Cal	Fat(g)	% Fat Cal	Sat Fat(g)	Chol(mg)	Sod(mg)
Per Serving	292	6.6	20	1.7	8	400

Andalusion Salad
Yield: 12 servings

2 cans artichoke hearts, lightly rinsed, drained and
    sectioned
2 cans hearts of palms, drained and sectioned
3 tomatoes, cut into thin wedges
One 3 1/4-ounce can pitted black olives, drained and
    halved
1 purple onion, thinly sliced
1 clove garlic, minced
1/4 cup vegetable oil
1/2 cup white vinegar
1/4 cup defatted chicken broth, less salt
1 teaspoon lemon juice
1 1/2 tablespoons Worcestershire sauce
1/3 cup sugar
2 tablespoon sweet basil
1/2 teaspoon black pepper
Red leaf lettuce

Combine all ingredients and marinate in an airtight container 24 to 48 hours. Stir a couple of times a day. This salad is better the longer it marinates, up to 3 to 4 days, before serving. Drain vegetables well and serve on a bed of red leaf lettuce on individual serving plates.

Karen Brannon Deumite

	Cal	Fat(g)	% Fat Cal	Sat Fat(g)	Chol(mg)	Sod(mg)
Per Serving	77	4	45	0.5	trace	164

Nutrition Note

Andalusion Salad
Olive oil is especially good in this salad and is authentic to its name, but any good vegetable oil may be used. Nutrition information is based on at least 1/2 the marinade, about 1/2 cup, drained and discarded.

Marinated Corn *with Artichokes*
Yield: 6 servings

One 6-ounce jar marinated artichoke hearts, cut in pieces
One 17-ounce can whole kernel corn, rinsed and drained
1 large stalk celery, diced
1/2 green pepper, diced
2 ounces sliced black olives
1 green onion, sliced thinly
1 medium tomato, cut in chunks
1 tablespoon lemon juice
3/4 teaspoon garlic powder
1 teaspoon basil
1/2 teaspoon coarsely ground black pepper

Drain artichokes, reserving marinade. Place marinated artichokes in a bowl. Combine with corn, celery, green pepper, black olives, green onion and tomato. Combine artichoke marinade with lemon juice, garlic powder, basil and pepper. Pour over artichoke/corn mixture, tossing lightly. Cover and chill several hours (preferably overnight) to blend flavors, tossing once or twice.

Karen Brannon Deumite

	Cal	Fat(g)	% Fat Cal	Sat Fat(g)	Chol(mg)	Sod(mg)
Per Serving	120	5.4	38	0.8	0	338

Marinated Crabmeat Salad
Yield: 4 servings

1 medium onion, finely chopped
1 pound lump crabmeat
1/8 teaspoon salt
1/4 teaspoon pepper
1/3 cup oil
1/3 cup apple cider vinegar
1/3 cup ice water

In a dish that can be covered and refrigerated, layer half of the chopped onion. Then layer the crabmeat. Sprinkle with salt and pepper. Top with the remaining onion. Mix oil, vinegar, and ice water. Pour over the crabmeat and onion. Cover and marinate overnight. Toss gently before

One Step Further

Marinated Corn with Artichokes
More fat and calories can be cut by discarding the marinade and adding low calorie/low fat Italian dressing (about 4 tablespoons). Sodium can be trimmed further by using no-salt-added canned or frozen corn, saving 150 to 200mg per serving!

Nutrition Note

Marinated Crabmeat Salad
Nutritional information is based on at least 1/2 of the marinade drained off and discarded.

serving and then drain well. Serve on lettuce with tomato wedges and fresh parsley.

Mrs. Robert V. McAnelly

	Cal	Fat(g)	% Fat Cal	Sat Fat(g)	Chol(mg)	Sod(mg)
Per Serving	201	10.9	49	1.4	108	309

Fresh Spinach *with Strawberries and Pecans*
Yield: 8 servings

Poppy Seed Dressing
2/3 cup white vinegar
1 1/2 cups sugar
1 cup chopped green onions
1 teaspoon salt
2 teaspoons dry mustard
2/3 cups salad oil
1 1/3 cups defatted chicken broth, less salt
3 tablespoons poppy seeds

Caramelized Pecans
1/2 cup sugar
1/2 cup chopped pecans

Salad
2 bunches fresh spinach
6 stalks celery, sliced
1 pint sliced strawberries

Mix first 5 ingredients in a blender. Slowly add oil and chicken broth. Stir in poppy seeds. Cook pecans and sugar until browned on low temperature in a heavy skillet. Cool immediately. (Dressing and caramelized pecans can be made 1 to 4 days ahead.) Mix spinach, celery, and strawberries. Toss with one cup of dressing. Garnish each serving with 1 tablespoon of the caramelized pecans. Extra dressing, even a week later, is great over fresh fruit.

Carole Wimberly (Mrs. Kenneth)

	Cal	Fat	% Fat Cal	Sat Fat	Chol	Sod
Per Serving	210	10.5	41	1.1	trace	186

Nutrition Note

Fresh Spinach
Although this salad is still moderately high in fat, it has less than 1/2 the fat, saturated fat and calories found in the original.

Sensation Salad

Yield: 1 1/4 cups dressing, 20 servings of 1 tablespoon each

1/2 teaspoon plain gelatin
4 tablespoons cold water, divided
3 tablespoons lemon juice
2 tablespoons wine vinegar
1/2 cup defatted chicken broth, less salt
3 garlic cloves, pressed
1/4 teaspoon salt
Pinch red pepper
1/2 teaspoon grated black pepper
1 bunch parsley, chopped
2 tablespoons olive oil
3 pounds mixed lettuce greens
3/4 cup freshly grated Romano cheese
1/4 cup crumbled bleu cheese

Sprinkle gelatin over 2 tablespoons of cold water. Let stand about 1 minute. Combine remaining water, lemon juice, vinegar, broth, garlic, salt, peppers and several tablespoons of parsley. Bring to a boil. Remove from heat and stir in gelatin mixture and olive oil. Chill. Whisk before tossing over lettuce and remaining parsley. Sprinkle cheeses and toss again. Add freshly grated black pepper to taste. Enough dressing for 3 pounds (20 cups) of mixed lettuce greens.

Mrs. James F. Pierson, Jr.
River Road Recipes II, page 38

Original Recipe

	Cal	Fat(g)	% Fat Cal	Sat Fat(g)	Chol(mg)	Sod(mg)
Per Serving	138	13.1	85	2.9	8	187

Lightened Recipe

	Cal	Fat(g)	% Fat Cal	Sat Fat(g)	Chol(mg)	Sod(mg)
Per Serving	50	3.3	59	1.4	7	132

Nutrition Nibble

Salad greens and vegetables are low fat and low-calorie items. The items we add to enhance taste become the major source of fat and calories and will make the percentage of fat seem unusually high. Classic salad items high in fat include cheeses, nuts, avocados, olives and, of course, the salad dressing. Some of our lightened salads appear proportionately high in fat; however, they are lower in fat than the original versions.

One Step Further

Sensation Salad
This version has only 1/4 the fat of the original. To trim further, omit bleu cheese and reduce Romano cheese to 1/2 cup, trimming off close to 1gm fat from each serving and 40mg sodium.

Marinated Shrimp and Rotini *with Anise*
Yield: 8 servings

1 1/2 pounds boiled and peeled shrimp
1/4 cup chopped celery
1/4 cup ripe olives
1/4 cup pimento-stuffed olives
One 4-ounce can mushrooms
1 package frozen snow peas, thawed
1/4 teaspoon anise seed
1 teaspoon white wine
One 8-ounce bottle low fat/low calorie Italian dressing
1/2 cup freshly grated Parmesan cheese
1 cup dry rotini pasta, boiled and cooled
Parsley to taste

Mix all ingredients. Sprinkle extra cheese on top to taste.

Laura Clark

	Cal	Fat(g)	% Fat Cal	Sat Fat(g)	Chol(mg)	Sod(mg)
Per Serving	233	8	31	2.1	138	805

Smoked Chicken Salad
Yield: 4 1/2 dozen tea sandwiches or 2 2/3 cups filling or spread

6 boneless chicken breast halves, smoked and skinned
1 cup low fat mayonnaise
3 stalks celery, minced
2 tablespoons minced green onion
1 teaspoon light Creole seasoning
1/4 teaspoon black pepper
26 slices whole wheat bread

Blend chicken with mayonnaise. Add celery, green onions, Creole seasoning and pepper. Refrigerate. Spread mixture on half the bread and top with remaining bread. Cut each sandwich into four pieces. Or may serve on a bed of salad greens or stuff inside a tomato.

Lisa Town

	Cal	Fat(g)	% Fat Cal	Sat Fat(g)	Chol(mg)	Sod(mg)
Per Serving	61	2.1	30	0.4	8	132

One Step Further

Smoked Chicken Salad
Cut the fat by 1/3 by replacing 1/2 the mayonnaise with nonfat plain yogurt.

Chilled Apple Rice Salad *with Pecans*
Yield: 6 servings

3 cups chilled cooked rice, no salt added
2 tablespoons golden raisins
2 tablespoons chopped parsley
1 Granny Smith apple, chopped in bite-size pieces
1/4 cup chopped toasted pecans
1 green onion, minced (including green portion)
Salad greens for garnish

Dressing
3 tablespoons olive oil
1/3 cup defatted chicken broth, less salt
1/3 cup red wine vinegar
1 tablespoon fresh lemon juice
1 clove garlic, minced
1 tablespoon sugar
1 teaspoon curry powder
1/4 teaspoon salt
1/8 teaspoon freshly ground black pepper
Dash of red pepper

Mix together salad ingredients. Chill. Combine dressing ingredients. Just before serving, dress and toss salad.

Donna West

	Cal	Fat(g)	% Fat Cal	Sat Fat(g)	Chol(mg)	Sod(mg)
Per Serving	270	10.3	34	1.3	<1	130

Nutrition Nibble

Chicken, seafood or other broths can be used in recipes to replace or decrease the amount of oil used to sauté ingredients and for other purposes.

Chicken and Potato Salad *with Pesto & Red Pepper*
Yield: 6 servings

1 1/2-2 pounds boneless, skinless chicken breast halves
1 pound red potatoes
1/2 teaspoon salt, divided
1 or 2 red bell peppers, cut in thin strips

Pesto
1/2 cup fresh basil leaves
2 cloves garlic
2 tablespoons olive oil
1/3 cup defatted chicken broth, less salt
1/4 cup white wine vinegar
3 tablespoons freshly grated Parmesan cheese
3/4 teaspoon oregano
1/4 teaspoon freshly ground pepper (more if desired)
White wine or salt-free seasoning for poaching water

Poach chicken breasts in simmering water seasoned with white wine or salt-free seasoning for 15 minutes. Wrap tightly and chill. Cook potatoes in boiling water, seasoned with 1/4 teaspoon salt, for 15 minutes; cool and remove skin. Cube chicken and potatoes and place in large bowl with red pepper strips. **Pesto:** In food processor combine basil, garlic, oil, chicken broth, vinegar, cheese and oregano. Puree until smooth. Season with remaining salt and pepper. Pour over chicken salad to coat. Serve slightly chilled or at room temperature.

Gail Erickson Schroeder

	Cal	Fat(g)	% Fat Cal	Sat Fat(g)	Chol(mg)	Sod(mg)
Per Serving	266	8.6	29	2.2	73	338

Three Bean Salad

Yield: 10 servings

Dressing

1/4 cup defatted chicken broth, less salt
2 tablespoons olive oil
Juice of 2-3 lemons (1/2 cup)
2 tablespoons wine vinegar
1 teaspoon paprika
1/4 teaspoon salt
1 teaspoon minced garlic
1/2 teaspoon dry mustard
2 teaspoons sugar
1/2 teaspoon white pepper

Salad

One 18-ounce can kidney beans
One 18-ounce can garbanzo beans
One 18-ounce can black beans
4 green onions, sliced
1/2 cup chopped green or red bell pepper
3 tablespoons chopped parsley
2/3 cup chopped celery

Place dressing ingredients in glass jar and mix. Let stand for 45 minutes. Shake again when ready to use. Drain beans and rinse with cold water, draining again. Combine with onions, pepper, parsley, and celery. Add dressing and toss. Cover and chill. This salad will keep in refrigerator for 3 to 4 days. For a different angle on this dish, place a mound of water-packed tuna in center of beans. Garnish with tomato wedges, onion slices, and/or olives.

Mary Sue Slack

	Cal	Fat(g)	% Fat Cal	Sat Fat(g)	Chol(mg)	Sod(mg)
Per Serving	221	6.8	27	1.7	3	453

Nutrition Nibble

Oil-based salad dressings can be lightened by replacing some or all of the oil with broth, fruit or vegetable juices and wine. Using flavored oils helps a smaller quantity of oil lend more flavor. Every tablespoon of oil trimmed from the dressing saves 120 calories and over 13gm fat.

One Step Further

Three Bean Salad
Use freshly cooked dried or frozen beans to reduce the sodium further. Omit salt and save 53mg per serving.

Breads

1950s

In 1951, Puppet Theater began as an experimental one-man puppet show for first and second graders, allowing children who might never see a play to experience live theater. Puppet Theater continued as a League project for 30 years, enriching the lives of two generations of Baton Rouge children.

As the country entered into post-war prosperity, the Junior League of Baton Rouge changed its focus from wartime projects to topics of a lighter note—entertainment with an educational twist. It was the age of television, and shows such as "The Honeymooners," "I Love Lucy," "Gunsmoke," "What's My Line" and "Dragnet" were becoming American favorites. The Junior League got into the act with public service announcements developed in 1953-1955 to let the community know about programs of interest.

Grandma's Blueberry Brunchcake

Yield: 16 servings

1/3 cup tub margarine
3/4 cup sugar
1 whole egg plus 4 egg whites, lightly beaten
1 teaspoon baking powder
1/4 teaspoon salt
1 1/2 teaspoons soda
1 1/2 teaspoons almond extract
1 teaspoon vanilla extract
1/2 cup light sour cream
3/4 cup nonfat plain yogurt
2 cups unbleached white flour, sifted
2 cups fresh or frozen blueberries

Topping
2 tablespoons tub margarine
3/4 cup brown sugar
1/4 cup flour
1/2 teaspoon cinnamon

Preheat oven to 350 degrees. Cream margarine and sugar. Add egg, egg whites, baking powder, salt, soda and extracts. Blend together sour cream and yogurt. Alternating, add flour and sour cream mixture. Fold in blueberries. Do not over mix. Pour into a cake pan approximately 9x13x2 inches well sprayed with vegetable oil cooking spray. For the topping, cream margarine and brown sugar. Add flour and cinnamon to get a semi-dry and lumpy mixture. Sprinkle on top of the batter. Bake for 30 minutes or until a toothpick inserted in the center comes out clean. The topping should melt and partially sink into the batter.

Patty Young

Grandma never measures anything. So when I want one of her recipes, I have to go into the kitchen while she cooks, armed with a bevy of measuring tools. She scoops up a handful of flour. Then I coax her into dropping it into a measuring cup for that instant it takes me to document the amount. We then repeat the process with each pinch of seasoning, dollop of butter, splash of buttermilk. And despite all this scientific accuracy, it never tastes quite the same. Maybe it's her pots.

	Cal	Fat(g)	% Fat Cal	Sat Fat(g)	Chol(mg)	Sod(mg)
Per Serving	209	5.4	23	1.5	17	226

Apple and Banana Nut Muffins
Yield: 12 muffins

2 cups oat bran
1 tablespoon baking powder
1/3 cup sugar substitute
2 egg whites
2 tablespoons vegetable oil
3 tablespoons light syrup
1 cup skim milk
2 apples
2 ripe bananas
1/4 cup roasted pecans

Combine oat bran, baking powder, and sugar substitute. Mix egg whites, oil and syrup; beat until foamy. Add milk. In food processor chop apples, bananas and nuts. Mix with rest of ingredients in food processor until smooth. Pour into muffin tin that has been coated with vegetable spray. Bake at 400 degrees for 30 minutes.

Vickie B. Johnson

	Cal	Fat(g)	% Fat Cal	Sat Fat(g)	Chol(mg)	Sod(mg)
Per Serving	123	5.1	35	0.7	trace	103

Zucchini Bread
Yield: 2 loaves, 32 servings

1 whole egg plus 2 egg whites, slightly whipped
1 1/2 cups sugar
1/3 cup oil
2/3 cup nonfat plain yogurt
1 tablespoon vanilla
2 cups flour
1 tablespoon cinnamon
2 teaspoons soda
3/4 teaspoon salt
1/2 teaspoon baking powder
2 cups grated zucchini
1/3 cup chopped walnuts

Blend eggs, sugar, oil, yogurt and vanilla. In a separate bowl mix flour, cinnamon, soda, salt and baking powder

Nutrition Nibble

Toasted nuts: Spread nuts in single layer on a cookie sheet. Bake at 300 to 325 degrees for 5 to 10 minutes, until aromatic. Check and shake half way through; be sure not to burn. Cool and chop. This procedure enhances the flavor; less will taste like more.

Nutrition Note

Apple and Banana Nut Muffins

This recipe uses sugar substitute which is measured as sugar is measured. If using granulated sugar, use 1/3 cup (calories and carbohydrate content will increase some). Eight packages of sugar substitute may also be used instead. Omit the nuts and save an additional 1.5gm fat in every serving. This recipe is a good source of fiber.

and add to first mixture. Add zucchini and walnuts. Grease loaf pans and bake at 350 degrees for 45 minutes. **Variation:** Substitute 1 cup zucchini with 1/2 cup grated carrot, I large apple finely chopped and 1 tablespoon fresh orange zest.

Diane Foster

	Cal	Fat(g)	% Fat Cal	Sat Fat(g)	Chol(mg)	Sod(mg)
Per Serving	98	3.2	29	0.4	7	114

Apple Sausage Stuffing
Yield: 16 servings

1 pound lean pork sausage
1 cup chopped onion
1/2 cup chopped green onion
4 stalks celery, chopped
2 cloves garlic, minced
1 large Granny Smith apple, diced
1 cup diced dried apricots
1/3 cup currants
1/2 cup chopped parsley
7-8 cups crumbled french bread (16-ounce loaf)
Two 14.5-ounce cans defatted chicken broth, less salt
Poultry seasoning and ground sage to taste
1/3 cup pecans

Cook sausage, onion, green onion, celery and garlic until pink has gone from sausage. Drain sausage and vegetables on paper towels and pat top with towels to remove excess grease. Wipe skillet clean and return mixture to skillet. Add apple, apricots, currants and parsley to sausage mixture. Toss in crumbled french bread. Put in a 3-quart baking dish. Add 1 1/2 cans of chicken stock. Use extra stock if stuffing gets too dry. Add seasonings. Top with pecans. Bake 35 to 45 minutes at 350 degrees.

Mary R. Aycock

	Cal	Fat(g)	% Fat Cal	Sat Fat(g)	Chol(mg)	Sod(mg)
Per Serving	191	6	28	1.6	20	477

Nutrition Note

Apple Sausage Stuffing

This has less than 1/2 the fat and 1/3 the sodium of the original. To reduce both further, reduce or omit the sausage used.

Julie's "Jam-Dandy" Muffins
Yield: 10 muffins

1 2/3 cup all-purpose flour
1/2 cup sugar
2 teaspoons baking powder
1/4 teaspoon salt
1/4 teaspoon nutmeg or cinnamon
1/4 cup margarine
3/4 cup skim/low fat milk
1 egg
Jam or jelly, low sugar

In a medium bowl, combine flour, sugar, baking powder, salt and nutmeg. Cut in margarine until particles are fine. Add milk and egg; mix until thoroughly blended. Spoon into greased muffin tin. Put 1 teaspoon jam or jelly on top of each muffin; pressing slightly into batter. Bake at 400 degrees for 20 to 25 minutes.

Julie Mandich

	Cal	Fat(g)	% Fat Cal	Sat Fat(g)	Chol(mg)	Sod(mg)
Per Serving	175	5	27	1	22	185

Harvest Festival Muffins
Yield: 22 muffins

1/2 cup unsweetened applesauce
1/3 cup oil
2 egg whites plus 1 whole egg
1 1/2 cups sugar
2 1/2 cups flour
1 teaspoon soda
1 teaspoon salt
1 1/4 teaspoons baking powder
1 1/2 teaspoons cinnamon
1/2 cup chopped roasted pecans
3 cups chopped apples
4 ounces butterscotch chips (approximately 2/3 cup)

In a bowl combine applesauce, oil, eggs, and sugar. In another bowl mix flour, soda, salt, baking powder, cinnamon and then pour in the oil mixture. Stir in pecans and

Nutrition Note

Harvest Festival Muffins

This version has over 100 calories and 10gm less fat per serving than the original. For a tasty variation, omit the butterscotch and save 1.5gm fat—mostly saturated fat—per serving.

apples and pour batter into lined muffin cups. Sprinkle butterscotch chips over top of batter. Bake for 20 to 30 minutes at 350 degrees. Muffins are done when inserted toothpick comes out clean. These are best made the day before they are served.

Dot DeBossier

	Cal	Fat(g)	% Fat Cal	Sat Fat(g)	Chol(mg)	Sod(mg)
Per Serving	190	6.8	32	2.0	10	164

Butter Twists
Yield: 24 servings

3 tablespoons butter
1/4 cup tub margarine
1 cup warm water
1 package dry yeast
1 teaspoon sugar
1/3 cup sugar
3/4 teaspoon salt
1 egg plus 2 egg whites
4 cups flour

In a small saucepan heat butter until it is light brown and has a "nutty" smell. Stir in the margarine and set aside to cool. Place in large bowl the water, yeast and 1 teaspoon sugar. In a separate bowl combine remaining sugar, butter/margarine mixture and salt. Beat the eggs and add to the sugar, butter and salt mixture. Combine the two mixtures together and add flour. Mix well. Cover bowl and chill, refrigerating overnight. Four hours before you wish to bake, cut dough into 4 parts. Divide each part into 6 portions and roll into crescents or shape as you like. Place on vegetable oil sprayed tray and let rise for 4 hours. Bake at 350 degrees for 15 to 20 minutes. Freeze in plastic bag while still hot. When they are warmed they taste fresh baked.

Marilyn Dietz

	Cal	Fat(g)	% Fat Cal	Sat Fat(g)	Chol(mg)	Sod(mg)
Per Serving	117	3.3	25	1.3	13	113

One Step Further

Butter Twists

To cut cholesterol and saturated fat more, omit the butter and use a total of 1/2 cup of tub margarine. Tub margarine was used to replace a portion of the original butter to save cholesterol, fat and saturated fat. Heating the butter to a light brown intensifies the butter flavor, allowing us to use less.

Spinach Bread

Yield: 12 servings

One 10-ounce box frozen spinach
1/2 teaspoon garlic powder
2 tablespoons margarine, melted
1 loaf french bread
3/4 cup grated mozzarella cheese

Cook spinach and drain. Add garlic powder to taste. Add melted margarine. Slice bread down side and open. Spread on spinach mixture. Sprinkle cheese on top and bake at 375 degrees for 15 to 20 minutes.

Sherri C. McKay

	Cal	Fat(g)	% Fat Cal	Sat Fat(g)	Chol(mg)	Sod(mg)
Per Serving	145	4.5	28	1.3	4	277

Chive Bread

Yield: 1 loaf, 28 servings

1 package yeast
1/4 cup warm water
1/3 cup sugar, divided
1/4 cup potato flakes
1/2 cup tub margarine
1 1/4 teaspoons salt
1 1/4 cups scalded skim milk
1 egg
3 1/2 - 4 cups flour

Chive filling
1/3 cup chives
3/4 cup evaporated skim milk
1 egg white, beaten

Nutrition Nibble

Using evaporated skim milk to replace creams saves fat and calories. An added benefit is that it can be kept "fresh" on the shelf and ready to use for months!

Mix yeast, warm water, and 1 tablespoon of sugar. Set aside 5 minutes. With a heavy duty mixer, mix together potato flakes, remaining sugar, margarine, salt and milk. Add yeast mixture and egg. Add flour, one cup at a time. Knead 5 minutes. Place in bowl sprayed with vegetable oil cooking spray for at least 2 hours. In the meantime, make chive filling. Combine all the ingredients in a double boiler, and cook until thickened. When dough has risen, roll out into a 12x16-inch rectangle. Spread filling on dough and roll "jelly roll style" from the long edge. Shape into a spiral. Cut small slits on the top with scissors. Let rise again 1 hour. Bake at 350 degrees for 25 minutes.

Anne Marie Hicks

	Cal	Fat(g)	% Fat Cal	Sat Fat(g)	Chol(mg)	Sod(mg)
Per Serving	94	2.9	28	0.6	8	157

Pumpkin Waffles
Yield: 12 waffles, 6 servings of 2 each

1 large egg plus 2 egg whites, beaten
4 tablespoons brown sugar
1 cup evaporated skim milk
2 tablespoons vegetable oil
1/2 cup pumpkin puree, canned
2 teaspoons vanilla
1 cup all-purpose flour
2 teaspoons baking powder
1/4 teaspoon salt
1 1/2 teaspoons cinnamon
1/2 teaspoon nutmeg
1/4 teaspoon ginger
1/4 teaspoon cloves
1/2 cup finely diced apple
1/4 cup toasted walnuts

Beat together egg, egg whites, sugar, milk, oil, pumpkin and vanilla. Mix dry ingredients. Add to egg mixture. Do not over mix. Fold in apple and nuts. Make waffle with 3/4 cup of batter per waffle. Try topping with vanilla fla vored nonfat yogurt or spiced apples. Also try making with half whole wheat flour for a heartier flavor and added fiber.

Melanie Prejean Sullivan

	Cal	Fat(g)	% Fat Cal	Sat Fat(g)	Chol(mg)	Sod(mg)
Per Serving	252	8.8	31	1.2	37	268

One Step Further

Pumpkin Waffles
This version saves over 11gm fat per serving! To trim further, omit the walnuts and save close to 3gm more fat.

Corn Muffins
Yield: 12 muffins

1 cup yellow corn meal
3/4 cup whole wheat flour
4 teaspoons baking powder
1 teaspoon Worcestershire sauce
1 1/2 cups skim milk
3 packages artificial sweetener
2 eggs
2 cups frozen corn or one 16-ounce can of corn

Mix dry ingredients. Add liquid and blend. Add corn. Spray muffin tin with vegetable oil cooking spray. Bake at 425 degrees for 20 to 25 minutes.

Amy Dixon

	Cal	Fat(g)	% Fat Cal	Sat Fat(g)	Chol(mg)	Sod(mg)
Per Serving	115	1.2	9	0.3	36	130

Apricot Bread
Yield: 2 loaves, 32 servings

3 cups flour
2 teaspoons baking powder
1 teaspoon baking soda
1/2 teaspoon salt
1/3 cup corn oil
1 cup brown sugar
1 tablespoon orange rind, grated fresh OR
        1/2 tablespoon dried
1/2 teaspoon almond extract
3 eggs
1/3 cup light sour cream
1 cup applesauce, unsweetened
One 6-ounce package apricots, diced

Sift flour with baking powder, soda and salt; set aside. In large bowl, combine oil, sugar, orange rind, almond extract, eggs, sour cream and applesauce. Mix thoroughly. Add dry ingredients and stir until thoroughly mixed. Fold in apricots. Pour into 2 greased 8-inch loaf pans.

One Step Further

Corn Muffins

To cut the cholesterol content in half, use just 1 whole egg and 2 egg whites. To reduce cholesterol to less than 1mg per muffin, omit whole eggs and use 4 egg whites or 1/2 cup cholesterol-free egg substitute.

Apricot Bread

To reduce the cholesterol content to less than 8mg per serving, use only 1 whole egg and 4 egg whites. 3/4 cup of cholesterol-free egg substitute can replace the eggs and bring cholesterol to a mere 1mg per slice.

Bake at 350 degrees for 40 minutes or until tests done. Remove from pan at once and cool on racks. May be frozen.

Sharon Randall Lanius

	Cal	Fat(g)	% Fat Cal	Sat Fat(g)	Chol(mg)	Sod(mg)
Per Serving	115	3.2	24	0.6	21	87

Adam's Autumn Biscuits
Yield: 24 biscuits

2 1/2 cups all-purpose flour
1 tablespoon baking powder
1/2 teaspoon salt
3 tablespoons brown sugar
1 teaspoon orange zest
1 teaspoon cinnamon
1/4 teaspoon nutmeg
1/2 cup margarine, chilled and cut into small bits
One 16-ounce can unsweetened pumpkin puree
2 tablespoons 1% or less buttermilk
1/2 cup white raisins
1/2 cup brown sugar

Preheat oven to 400 degrees. Sift the flour, baking powder, salt, brown sugar, orange zest, cinnamon and nutmeg into a mixing bowl. Using a pastry blender or food processor, cut the margarine into the flour mixture until it resembles very coarse meal. Add pumpkin and raisins. Pat the dough into 1/2 inch thickness on a well-floured surface. Cut out using a floured 1-inch cutter. Place biscuits on baking sheet sprayed with vegetable oil cooking spray. Brush biscuits with milk and top with 1 teaspoon brown sugar per biscuit.

Adam C. Aycock

	Cal	Fat(g)	% Fat Cal	Sat Fat(g)	Chol(mg)	Sod(mg)
Per Serving	121	3.9	29	0.8	trace	129

The ingredients may seem simple and humble. But the biscuits that come from Louisiana's ovens are anything but. Louisiana's culinary alchemists can indeed turn lead into gold. Golden towers of light flaky pastries that belie their humble beginnings.

97

Savory Sweet Potato Dressing
Yield: 12 servings

1/2 bunch celery, chopped
1 bunch green onions, chopped
4 medium onions, finely chopped
1/2 pound each ground round and ground lean pork
Pepper to taste
4 large sweet potatoes, peeled and boiled (2 pounds raw)
2/3 cup defatted chicken broth, less salt
1/2 loaf french bread, dampened and shredded

Brown the first 3 vegetables and meat together. Add pepper if desired. Drain in a colander to remove grease, pat with paper towels. Wipe pan with a paper towel, then return the drained meat mixture to the pan. Add the cooked and mashed sweet potatoes, along with chicken broth. Blend together. Then add shredded french bread and bake in a 300-degree oven for 1 1/2 hours.

Myrtle Levert

	Cal	Fat(g)	% Fat Cal	Sat Fat(g)	Chol(mg)	Sod(mg)
Per Serving	197	4.2	19	1.3	23	182

Ham and Cheese Brunch Rolls
Yield: 24 rolls

One 25-ounce package frozen Parkerhouse-style rolls
1 cup finely chopped ham, well trimmed OR 95% fat free
1/2 cup grated reduced fat sharp cheddar cheese
3 tablespoons grainy brown mustard
2 teaspoons prepared horseradish
1 teaspoon Worcestershire sauce

Allow the roll dough to thaw. Spread each roll into a 3" diameter circle. Combine the remaining 5 ingredients to make the filling. Put 1 heaping teaspoon of filling in the center of the circle. Bring the edges of the dough together to encase the filling in a ball of dough. Place each roll seam side down in a muffin pan sprayed with vegetable oil cooking spray. Allow the rolls to rise until doubled in size. Bake for 15 minutes at 350 degrees.

Sharon Randall Lanius

	Cal	Fat(g)	% Fat Cal	Sat Fat(g)	Chol(mg)	Sod(mg)
Per Serving	96	2.3	22	0.8	6	262

One Step Further

Ham and Cheese Brunch Rolls

These are moderate in sodium content. To reduce sodium try low sodium ham and a lower salt roll dough.

Sweet Potato Coffee Cake

Yield: 16 servings

2 teaspoons cinnamon
2 1/4 cups flour
1 1/2 teaspoons baking powder
1 teaspoon baking soda
1/2 teaspoon salt
1/2 cup tub margarine
1/2 cup brown sugar
1/2 cup sugar
2 egg whites plus 1 whole egg
1/2 cup light sour cream
2/3 cup cooked and mashed sweet potato
3/4 cup nonfat yogurt
2 teaspoons vanilla
Nut topping
1 tablespoon melted tub margarine

Nut Topping

1/3 cup brown sugar
2 tablespoons sugar
2 tablespoons wheat germ
1 teaspoon cinnamon
1/2 teaspoon nutmeg
1/2 cup chopped nuts

Combine first 5 dry ingredients. In a mixer, beat 1/2 cup margarine and sugars until well blended, adding eggs 1 at a time. Add sour cream, sweet potato, yogurt and vanilla. Gradually add dry ingredients. Prepare a 10-inch tube or bundt pan with vegetable oil cooking spray and dust with flour. Combine nut topping ingredients. Spread 1/2 of batter into pan, covering with 1/2 of nut topping. Spread remaining batter over topping. Stir 1 tablespoon margarine into remaining nut topping. Sprinkle over batter. Bake at 350 degrees for 50 to 60 minutes or until toothpick comes out clean. Cool 10 minutes.

Betsy Harper

	Cal	Fat(g)	% Fat Cal	Sat Fat(g)	Chol(mg)	Sod(mg)
Per Serving	247	8.9	32	1.9	17	253

The tiny community of Paincourtville boasts one of Louisiana's most beautiful small churches. . . . St. Elizabeth. And one of its best church fairs . . . the Harvest Festival. Every fall is a homecoming for the folks who have scattered far from the banks of Bayou LaFourche. And every fall they're welcomed by tables piled with the kinds of wonderful pastries that could only come from the small town parishioners who offer up their kitchens in tribute to their faith.

Perfectly Easy Popovers
Yield: 8 muffins

3/4 cup egg substitute OR 1 whole egg and 4 egg whites
1 1/4 cups skim milk
1 tablespoon melted diet margarine
1 1/4 cups white or blended grain flour
1/4 teaspoon salt

Put all ingredients in a large bowl and mix until just blended. Half fill muffin tins or popover pan sprayed with non-stick vegetable oil cooking spray. Place in center of cold oven and set the heat for 450 degrees. Bake for 15 minutes, then reduce heat to 350 degrees and bake for another 15 to 20 minutes. To be sure it's done, test one by removing it from the pan; it should be crisp outside and moist and tender inside. For whole-wheat popovers: use 2/3 cup whole-wheat flour and 1/3 cup white flour instead of all white flour. (Whole-wheat popovers will not rise as high as regular popovers.)

Susan Saurage-Altenloh

	Cal	Fat(g)	% Fat Cal	Sat Fat(g)	Chol(mg)	Sod(mg)
Per Serving	112	1.9	16	0.4	0	135

Banana Pecan Pancakes
Yield: 6 servings of three 3-inch pancakes

1/2 cup whole wheat flour
1/2 cup all-purpose flour
1 tablespoon sugar
2 teaspoons baking powder
1/4 teaspoon salt
3/4 teaspoon baking soda
2 egg whites OR 1/4 cup egg substitute
1/4 cup water
1/2 cup low fat buttermilk
1 tablespoon vegetable oil
2 bananas, chopped (approximately 1 1/2 cups)
1/4 cup chopped roasted pecans

Mix dry ingredients. Beat egg whites, water and buttermilk 30 seconds. Whisk together dry and liquid ingredients

Nutrition Note

Perfectly Easy Popovers

The secret in making good popovers is to start them in a cold oven. They rise 2 to 3 inches over the top of the pan before "popping over." Serve immediately with light cream cheese and sugarless fruit spread or honey. Try blended low fat ricotta cheese for a lower fat alternative to low fat cream cheese.

One Step Further

Banana Pecan Pancakes

This version saves 6gm fat and over 50 calories per serving from the original. Omit the nuts and save an additional 3gm fat and 30 calories per serving.

with the oil long enough to eliminate lumps. Fold in chopped bananas. Place batter on hot nonstick pancake grill treated with vegetable oil cooking spray. Place roasted pecans onto the uncooked surface and cook until bubbles appear. Turn and cook 3 more minutes.

Mark Waggenspack

	Cal	Fat(g)	% Fat Cal	Sat Fat(g)	Chol(mg)	Sod(mg)
Per Serving	184	6.5	31	0.8	<1	329

Joggers Bran Muffins
Yield: 21 muffins

1 cup sugar
1 whole egg plus 2 egg whites, well beaten
1/3 cup oil
2 1/2 cups flour
2 teaspoons soda
1/4 teaspoon salt
2 1/2 cups low fat buttermilk
4 cups bran cereal with raisins
Additional raisins, optional
1/2 cup toasted pecans or walnuts

Mix sugar, egg, egg whites and oil together in large bowl. Sift together in another bowl flour, soda, and salt. Alternating, add flour mixture and buttermilk to sugar mixture. Fold in cereal to make a loose mixture. If desired you can add more raisins or currants and 1/2 cup chopped pecans or walnuts. Bake at 350 degrees for 20 to 30 minutes. Recipe will keep up to 6 weeks in refrigerator in covered container. Take out as much as needed and bake. For an interesting variation, try adding crystallized ginger or lemon zest.

Kay Platte

	Cal	Fat(g)	% Fat Cal	Sat Fat(g)	Chol(mg)	Sod(mg)
Per Serving	183	6.0	29	0.9	11	210

One Step Further

Joggers Bran Muffins
Replace the egg with 2 additional whites or omit egg and egg whites and use 1/2 cup egg substitute to save an additional 10mg cholesterol per serving. Omit nuts and save close to 2gm fat per serving.

101

Morning Mabels Muffins
Yield: 18 muffins

2 cups flour
1 cup sugar
2 teaspoons soda
1/2 teaspoon baking powder
2 teaspoons cinnamon
1/4 teaspoon nutmeg
1/4 teaspoon salt
2 cups grated carrots
2 large Granny Smith apples, diced
1/2 cup lightly toasted pecans
3/4 cup white raisins
1/4 cup lightly toasted coconut
2 tablespoons vanilla
1 egg plus 4 egg whites, beaten
1/3 cup oil
1/3 cup unsweetened applesauce

Mix dry ingredients. Stir in by hand carrots, apples, pecans, raisins and coconut. Blend wet ingredients. Add to mixture. Don't over stir. Fill muffin tins sprayed with non-stick vegetable oil cooking spray. Bake 20 to 22 minutes at 350 degrees.

Carolyn Bercier Wilkinson

	Cal	Fat(g)	% Fat Cal	Sat Fat(g)	Chol(mg)	Sod(mg)
Per Serving	204	7	30	1.2	12	154

One Step Further

Morning Mabels Muffins

Eliminate cholesterol content by omitting the whole egg and using a total of 6 egg whites (or 3/4 cup) or use 3/4 cup egg substitute in place of egg and egg whites.

Cheese-Chive Biscuits
Yield: 2 dozen biscuits

2 cups all-purpose flour
1 tablespoon baking powder
3/4 teaspoon salt
1/4 cup tub margarine, well chilled
1/2 cup grated reduced fat sharp cheddar cheese
1/4 cup chopped fresh chives
1 cup skim milk
1 tablespoon tub margarine, melted

Preheat the oven to 450 degrees. In a large bowl, mix the flour, baking powder, and salt with a fork. With a pastry cutter, cut in the cold margarine until the mixture resembles coarse crumbs. Stir in the grated cheese and chives. Add the milk and stir just until the mixture forms a soft dough that pulls away from the side of the bowl. Turn the dough out onto a lightly floured surface; knead quickly to mix the dough thoroughly. Roll the dough out until 1/2 inch thick. Cut out biscuits with a floured biscuit cutter and place on an ungreased cookie sheet. Brush tops with melted margarine mixed with 2 teaspoons of water. Bake until golden brown, about 12 to 15 minutes.

Margo Bouanchaud, Unique Cuisine

	Cal	Fat(g)	% Fat Cal	Sat Fat(g)	Chol(mg)	Sod(mg)
Per Serving	65	2.3	33	0.6	2	158

Nanny's Coffee Cake
Yield: 12 servings

1/4 cup vegetable oil
1 cup sugar
1 egg and 2 egg whites, well beaten
1 cup light sour cream
1 teaspoon vanilla
2 cups flour
1 teaspoon baking powder
1 teaspoon baking soda
1/3 cup brown sugar
1/3 cup sugar
2 teaspoons cinnamon
1 1/2 tablespoons margarine
1 tablespoon water

Cream well the oil, sugar and eggs. Mix with the sour cream, vanilla, flour, baking powder and baking soda. Pour into a greased and floured 9-inch square pan. Blend brown sugar, sugar, cinnamon, margarine and water. Sprinkle this mixture over top of cake batter. Bake at 325 degrees for 45 minutes or until done.

Joan McLaughlin Surso
In loving memory of Mrs. Thomas (Nanny) Clark

	Cal	Fat(g)	% Fat Cal	Sat Fat(g)	Chol(mg)	Sod(mg)
Per Serving	266	9	30	2.5	26	134

One Step Further

Nanny's Coffee Cake

To cut cholesterol content to less than 9gm per serving, omit the whole egg and use a total of 1/2 cup egg whites or egg substitute.

Apple Nut Bread
Yield: 1 loaf, 16 servings

1/4 cup corn oil
3/4 cup sugar
4 egg whites OR 1/2 cup egg substitute
2 cups flour
1 teaspoon each baking soda and baking powder
1/4 teaspoon salt
1 1/2 cups diced apples, with peel
1/4 cup applesauce
1/3 cup pecans
1 teaspoon vanilla
1 tablespoon each sugar and cinnamon

Mix all ingredients except sugar and cinnamon, do not beat. Scoop into an ungreased loaf pan. Sprinkle sugar and cinnamon mixture over top. Bake at 350 degrees for 1 hour. Remove pan and set aside until cool. Remove carefully. Bananas will substitute nicely for apples.

Helen Lamont Worthen (Mrs. Mark S.)

	Cal	Fat(g)	% Fat Cal	Sat Fat(g)	Chol(mg)	Sod(mg)
Per Serving	152	5.1	30	0.6	0	117

Whole Wheat Yeast Muffins
Yield: 12 muffins

1 package dry yeast
1 cup warm water
1 teaspoon salt
2 tablespoons canola oil
1/4 cup brown sugar
1 1/4 cups whole wheat flour
1/4 cup wheat germ
1/2 cup oatmeal (old fashioned)

Dissolve yeast in water; let stand 5 minutes. Whisk in salt, oil and sugar. Briskly stir in whole wheat flour. Mix in remaining ingredients. Cover with towel and let rise 2 hours in a warm place. Stir down, divide batter into muffin tin coated with vegetable spray. Let rise 1 hour. Bake at 400 degrees for 15 minutes.

Susan Giglio

	Cal	Fat(g)	% Fat Cal	Sat Fat(g)	Chol(mg)	Sod(mg)
Per Serving	103	2.9	25	0.3	0	181

One Step Further

Apple Nut Bread
Omit nuts and save
2gm fat per serving.

Vegetables

1960s

1960
- Baton Rouge Speech and Hearing Foundation
- Louisiana Arts and Science Center

1964
- Baton Rouge Association for Retarded Children
- City Beautification

1965
- Baton Rouge Area Council on Alcoholism

1968
- Community Volunteer Bureau
- Handbook for the Handicapped

1969
- Baton Rouge Goals Congress
- East Baton Rouge Parish Family Court Volunteer Program
- Historical Preservation
- Keyettes Sponsorship

Musicals dominated the American theater in the '50s. "Oklahoma," "South Pacific," "Annie Get Your Gun," "My Fair Lady," "The Music Man" and "West Side Story," inspired the League to get the students of Baton Rouge involved in a series of Youth Concerts within the school system—and brought the great songs of the '50s and '60s to the stages of Baton Rouge as well as New York.

Seafood Stuffed Mirlitons
Yield: 16 stuffed halves

8 medium mirlitons
1/3 cup minced onions
2/3 cup chopped green onions
3 cloves garlic, minced
1/4 cup chopped parsley
2 tablespoons vegetable oil
2/3 cup defatted chicken or seafood broth, less salt
2 pounds raw shrimp, peeled and chopped
3/4 cup fresh bread crumbs, divided
1/2 teaspoon salt
1/2 teaspoon pepper
1/8 teaspoon Tabasco sauce
1/4 teaspoon liquid crab boil
1 egg, beaten
1 pound lump crabmeat

Cover mirlitons with water and boil until tender, about 1 hour. Cool and cut in half lengthwise. Scoop out tender pulp and reserve. Discard seeds and set shells aside for stuffing. Sauté onions, green onions, garlic, and parsley in oil for 5 minutes or until onions are clear. Add broth and shrimp and cook for 5 minutes. Add mirliton pulp, 1/2 cup bread crumbs, salt, pepper, Tabasco sauce, and crab boil and cook for 10 minutes. Add 1/4 cup more chicken or seafood broth if mixture is dry. Remove from heat and stir thoroughly. Add egg, return to heat, and cook 1 minute. Fold in handpicked lump crabmeat. Fill the mirliton shells and sprinkle with remaining bread crumbs. Bake at 375 degrees for 10 to 15 minutes or until bread crumbs are brown. May be prepared ahead of time as they freeze well.

Michelle Bienvenu

	Cal	Fat(g)	% Fat Cal	Sat Fat(g)	Chol(mg)	Sod(mg)
Per Serving	**150**	**3.7**	**22**	**0.6**	**121**	**277**

This is an excellent main dish for company. Mirlitons have a delicate flavor. This tastes similar to stuffed eggplant but better. Mirlitons are also known as chayote squash and as vegetable pears.

Michelle Bienvenu

Every summer our neighbor would plant a mirliton vine in her front yard. And all summer long it meandered across the lawn, propped up at random spots along the way by tomato stakes. After a while it grew as much in our imaginations as in her yard, until it became a terrifying leafy roller coaster. And then one day she would pick the mirlitons. And the next day the vine would be gone. And summer would be over.

Okra and Tomato Creole

Yield: 10 servings

8 cups sliced fresh okra (2 pounds)
2 cups peeled and chopped fresh tomatoes
1 cup chopped onion
3/4 cup chopped bell pepper
3/4 teaspoon salt
1 teaspoon red pepper

Spray a 4-quart dish with vegetable oil cooking spray. Combine all ingredients. Bake at 350 degrees uncovered for 1 hour. Stir about 3 times during the baking.

Glenda McCarty

	Cal	Fat(g)	% Fat Cal	Sat Fat(g)	Chol(mg)	Sod(mg)
Per Serving	46	0.4	6	trace	0	169

Tex Mex Black Beans

Yield: 10 servings of 1/2 cup each

1 pound black beans, soaked in cold water overnight
1 medium onion, chopped
2 green onions, chopped
1/2 green pepper, chopped
1/2 red pepper, chopped
4 cloves garlic, minced
One 16-ounce can tomatoes with peppers, drained
1 1/2 tablespoons red wine vinegar
1 tablespoon dried oregano
1 tablespoon ground cumin
3 tablespoons minced fresh coriander leaves
1/2 teaspoon salt
1/2 teaspoon pepper

Drain beans; rinse and drain 3 times. Place in large saucepan or stockpot with water to cover. Heat to boiling, skim and lower heat to simmer for 1 1/2 hours with pot partially covered. Add water if necessary to keep beans moist and stir occasionally. Meanwhile, sauté onions, green onions, peppers and garlic for 5 minutes in a skillet sprayed with vegetable oil cooking spray. Add tomatoes,

One Step Further

Tex Mex Black Beans

Omit salt and save over 100mg sodium per serving.

vinegar, oregano, cumin, coriander, salt and pepper and cook for 5 minutes. Remove from heat and add to beans. Simmer uncovered for 30 minutes until thickened. Serve over rice. When reheating beans, use low heat and add water if necessary. Do not scorch. Served over rice, this makes an excellent meatless meal. Good high fiber, low fat dish.

Helen House Boyer

	Cal	Fat(g)	% Fat Cal	Sat Fat(g)	Chol(mg)	Sod(mg)
Per Serving	147	1	5	0.2	0	246

Spinach Enchiladas may be served as part of a Mexican dinner, but I frequently use it to jazz up an otherwise "plain" dinner such as sliced ham, pork chops or baked chicken.

Spinach Enchiladas

Yield: 6 servings

1 10-ounce package frozen spinach
1 10 3/4-ounce can light cream of chicken soup
1/2 cup light sour cream
1/2 cup nonfat plain yogurt
1 tablespoon flour
1 teaspoon lemon juice
One 4-ounce can chopped green chilies, lightly rinsed
    and drained
2 green onions, chopped
1/2 cup grated Monterey Jack cheese
1 cup grated skim mozzarella cheese
6 flour tortillas

Cook spinach according to package directions. Drain thoroughly. Mix spinach with soup, sour cream, yogurt, flour, lemon juice and chilies. Set aside. Stir green onions with grated cheese. Place about 2 tablespoons of the cheese mixture on each tortilla. Roll and place seam side down into a glass 9x12-inch baking dish generously sprayed with vegetable oil cooking spray. Top with spinach sauce. Bake at 350 degrees for 20 to 30 minutes until just bubbly. Do not overcook or the tortillas will become tough. May be reheated in microwave.

Susan Samuel Travis

	Cal	Fat(g)	% Fat Cal	Sat Fat(g)	Chol(mg)	Sod(mg)
Per Serving	267	11	37	6.3	32	609

One Step Further

Spinach Enchiladas
Save another 2.4gm fat per serving by omitting the reduced fat sour cream and using a fat-free sour cream or nonfat plain yogurt.

Sweet Potatoes and Apples
Yield: 10 servings

8 sweet potatoes, partially boiled and thinly sliced
8 Granny Smith apples, peeled and thinly sliced
1 stick light margarine or 1/3 cup tub margarine
1 1/2 tablespoons cinnamon
2 teaspoons nutmeg
1 cup dark brown sugar
1/2 cup apple juice

Layer sweet potatoes and apples, alternating margarine, spices, sugar and apple juice in a 9x13-inch casserole dish. Cover with foil and bake at 350 degrees for 30 minutes or until apples are tender.

Margaret Gremillion

	Cal	Fat(g)	% Fat Cal	Sat Fat(g)	Chol(mg)	Sod(mg)
Per Serving	274	5.4	17	1.0	0	58

Tomatoes Rockefeller
Yield: 6 servings of 2 slices each

Two 10-ounce packages frozen chopped spinach
1 teaspoon each oregano and basil
2 cups plain bread crumbs
2 bunches green onions, chopped
1 1/2 cups of egg substitute
2 tablespoons melted margarine
1/2 cup freshly grated Parmesan cheese
2 teaspoons Worcestershire sauce
1 teaspoon minced garlic
1/2 teaspoon black pepper
1 teaspoon thyme
1/4 teaspoon Tabasco sauce
2 tablespoons parsley
3 tablespoons flour
1/3 cup defatted chicken broth, less salt
1/3 cup white wine
12 thick tomato slices

Cook spinach according to directions; do not drain. Add remaining ingredients except tomatoes. Place tomato slices

Nutrition Note

Tomatoes Rockefeller
Very colorful and delicious dish with 1/3 less calories, 20gm less fat, 14gm less saturated fat – the "bad" fat – and less than 2/3 the sodium of the original.

in a single layer on a baking dish sprayed with vegetable oil cooking spray. Place a mound of spinach mixture on each tomato slice. Bake at 350 degrees for about 15 minutes or until topping sets a bit. Topping freezes well and may be thinned with a little wine or chicken broth to cover more slices.

Ashley Hamilton Higginbotham

	Cal	Fat(g)	% Fat Cal	Sat Fat(g)	Chol(mg)	Sod(mg)
Per Serving	300	9.3	27	3.1	10	628

Okra Stew
Yield: 10 servings

One 8-ounce package frozen baby lima beans
1 tablespoon oil
1 pound fresh okra, sliced crosswise, OR
　One 16-ounce package frozen okra
1/2 pound smoked turkey sausage, reduced fat
1 cup chopped onions
1/2 cup chopped bell pepper
1/2 cup chopped green onions
2 cloves garlic, minced
1/4 teaspoon salt
1/2 teaspoon pepper
1/2 pound shrimp, peeled and deveined
One 16-ounce can tomatoes, chopped

Cook lima beans until soft. Meanwhile, in a large skillet, place oil, okra, sausage and all seasonings. Cook on medium heat until okra is tender crisp and, if fresh, until all traces of "slime" have been removed. Add shrimp and cook on low heat until shrimp are done, about 5 minutes. Add tomatoes, cook 10 minutes, then add the lima beans and simmer an additional 15 minutes. Serve over rice.

Mary Elizabeth Cash

	Cal	Fat(g)	% Fat Cal	Sat Fat(g)	Chol(mg)	Sod(mg)
Per Serving	127	3.5	24	0.8	49	370

Nutrition Note

Okra Stew
Use a 16-ounce package of lima beans to increase the fiber and protein; then serve over rice as an excellent low fat entrée.

One Step Further

Okra Stew
Reduce sodium by an additional 120mg by using no-salt-added tomatoes and omitting salt. Add 1 teaspoon basil and 1/4 cup fresh parsley.

Corn Pudding

Yield: 8 servings

One 16-ounce bag frozen cut corn
1/2 cup egg substitute
1 1/2 cups skim milk
1/4 cup sugar
1/4 teaspoon salt

Pour all ingredients into blender. Blend until slushy. Pour into a 2-quart casserole dish which has been sprayed with vegetable oil cooking spray. Bake in 350-degree oven in a pan of hot water (like cooking custard) for 1 1/4 hours or until a knife inserted comes out clean. For a somewhat richer flavor, without adding fat, use evaporated skim milk in place of the fresh skim milk.

Suzanne Voorhies Kennon

	Cal	Fat(g)	% Fat Cal	Sat Fat(g)	Chol(mg)	Sod(mg)
Per Serving	102	1	9	0.2	1	120

Zucchini Boats with *Spinach*

Yield: 8 servings

One 10-ounce package frozen chopped spinach
4 medium zucchini
3 tablespoons finely chopped onions
2 tablespoons melted margarine
3 tablespoons all-purpose flour
1 1/2 cups evaporated skim milk
1/2 cup shredded low fat Swiss or mozzarella cheese
1/2 teaspoon salt
1/4 teaspoon white pepper
5 drops Tabasco sauce
1 tablespoon Parmesan cheese

Cook spinach according to package directions, drain and press dry. Set aside. Cook zucchini in boiling salted water for 5 minutes. Drain and trim off stems. Cut zucchini in half lengthwise; remove and reserve pulp, leaving 1/4-inch-thick shells. Drain shells and set aside. Sauté onion in margarine in a saucepan. Reduce heat to low; add flour, and stir until smooth; cook 1 minute, stirring constantly.

Nutrition Note

Zucchini Boats with Spinach

Omit salt and save over 130mg sodium per serving.

One Step Further

Corn Pudding

Omit the salt and save another 67mg sodium for each serving. If you do not have egg substitute, use 2 eggs which will add 0.7 grams of fat and 54mg cholesterol per serving.

Gradually add milk; cook over medium heat, stirring constantly, until thick and bubbly. Add spinach, zucchini pulp, cheese, salt, pepper, and hot sauce. Place zucchini shells in a 12x8x2-inch baking dish. Spoon spinach mixture into shells; sprinkle with Parmesan cheese. Bake, uncovered, at 350 degrees for 15 minutes or until thoroughly heated.

Michele Bienvenu

	Cal	Fat(g)	% Fat Cal	Sat Fat(g)	Chol(mg)	Sod(mg)
Per Serving	116	4.5	33	0.8	6	272

Aunt Tillie's Green Beans
Yield: 10 servings

Two 1-pound packages frozen french-style green beans
1 1/2 tablespoons tub margarine or oil
2 tablespoons flour
1/4 teaspoon salt
1 teaspoon sugar
1/2 teaspoon pepper
1/4 teaspoon paprika
2 tablespoons grated onion
3/4 cup light sour cream
3 ounces grated reduced fat Swiss cheese
1 cup bread crumbs

Steam or cook beans until just crisp, drain thoroughly. In saucepan, melt margarine over low heat. Blend in flour, salt, sugar, pepper, paprika, onion and sour cream. When smooth and thickened, remove from heat and fold in beans. Pour into 2 1/2-quart casserole sprayed with vegetable oil cooking spray. Sprinkle cheese over top, cover with bread crumbs and spray with vegetable oil cooking spray. Bake for 30 minutes at 350 degrees.

Lynda Hiltz Daniel

	Cal	Fat(g)	% Fat Cal	Sat Fat(g)	Chol(mg)	Sod(mg)
Per Serving	139	6.1	39	3.2	14	185

We don't know who "Aunt Tillie" is, but her beans have been a family favorite for years. We always serve these on holidays and special occasions.

Lynda H. Daniel

Spinach Madeline

Yield: 6 servings

2 packages frozen chopped spinach
2 tablespoons tub margarine
2 tablespoons plus 1 teaspoon flour
3 tablespoons chopped onion
2/3 cup reserved vegetable liquid
3/4 cup evaporated skim milk
1/2 teaspoon black pepper
1/2 teaspoon garlic powder
2 teaspoons minced jalapeños
1/2 teaspoon ground celery seed
1 teaspoon Worcestershire sauce
Red pepper to taste
4 ounces light Velveeta cheese, cubed

Cook spinach according to directions on package. Drain and reserve liquid. Melt margarine in saucepan over low heat. Add flour, stirring until blended, but not brown. Add onion and cook until soft but not brown. This mixture will be coarse-looking at this point. While stirring constantly, slowly add reserved spinach liquid. To avoid lumps be sure to constantly stir until smooth. Gradually add milk. Continue stirring; cook until smooth and thick. Add seasonings and cheese, stir until melted. Combine with cooked spinach. This may be served immediately or put into a casserole and topped with buttered bread crumbs. The flavor is improved if latter is done and kept in refrigerator overnight. This may also be frozen.

Madeline Noland Reymond
River Road Recipes, *page 63*

Original Recipe

	Cal	Fat(g)	% Fat Cal	Sat Fat(g)	Chol(mg)	Sod(mg)
Per Serving	219	16.3	65	10.1	45	1088

Lightened Recipe

	Cal	Fat(g)	% Fat Cal	Sat Fat(g)	Chol(mg)	Sod(mg)
Per Serving	130	5.8	39	2.3	10	482

114

Florentine Burrito

Yield: 8 servings

1 1/2 cups shredded low moisture part skim mozzarella
     cheese, divided
One 10-ounce box frozen chopped spinach, thawed
     and squeezed dry
One 10-ounce box frozen sweet corn, thawed and
     drained
1 small onion, finely chopped
1 teaspoon Italian seasoning
1 teaspoon lemon-pepper, no salt
One 15-ounce container light ricotta cheese OR low fat
     cottage cheese
1 egg
Eight 8-inch flour tortillas
One 14-ounce can Italian styled stewed tomatoes,
     chopped and drained
One 8-ounce can tomato sauce, no salt added
1 clove garlic, crushed
1 teaspoon dried basil OR 1 tablespoon fresh basil
1 teaspoon Tabasco sauce
1/4 cup shredded Parmesan cheese

Mix 3/4 cup mozzarella cheese, spinach, corn, onion,
Italian seasoning, lemon-pepper, ricotta and egg. Place
about 1/3 to 1/2 cup mixture down center of each tortilla.
Roll tightly; arrange seam down in 13x9-inch or two 8x8-
inch pans sprayed with vegetable spray. Mix tomatoes,
tomato sauce, garlic, basil and Tabasco sauce; spoon over
filled tortillas. Sprinkle with remaining mozzarella and
Parmesan cheese. Bake at 375 degrees for 30 minutes.
Recipe may be prepared, cooked and frozen. Thaw before
reheating. Big eaters may want 2 of these, but most people
are satisfied with 1.

Ashley Hamilton Higginbotham

	Cal	Fat(g)	% Fat Cal	Sat Fat(g)	Chol(mg)	Sod(mg)
Per Serving	278	8.6	27	4.5	49	478

One Step Further

Florentine Burrito
Using 2 egg whites or
1/4 cup egg substitute
will trim off 27mg cho-
lesterol. As an entree,
this dish with the whole
egg has only moderate
cholesterol content.

115

No Gain Potatoes

Yield: 6 servings

6 medium red potatoes, sliced thick
1 medium purple onion, sliced thin
1/2 bell pepper, chopped
4 cloves garlic, minced
1/2 teaspoon light Creole seasoning
1 tablespoon margarine
1 cup water

Spray a 9x13-inch pan with vegetable oil cooking spray. Layer the potatoes, onion, bell pepper. Add garlic and Creole seasoning. Dot with margarine. Add the water to the pan. Cover and bake 1 1/2 hours at 350 degrees. Remove cover and bake 30 minutes more to brown the top.

Amy Brassett

	Cal	Fat(g)	% Fat Cal	Sat Fat(g)	Chol(mg)	Sod(mg)
Per Serving	169	2.1	11	0.4	0	55

Vegetable Chili

Yield: 8 servings

1 large eggplant, cut into 1-inch chunks
2 tablespoons olive oil, divided
2 onions, chopped
3 cloves garlic, chopped
2 red bell peppers, chopped
2 zucchini, diced
1 jalapeño pepper, minced
One 10-ounce can stewed tomatoes
3 fresh tomatoes, chopped
1/2 cup red wine
2 tablespoons chili powder
1 tablespoon ground cumin
2 teaspoons oregano
One 16-ounce can kidney beans
One 16-ounce can white beans

Preheat oven to 350 degrees. Put eggplant in a small shallow baking pan sprayed lightly with vegetable oil cooking

Nutrition Note

No Gain Potatoes
To speed this up, microwave for 12 to 16 minutes stirring every 3 to 4 minutes, until potatoes are tender. Finish in oven until brown on top.

spray and toss with one tablespoon of olive oil. Cover with foil and bake 30 minutes, stirring once. Meanwhile, heat remaining tablespoon oil in large pot. Add onions and garlic and cook 5 minutes. Add next 3 ingredients. Cook 5 minutes. Add next 6 ingredients. Cook 10 minutes. Add cooked eggplant and beans. Cook 20 minutes on simmer. The vegetables can be chopped the night before and stored in air-tight containers to save time. Can be garnished with grated cheese, chopped green onions, chopped parsley, light sour cream, or chopped cilantro.

Donna Maddox Saurage

	Cal	Fat(g)	% Fat Cal	Sat Fat(g)	Chol(mg)	Sod(mg)
Per Serving	230	4.7	17	0.9	0	368

Carolyn's Green Beans *with Creamy Sauce*
Yield: 12 servings

Three 16-ounce cans whole green beans, vertical pack
    preferred
8 ounces low fat ricotta cheese
2/3 cup light sour cream
1/3 cup reduced fat mayonnaise
1 tablespoon wine vinegar
1 tablespoon tarragon vinegar
2 tablespoons anchovy paste
2 or 3 green onions, chopped
1/4 cup fresh chopped parsley
1/4 teaspoon salt
1/4 teaspoon pepper

Drain beans, wash well, and drain again. Place in 3-quart rectangular serving dish. Cream together ricotta cheese, sour cream and mayonnaise until smooth and creamy. Add all other ingredients to this mixture and pour over beans. Refrigerate overnight. Serve from dish or in lettuce cups.

Mrs. Thomas B. Pugh, II

	Cal	Fat(g)	% Fat Cal	Sat Fat(g)	Chol(mg)	Sod(mg)
Per Serving	75	4.3	46	1.8	9	329

One Step Further

Carolyn's Green Beans with Creamy Sauce
This version has less than 1/2 the calories found in the original and less than 1/4 the fat! To trim off more fat, use a fat-free mayonnaise or replace the mayonnaise with non-fat yogurt and a twist of fresh lemon. To cut out over 200mg sodium per serving, try fresh steamed beans or no-salt-added canned beans.

Potatoes Supreme
Yield: 12 servings

9 medium potatoes
1/4 cup margarine
2 cups evaporated skim milk
1 1/2 teaspoons salt
1/4 cup grated sharp low fat cheddar cheese
1 cup light sour cream
1/4 pound Canadian bacon, chopped and cooked
    crisp

Boil whole potatoes until tender. Chill 24 to 48 hours. Remove skin and grate. Heat margarine, milk, salt, and cheese on stove. Stir until cheese is melted. Mix in grated potatoes. Pour into 2-quart casserole. Bake at 350 degrees for 1 hour. Remove from oven and top with sour cream and crumbled Canadian bacon. Return to oven and bake an additional 10 minutes.

Lynn Kilgore

	Cal	Fat(g)	% Fat Cal	Sat Fat(g)	Chol(mg)	Sod(mg)
Per Serving	240	6.8	25	2.8	16	484

Mama's Eggplant Casserole
Yield: 6 servings

1 large or 2 small eggplants, peeled and chopped
1/2 cup chopped celery
1/4 cup chopped bell pepper
1/2 cup chopped onion
2 tablespoons tub margarine
1 egg, beaten
1/2 of a 10 3/4-ounce can cream of mushroom soup,
    less salt/low fat
3/4 cup grated reduced fat American cheese, divided
3/4 cup bread crumbs OR herb stuffing mix, divided
1/4 cup chopped parsley
1/4 cup chopped green onion

Boil eggplant with celery, bell pepper and onion in small amount of water until tender, about 15 minutes. Drain, add margarine and let cool. Add egg, soup, 1/2 the cheese,

Nutrition Note

Mama's Eggplant Casserole

Still moderate in fat content but less than 1/2 of that found in the original. By using 2 egg whites or 1/4 cup egg substitute, cholesterol content can be reduced to less than 8mg per serving. This has almost 1/3 less sodium than the original. Caution: the herb stuffing mix will raise the sodium content.

1/2 the bread crumbs, parsley and green onions. Mix well and pour into a greased 2-quart casserole. Top with remaining bread crumbs. Bake at 350 degrees for 25 minutes. Top with remaining cheese and bake 5 more minutes.

Kate Brady

	Cal	Fat(g)	% Fat Cal	Sat Fat(g)	Chol(mg)	Sod(mg)
Per Serving	176	8	40	2.6	43	495

Carrot Soufflé
Yield: 6 servings

1 pound carrots
2 tablespoons tub margarine
1/3 cup defatted chicken broth, less salt
2/3 cup sugar
3/4 cup egg substitute OR 4 egg whites
1/4 cup sifted flour
1 teaspoon baking powder
1 tablespoon plus 1 teaspoon vanilla
1 1/2 teaspoon cinnamon
1/2 teaspoon nutmeg

Clean, peel and cook carrots until tender. In food processor, blend carrots and margarine, then gradually add chicken broth and blend until smooth. Add sugar, then egg substitute. Sift together dry ingredients. Add rest of ingredients. Pour mixture into a 1-quart soufflé dish that has been sprayed with vegetable oil cooking spray. Bake in preheated 350 degree oven for 50 minutes or until set. Will double well for larger groups.

Mary R. Aycock

	Cal	Fat(g)	% Fat Cal	Sat Fat(g)	Chol(mg)	Sod(mg)
Per Serving	190	4.1	19	1.0	1	216

Nutrition Note

Carrot Soufflé
This modified recipe trimmed off over 100 calories, 14gm fat and 9gm saturated ("bad") fat per serving from the original.

Sweet Potato Pone
Yield: 8 servings

4 large fresh sweet potatoes, peeled and grated
2 tablespoons melted margarine
1/3 cup cane syrup
1 1/2 cups canned evaporated OR regular skim milk
3/4 cup egg substitute OR 3 egg whites
3/4 cup sugar
2 teaspoons cinnamon
1/2 teaspoon nutmeg
Grated peel from 1 small orange

Mix all ingredients in a large skillet. Cook on low heat until it has thickened somewhat. Put in a 9x13-inch glass baking dish, sprayed lightly with vegetable oil cooking spray (preferably butter flavored). Bake at 325 degrees for 1 hour or until firm and tender and brown around the edges.

Augusta Waggenspack

	Cal	Fat(g)	% Fat Cal	Sat Fat(g)	Chol(mg)	Sod(mg)
Per Serving	280	4.2	14	0.9	2	132

Onions Monterey
Yield: 8 servings

3 large Vidalia onions
1 tablespoon margarine
1/4 cup skim milk
1/2 cup grated Monterey Jack cheese
1/4 teaspoon salt
1/2 teaspoon pepper
8 white unsalted soda crackers, toasted and crushed

Peel and thinly slice onions. Layer in a flat bottom microwavable dish. Dot with margarine. Cover with plastic wrap and microwave on high for 3 minutes. Stir, add milk, cover again and microwave on high 5 to 7 minutes more. Stir in cheese, salt, and pepper. Cover and let stand for 5 minutes. Top with cracker crumbs.

Mrs. Robert V. McAnelly

One Step Further

Onions Monterey
May reduce 1gm more fat per serving if you use a reduced fat Monterey Jack cheese.

	Cal	Fat(g)	% Fat Cal	Sat Fat(g)	Chol(mg)	Sod(mg)
Per Serving	83	4.2	45	1.7	6	145

Cranberry Carrots
Yield: 6 servings

1 pound baby carrots
1/2 cup water
1/4 cup jellied cranberry sauce
2 tablespoons light margarine OR 1 tablespoon tub
        margarine
1/4 teaspoon cinnamon
1/2 teaspoon orange peel

Place carrots and water in a microwave container. Cover and cook on high until just tender; drain and set aside. In the same container, melt the cranberry sauce and margarine on 80% power. Add the seasonings. Pour sauce over carrots and mix well. Serve warm.

Sharon Randall Lanius

	Cal	Fat(g)	% Fat Cal	Sat Fat(g)	Chol(mg)	Sod(mg)
Per Serving	58	2.1	32	0.4	0	54

Zesty Dijon Green Beans
Yield: 12 servings of 1/2 cup each

Three 16-ounce cans whole green beans
2 teaspoons garlic powder
1 1/2 tablespoons melted margarine
2 tablespoons white wine
3 tablespoons dijon mustard
3 tablespoons Worcestershire sauce

Drain 1/2 the liquid from canned beans. Place beans, remaining liquid and garlic powder in a pan. Cook on medium heat for 20 minutes and drain. Combine margarine, wine, mustard and Worcestershire sauce and add to beans. Marinate in refrigerator 6 to 12 hours. Warm before serving.

Shelley Alexander

	Cal	Fat(g)	% Fat Cal	Sat Fat(g)	Chol(mg)	Sod(mg)
Per Serving	46	2.1	39	0.4	0	410

One Step Further

Zesty Dijon Green Beans
Frozen or fresh green beans can reduce sodium by over 200mg per serving.

Squash Supreme
Yield: 8 servings

2 pounds yellow squash and/or zucchini
1 large onion, chopped
1 tablespoon light margarine OR 2 teaspoons tub
    margarine
1/4 teaspoon salt
1/4 teaspoon pepper
1/2 teaspoon tarragon
1/2 cup grated low fat mozzarella cheese
1 tomato, cubed
2 tablespoons freshly minced parsley

Slice and sauté squash and onion in margarine in a non-stick skillet until barely tender. Add seasonings and cheese and continue to cook until vegetables are soft. Toss in the tomato just prior to serving. Taste before adding salt. Garnish with parsley.

Mrs. Charles Spaht

	Cal	Fat(g)	% Fat Cal	Sat Fat(g)	Chol(mg)	Sod(mg)
Per Serving	57	2.2	32	1.0	5	117

Butternut Squash
Yield: 6 servings

2 medium butternut squash
2 cups peeled and chopped Golden Delicious apples
1/2 cup chopped Vidalia onions
2 tablespoons light margarine OR 1 tablespoon tub
    margarine
1/4 cup lemon juice
1/3 cup brown sugar
1/2 teaspoon cinnamon
1/4 cup raisins

Cut the squash in chunks and remove seeds. Boil until tender, then drain and peel. At this point, it may be mashed and frozen for future preparation. Sauté chopped apples and onions together in margarine until tender. Mix with squash and add the remaining ingredients. Put in a 2-quart casserole and bake 20 minutes at 325 degrees.

Mrs. Glenn S. Darsey (Katherine)

	Cal	Fat(g)	% Fat Cal	Sat Fat(g)	Chol(mg)	Sod(mg)
Per Serving	144	2.2	14	0.4	0	25

Nutrition Note

Squash Supreme
If you omit the salt, you save over 65mg sodium per serving.

Greek Artichoke Spinach Casserole
Yield: 12 servings

Two 14-ounce cans artichoke hearts
1 pound fresh mushrooms, sliced
1/3 cup defatted chicken broth, less salt
1 1/2 tablespoons margarine
2 tablespoons flour
1 cup evaporated skim milk
Four 10-ounce packages chopped spinach, thawed and
     well drained
One 16-ounce can chopped tomatoes, no salt added,
     well drained
1 cup light sour cream
1/2 cup low calorie mayonnaise/salad dressing
3 tablespoons lemon juice
1/4 teaspoon salt
1/4 teaspoon pepper
1/2 teaspoon garlic powder
Paprika

Arrange artichoke hearts in 3-quart baking dish. Sauté mushrooms in chicken broth until done. Remove mushrooms, add margarine, gradually add flour and stir until smooth. Gradually add milk to this mixture to make a white sauce, then add mushrooms, spinach, and tomatoes, blending well. Pour over the artichoke hearts. Blend sour cream and mayonnaise, slowly add the lemon juice and remaining seasonings. Spread this over the spinach mixture. Sprinkle with paprika. Bake uncovered for 30 minutes at 350 degrees.

Nadine Benton

	Cal	Fat(g)	% Fat Cal	Sat Fat(g)	Chol(mg)	Sod(mg)
Per Serving	116	5.6	41	2.1	11	296

This is one dish we always serve during the holidays, the red of the tomatoes and the green of the spinach make it festive.

Nadine Benton

Nutrition Nibble

Chicken, seafood or other broths can be used in recipes to replace or decrease the amount of oil used to sauté ingredients and for other purposes.

Nutrition Note

Greek Artichoke Spinach Casserole
This recipe has less than 1/4 the fat, saturated fat and cholesterol and less than 1/2 the calories of the original recipe.

123

Orange Garlic Roasted Potatoes
Yield: 4 servings

2 teaspoons extra virgin olive oil
1 teaspoon grated orange peel
1/2 teaspoon dried sage
1/4 teaspoon ground pepper
1/4 teaspoon garlic powder
3 medium red potatoes, cut into wedges

Preheat oven to 425 degrees. Mix the first 5 ingredients, add potatoes and toss. Transfer to a baking sheet. Bake until crisp and brown, turning once, about 40 minutes.

Patty Young

	Cal	Fat(g)	% Fat Cal	Sat Fat(g)	Chol(mg)	Sod(mg)
Per Serving	114	2.4	18	0.3	0	7

Mom's Squash Casserole
Yield: 6 servings

1 pound sliced yellow squash
1/2 cup low fat ricotta cheese or light cream cheese
1 tablespoon tub margarine, melted
2 teaspoons lemon juice
1/2 cup chopped onions
3/4 teaspoon light Creole seasoning
1/4 teaspoon pepper
3/4 cup grated low fat sharp Cheddar cheese, divided
1 cup unsalted cracker crumbs, saltine style, divided
3 tablespoons fresh chopped parsley, optional

Steam squash for 5 minutes. Drain squash and reserve some of the liquid. In a food processor, blend ricotta cheese until smooth. Add 1 tablespoon of melted margarine and blend in. Mix squash with other ingredients, retaining 1/2 of the cheese and crumbs for the top of the casserole. Bake for 35 minutes at 350 degrees.

Karen Deumite

One Step Further

Mom's Squash Casserole

If on a more restricted sodium diet, further reduce the sodium content by using a salt-free Creole seasoning—saving another 80mg for each serving.

	Cal	Fat(g)	% Fat Cal	Sat Fat(g)	Chol(mg)	Sod(mg)
Per Serving	158	6.1	36	2.7	17	326

Oven Fried Potatoes

Yield: 1 serving

One 4-ounce potato
1/8 teaspoon light Creole seasoning

Boil, bake or microwave potato until done. Do not peel. Refrigerate until cold. Preheat oven to 400 degrees. Cut the potato into thick slices or french fry shapes. Place on nonstick cookie sheet or one lined in foil and sprinkle with light Creole seasoning. Bake for 10 minutes. Potatoes are done when they are lightly browned and puffy.

Celia Pope

	Cal	Fat(g)	% Fat Cal	Sat Fat(g)	Chol(mg)	Sod(mg)
Per Serving	123	0.12	1	trace	0	63

Golden Spaghetti Squash

Yield: 8 servings

One 2 1/2- to 3-pound spaghetti squash
2 tablespoons tub margarine, room temperature
2 tablespoons brown sugar
1/2 teaspoon cinnamon
1/4 teaspoon salt
1 tablespoon orange juice
1/4 cup chopped pistachios
1 orange, peeled and diced

Preheat oven to 375 degrees. Cut squash in 1/2 lengthwise. Using a spoon, scrape out seeds and loose strings. Place squash, cut side down, on a shallow baking pan. Bake 35 to 45 minutes or until tender. While baking, combine margarine, sugar, cinnamon, salt, juice and nuts in a bowl. Invert baked squash halves. Using a fork, pull spaghetti-like strands up. Divide the nut mixture between the 2 squash halves and lightly toss. Add orange pieces and toss again. Serve warm.

Elizabeth McKowen

	Cal	Fat(g)	% Fat Cal	Sat Fat(g)	Chol(mg)	Sod(mg)
Per Serving	99	4.6	40	0.7	0	155

One Step Further

Golden Spaghetti Squash
To trim fat further, omit the nuts and save over 2gm more fat per serving. Try with raisins.

125

Autumn Vegetables *with Horseradish Dill Sauce*
Yield: 10 servings

One 10-ounce box frozen brussels sprouts,
    steamed tender
1/2 pound baby carrots, steamed tender
1/2 pound snow peas, steamed tender
1/2 pound small new potatoes, steamed tender
2 tablespoons tub margarine
1/2 cup defatted chicken broth, less salt
1/3 cup horseradish, drained
1/4 cup balsamic vinegar
2 tablespoons dried dill
Juice of 1 lemon

Combine the cooked vegetables in a large serving dish. Heat the remaining ingredients together in a small saucepan and cook on medium heat for 5 minutes. Pour over the vegetables. Toss to coat and serve warm.

Michael James Romero

	Cal	Fat(g)	% Fat Cal	Sat Fat(g)	Chol(mg)	Sod(mg)
Per Serving	72	2	23	0.6	0	171

Southwest Corn
Yield: 6 servings

2 tablespoons tub margarine
1 green pepper, chopped
1 red pepper, chopped
1 onion, chopped
6 ears fresh corn, kernels cut from the cob
One 4-ounce can chopped green chiles, drained
2 tablespoons finely chopped cilantro
1/4 teaspoon salt
1/4 teaspoon pepper
Dash of hot sauce

Melt margarine in nonstick skillet and sauté the peppers and onion. Add the corn and seasonings. Cook 5 more minutes.

Patty Young

	Cal	Fat(g)	% Fat Cal	Sat Fat(g)	Chol(mg)	Sod(mg)
Per Serving	135	4	24	0.8	0	241

One Step Further

Southwest Corn
Save close to 3gm fat and 26 calories per serving by omitting the margarine and using defatted chicken broth to sauté or sweat the vegetables. Taste before adding salt — if omitted, you can save close to 90mg sodium per serving.

Pasta, Etc.

1970s

The 1960s were a time of questioning values, of fresh starts, of increased awareness of the needs of others. The Junior League projects of the 1960s centered on the handicapped citizens of Baton Rouge—those persons, both adults and children, who were physically challenged, sight or hearing impaired.

In 1960 the Junior League donated $7000 for the salary of the director of the Baton Rouge Speech and Hearing Foundation, starting an involvement that to date totals $177,000 and countless hours of volunteer work. A school was established to provide speech therapy for both children and adults in an effort to help children enter a mainstream school situation.

Never Fail Cheese Soufflé
Yield: 6 servings

6 egg whites
1/2 cup freshly grated Parmesan cheese, divided
3 tablespoons cornstarch
1/2 teaspoon salt
1/8 teaspoon nutmeg
1/8 teaspoon cayenne
1 1/4 cups skim milk or evaporated skimmed milk
1 1/2 cups egg substitute
1/2 cup grated low fat Swiss cheese
1/4 teaspoon salt
1/4 teaspoon cream of tartar

Separate egg whites and let warm to room temperature. Fold sheet of wax paper approximately 26 inches long lengthwise into thirds. Lightly spray one side of paper with vegetable oil cooking spray. Lightly spray soufflé dish. Place sprayed side of wax paper around top of soufflé dish to leave a rim of approximately 2 inches above and tie in place with a string. Dust lightly with Parmesan cheese. Set aside. Preheat oven. Mix cornstarch, 1/2 teaspoon salt, nutmeg and cayenne then blend with about 1/4 cup milk until a smooth paste is formed. Gradually stir in remaining milk and then heat over medium heat, stirring constantly. Bring to boil, reduce heat and stir constantly until mixture is thick and leaves bottom and sides of pan. Remove from heat. Beat egg substitute with wire whisk and gradually beat cooked mixture into egg substitute. Beat in remaining Parmesan cheese and Swiss cheese. Add 1/4 teaspoon salt and cream of tartar to egg whites and beat until stiff. Using whisk, fold 1/3 of egg whites into warm cheese mixture to combine well. Carefully fold remaining egg whites in until just combined. Pour into prepared soufflé dish and bake 40 minutes at 350 degrees or until soufflé is puffed and golden brown. Carefully remove collar before serving. This may be prepared up to 2 hours prior to baking but is best when baked immediately.

Brownie Jeffries

	Cal	Fat(g)	% Fat Cal	Sat Fat(g)	Chol(mg)	Sod(mg)
Per Serving	172	6.4	35	3.1	14	634

Helpful hints for inexperienced Jambalaya cooks: The best pot to use is a cast iron one—it should be heavy enough to prevent easy burning and should have a tight fitting lid.

Jambalaya should never be stirred—turn rather than stir after the rice has been added to prevent the grains of rice from breaking up.

Blair Lamendola
Gonzales, LA
Jambalaya Capital of
the World

Oriental Restaurant Rice

Yield: 8 servings of 1/3 cup each

2 cups cooked white rice
1 tablespoon plus 1 teaspoon ginger-garlic flavored oil
2 egg whites or 1/4 cup egg substitute
1/2 cup frozen peas, thawed and well drained
1/2 teaspoon chili powder
1/8 teaspoon white sugar
1/8 teaspoon black pepper
2 tablespoons reduced sodium soy sauce

Heat wok to medium high, ring with 1 tablespoon oil. Add rice and stir-fry until thoroughly heated. Clear space in the bottom center of wok by pushing rice onto wok's sides, add remaining oil, heat, then add egg in a stream. As egg cooks on bottom of wok, incorporate the rice. Continue until all egg is cooked. Add peas and seasonings; fluff together.

Susan Saurage-Altenloh

	Cal	Fat(g)	% Fat Cal	Sat Fat(g)	Chol(mg)	Sod(mg)
Per Serving	106	2.5	21	0.5	0	151

World Championship Jambalaya

Yield: 10 servings

1 large skinless hen cut in serving pieces OR
    3 pounds boneless well-trimmed lean pork
1 teaspoon salt
1 teaspoon garlic powder
1/2 teaspoon black pepper
1/4 teaspoon red pepper
2 tablespoons oil
4 medium onions, chopped
6 cups water
Tabasco sauce to taste
3 cups uncooked long grain rice
4 green onion tops, chopped

Season chicken or pork with salt, garlic, black pepper and red pepper and brown meat in oil in a heavy pot for approximately 30 minutes. Add onions and cook until limp. Blot off oil with paper towels, then add water and Tabasco sauce and bring to a boil. Stir in rice, cover and simmer for about 15 minutes or until rice is tender. Jambalaya should be turned, being sure to scoop from the bottom of the pot, about 5 times while rice is cooking. Add green onions to rice just before it is done.

Mr. Blair Lamendola

	Cal	Fat(g)	% Fat Cal	Sat Fat(g)	Chol(mg)	Sod(mg)
Per Serving	344	6.7	18	1.4	44	261

Fettuccine *with Chicken and Mushrooms*
Yield: 6 servings

6 ounces fettuccine, boiled and drained
2 teaspoons olive oil
1 pound skinless, boneless chicken, cut into
      1 1/2-inch pieces
1 cup sliced mushrooms, fresh or canned
1 tablespoon margarine
1 tablespoon flour
2 teaspoons parsley flakes
1/2 teaspoon onion powder
1/4 teaspoon salt
1/2 teaspoon black pepper
1 cup evaporated skim milk
1/4 cup grated Parmesan cheese

Toss fettuccine in olive oil and set aside. In a nonstick skillet, sauté chicken and mushrooms in 1 tablespoon margarine until cooked thoroughly. Stir in flour, parsley, onion powder, salt and pepper. Slowly blend in evaporated milk; cook until thickened. Remove from heat and add fettuccine and cheese.

Laura Clark

	Cal	Fat(g)	% Fat Cal	Sat Fat(g)	Chol(mg)	Sod(mg)
Per Serving	305	9.4	28	2.6	56	282

Arborio, an Italian short grain rice, is available at Italian markets as well as specialty food stores.

Larry Firmin

Creamy Risotto

Yield: 6 servings

1 tablespoon olive oil
1 tablespoon tub margarine
1 onion, chopped
1 teaspoon chopped garlic
1 cup arborio rice or medium grain rice
3 tablespoons dry white wine
3 1/2 cups defatted chicken stock, less salt
1/3 cup grated fresh Parmesan cheese
1/8 teaspoon saffron, optional
1/2 teaspoon basil
Black pepper for seasoning

Heat oil and margarine. Sauté vegetables 5 minutes. Add rice and stir 30 seconds. Add wine and stir 1 minute. Add stock, cheese, and spices. Simmer until rice is tender but slightly firm to bite, and mixture is creamy, about 25 minutes. Season with pepper. Serve with extra Parmesan cheese if desired.

Larry J. Firmin

	Cal	Fat(g)	% Fat Cal	Sat Fat(g)	Chol(mg)	Sod(mg)
Per Serving	**208**	**6.4**	**28**	**2.2**	**11**	**511**

Fiesta Quiche

Yield: 6 servings

Four 8 1/2-inch flour tortillas
1/2 cup shredded reduced fat sharp cheddar cheese
One 4-ounce can chopped green chilies, drained
1/4 cup chopped green onions
1/2 cup picanté sauce
1 cup egg substitute
1/3 cup skim milk
1/2 teaspoon chili powder
1/4 teaspoon black pepper
6 tomato slices
2 tablespoons light sour cream

Coat a 12-inch quiche pan with vegetable oil cooking spray. Layer the tortillas in the dish. Sprinkle cheese, chilies

One Step Further

Creamy Risotto

This recipe has a savings of over 5gm fat per serving when compared to the original. Omit the olive oil and margarine, sauté in the chicken broth to save an additional 3.7gm fat and 33 calories per serving. To cut sodium, use a sodium-free broth.

and green onions over the top. Spread the picanté sauce on next. Combine the egg substitute with the next 3 ingredients; pour into the dish. Bake at 350 degrees for 30 minutes. Cut into wedges to serve. Garnish each serving with a tomato slice and sour cream.

Kristl Story

	Cal	Fat(g)	% Fat Cal	Sat Fat(g)	Chol(mg)	Sod(mg)
Per Serving	160	5.4	30	2	9	380

Basil Vegetable Pasta
Yield: 10 servings

2 tablespoons olive oil
6 cloves garlic, chopped
Two 14 1/2-ounce cans Italian-style tomatoes with juice
1 teaspoon oregano
1/2 teaspoon fresh black pepper
1/2 teaspoon cayenne
One 8-ounce package fresh mushrooms, sliced
2 zucchini, sliced
1/4 teaspoon salt
12 fresh basil leaves, chopped
1 tablespoon fresh parsley
1 pound angel hair pasta, cooked

Cook garlic in olive oil on medium heat about 5 minutes or until it is pale gold. Quarter tomatoes and add with juice to garlic; reduce heat to low. Cook about 20 minutes. Season with oregano, pepper and cayenne. Add mushrooms and zucchini and simmer 10 minutes. Add more pepper if desired and salt, if needed. Remove from heat, add basil and parsley and toss with pasta.

Sugar McAdams

	Cal	Fat(g)	% Fat Cal	Sat Fat(g)	Chol(mg)	Sod(mg)
Per Serving	222	3.8	15	0.5	0	246

It's a south Louisiana tradition to serve these wonderful garlicky grits along with New Orleans grillades at brunches celebrating engagements and christenings or at midnight breakfast parties after Mardi Gras balls.

Cabbage Rice Casserole
Yield: 8 servings

1 pound ground turkey
1 medium onion, chopped
1/2 cup raw long grain rice
1 tablespoon parsley flakes
1 teaspoon black pepper
1/4 teaspoon red pepper
1 teaspoon garlic powder
1 teaspoon light Creole seasoning
1 small head cabbage, chopped (about 6 cups)
2 1/2 cups spicy hot tomato vegetable juice

Crumble ground turkey into a 2 1/2- or 3-quart microwavable casserole dish. Add onion. Microwave on high, uncovered, 5 to 6 minutes or until meat is set, stirring once. Drain. Mix in rice, seasonings, and cabbage. Pour vegetable juice over all. Cover with casserole lid. Microwave on high 9 to 10 minutes or until boiling, stirring once. Set microwave on 50% power for 20 to 25 minutes or until rice is tender, stirring once.

Celia Page

	Cal	Fat(g)	% Fat Cal	Sat Fat(g)	Chol(mg)	Sod(mg)
Per Serving	156	4.6	26	1.2	21	556

Garlic Cheese Grits
Yield: 8 servings

1 cup uncooked grits
3 3/4 cups water
1/2 teaspoon salt
1/3 cup skim milk
3 tablespoons tub margarine
1/2 teaspoon garlic powder
4 ounces light Velveeta cheese
1 cup grated reduced fat sharp cheddar cheese
1 tablespoon Worcestershire sauce

Cook the grits in the salted water. Once cooked, stir in milk and cook a few more minutes. Then add the margarine, garlic, Velveeta cheese, sharp cheddar cheese and

One Step Further

Cabbage Rice Casserole

To reduce the sodium, replace the vegetable juice with a reduced sodium version and add 8 drops of Tabasco sauce.

Worcestershire sauce. Stir until the margarine and cheese have melted. Put in a casserole sprayed with vegetable oil cooking spray and sprinkle with paprika. Bake in preheated 350 degree oven for 15 to 20 minutes. Use as main supper dish or starch.

Mrs. J.L. Hochenedel
River Road Recipes, page 56

Original Recipe

	Cal	Fat(g)	% Fat Cal	Sat Fat(g)	Chol(mg)	Sod(mg)
Per Serving	219	16.3	65	10.1	45	1088

Lightened Recipe

	Cal	Fat(g)	% Fat Cal	Sat Fat(g)	Chol(mg)	Sod(mg)
Per Serving	177	7.3	37	3.1	16	510

Oriental Rice Casserole
Yield: 8 servings

2 1/4 cups boiling water
1/2 cup wild rice
1/2 cup long grain white rice
1 cup chopped onion
1 cup chopped celery
1 tablespoon vegetable oil
1/4 cup defatted chicken broth, less salt
One 3-ounce can mushrooms, sliced
One 5-ounce can water chestnuts rinsed, sliced
1/3 cup sliced toasted almonds
2 tablespoons reduced sodium soy sauce

To the boiling water, add the wild rice. Reduce to simmer, cover and cook 20 minutes. Bring back to a boil and add the white rice. Reduce heat again, cover and cook 20 more minutes. In a separate pan, sauté the onion and celery in the oil until tender. Add chicken broth and continue to sauté. Mix with all the rest of the ingredients in a 2-quart casserole. Cover and bake 20 minutes at 350 degrees.

Laura Clark

	Cal	Fat(g)	% Fat Cal	Sat Fat(g)	Chol(mg)	Sod(mg)
Per Serving	157	4.5	25	0.5	0	215

One Step Further

Oriental Rice Casserole
Omitting the almonds trims off an additional 2.5gm fat per serving. Sautéing the vegetables in chicken broth and omitting the oil can save 1.7gm fat per serving.

Crabmeat Pasta

Yield: 10 servings

One 6-ounce package curly egg noodles
One 6-ounce package spinach noodles
1 small onion, chopped
1 stalk celery, chopped
1 tablespoon olive oil
1 clove garlic, minced
1/4 teaspoon salt
1/8 teaspoon cayenne pepper
1/8 teaspoon paprika
2 cups skim OR 1% low fat milk, divided
1 teaspoon cornstarch
1 tablespoon tub margarine
1 egg, beaten
2 egg whites, beaten OR 1/4 cup egg substitute
2 tablespoons lemon juice
1/2 cup Parmesan cheese
1/4 cup dried parsley
1/8 cup dried basil
8 ounces lump crabmeat

Cook both packages of noodles according to the package directions, drain and set aside. Sauté the onion and celery in olive oil for 5 minutes. Add the garlic, salt, pepper and paprika and cook 3 or 4 minutes more, set aside. Slowly stir 1/2 cup of the milk into the cornstarch until smooth. Place in a saucepan, add the margarine, remaining milk, eggs, and lemon juice. Cook over low heat. Stir until it thickens. Add the Parmesan cheese, parsley, basil, onions, celery, crabmeat and cooked noodles. Toss together until noodles are coated with sauce and warmed thoroughly.

Gaye Bennett

Nutrition Nibble

Evaporated skim milk will thicken as it cooks and once cooked is richer tasting than plain milk. This makes it an ideal fat-free replacement for half-and-half and heavy creams in sauces, soups and dishes such as fettuccine alfredo.

One Step Further

Crabmeat Pasta

Omit the salt and save another 55mg sodium per serving. Save close to another 2.5gm fat per serving by omitting the margarine and olive oil and sautéing in defatted chicken broth.

	Cal	Fat(g)	% Fat Cal	Sat Fat(g)	Chol(mg)	Sod(mg)
Per Serving	228	6.1	24	1.9	76	292

Vegetable Couscous
Yield: 10 servings

1 tablespoon olive oil
1 clove garlic, minced
1 large onion, chopped
1 large red bell pepper, cut in long strips
4 carrots, peeled and sliced into long strips
2 yellow squash, cut into chunks
2 1/4 cups defatted chicken stock, less salt
1 cup golden raisins
1/2 teaspoon cinnamon
1/4 teaspoon tumeric
1/8 teaspoon saffron, optional
1/4 teaspoon salt
1/4 teaspoon each black and white pepper
1 1/2 cups couscous

Heat olive oil in large saucepan. Sauté garlic and onion 5 minutes. Add bell pepper and carrots, cook 5 minutes (add a little stock if needed while sautéing), add squash and cook an additional 5 minutes. Add stock, raisins, spices, salt and peppers. Bring to boil and slowly add couscous. Cover, remove from heat and let stand for 10 minutes before serving.

Claude Barrilleaux

	Cal	Fat(g)	% Fat Cal	Sat Fat(g)	Chol(mg)	Sod(mg)
Per Serving	205	2.1	9	0.4	3	222

Cheese and Herb Tortellini *with Smoked Chicken*
Yield: 12 servings

1/2 cup red wine vinegar
8 shakes Tabasco sauce
Two 2 1/2-pound fresh smoked chickens, skinned,
    deboned and cubed
4 green onions, chopped
1 red bell pepper, coarsely chopped
1 yellow bell pepper, coarsely chopped
3/4 cup raisins
1 cup green grapes
1 cup red grapes
1 1/2 tablespoons Italian seasoning (herb blend) OR 1
    teaspoon each marjoram, thyme and rosemary mixed
    with 1/2 teaspoon each basil, oregano and savory
2-3 teaspoons dill weed
2 1/2 tablespoons garlic powder
1 1/2 teaspoons celery seed
1/4 teaspoon salt
1/4 teaspoon pepper
Juice of 3 lemons
3/4 cup canola oil poppyseed dressing
Three 9-ounce packages fresh light cheese and herb
    tortellini, cooked

Combine wine vinegar and Tabasco sauce. Mix with all
other ingredients except tortellini. Add tortellini and toss.
Refrigerate several hours. Allow to reach room temperature
and serve. Makes a meal in one; just add a crusty bread
and a steamed vegetable.

Amy Dixon

Nutrition Note

**Cheese and Herb
Tortellini with
Smoked Chicken**
If commercial smoked
chickens are used,
sodium content per
serving would increase
by 200 to 300mg sodi-
um. Over 250mg sodi-
um per serving was
saved when a Greek
seasoning was
replaced by the Italian
seasoning blend, as
well as a little more
garlic and pepper.

	Cal	Fat(g)	% Fat Cal	Sat Fat(g)	Chol(mg)	Sod(mg)
Per Serving	463	15.6	30	3.2	89	503

Linguini with Tomato and Seafood Sauce
Yield: 12 servings

2 onions, chopped
2 cloves garlic, chopped
2 tablespoons olive oil
8 large tomatoes, peeled, seeded, and chopped
1/2 teaspoon granulated sugar
1/2 cup chopped fresh basil
1/4 cup chopped fresh oregano
1/4 teaspoon salt
1/2 teaspoon freshly ground black pepper
1/2 teaspoon Tabasco sauce
1 cup dry vermouth
3/4 pound each peeled and deveined shrimp and scal-
    lops OR
1 1/2 pounds peeled, deveined shrimp
2 tablespoons minced parsley
1 pound linguini
3 ounces freshly grated Parmesan cheese

Cook onions and garlic in olive oil until soft. Add tomatoes, sugar, basil, oregano, salt, pepper and Tabasco sauce. Simmer, partially covered, for 25 minutes. Bring vermouth to a boil; add seafood and simmer 3 minutes. Add to tomato sauce with parsley and simmer 5 minutes uncovered or until seafood is cooked. Cook linguini in boiling, lightly salted water. Drain and top with sauce. Sprinkle with Parmesan cheese. Although canned tomatoes and dry herbs may be substituted for fresh, the dish is best prepared in summer with fresh ingredients.

Ashley Hamilton Higginbotham

My son, Scott, pasta lover and sometimes long distance runner, helped me work out this recipe. I always taste to adjust seasonings.

Ashley H.
Higginbotham

	Cal	Fat(g)	% Fat Cal	Sat Fat(g)	Chol(mg)	Sod(mg)
Per Serving	**294**	**5.7**	**17**	**1.8**	**58**	**264**

Pasta Provisional

Yield: 12 servings

1 pound vermicelli or angel hair pasta
1 small onion, chopped
1 pound peeled, deveined shrimp
1/4 cup light margarine OR 2 tablespoons olive oil
1 yellow squash, sliced
1 green zucchini squash, sliced
1 cup fresh broccoli florets
1 cup fresh cauliflower florets
1/4 cup chopped green pepper
1/4 cup chopped red pepper
1/4 cup chopped yellow pepper
1 carrot, chopped
1/4 teaspoon salt
1/4 teaspoon Creole seasoning
Juice of 1 lemon (1/4 cup)
1/4 cup freshly grated Parmesan or Romano cheese

Prepare pasta and set aside. In a skillet, sauté onions and shrimp in margarine or olive oil. Add all your vegetables at once, cooking on a medium to medium-high heat for 5 minutes. Add seasonings and lemon juice. Serve over pasta. A little Parmesan or Romano cheese sprinkled on top is good!

Marsha Town

	Cal	Fat(g)	% Fat Cal	Sat Fat(g)	Chol(mg)	Sod(mg)
Per Serving	221	3.8	15	1.0	60	202

Curry Artichoke Rice

Yield: 12 servings

2 boxes less-salt chicken rice and vermicelli mix
Three 6-ounce jars marinated artichoke hearts, drained
    and chopped, 2 tablespoons marinade reserved
12 stuffed olives, chopped
1 medium bell pepper, chopped
8 green onions, chopped
1 teaspoon curry powder
2/3 cup reduced fat mayonnaise

Cook rice and vermicelli mix as directed. Mix all the ingredients together in a serving bowl and serve at room tem-

One Step Further

Curry Artichoke Rice

Reduce the fat content by 2gm per serving by using only 1/3 cup low fat mayonnaise and 1/3 cup plain nonfat yogurt with 1 teaspoon of flour stirred in.

perature. Also good as a dinner entree when you add 2
cups of cooked lean chicken, lean ham, etc.

Debbie Heroman

	Cal	Fat(g)	% Fat Cal	Sat Fat(g)	Chol(mg)	Sod(mg)
Per Serving	188	7.3	35	2	0	569

Rispishadia
Yield: 14 servings

One 2 1/2-pound skinless chicken
1 teaspoon salt
1/4 teaspoon red pepper
1/4 teaspoon cinnamon
2 tablespoons margarine
One 12-ounce package vermicelli, broken into 1-inch
    pieces
2 cups rice
1/2 teaspoon salt
1/8 teaspoon cayenne
1/8 teaspoon cinnamon

Boil chicken in enough water (seasoned with next 3 ingredients) to reserve 7 cups of broth. Debone chicken and cut
into bite-size pieces. Chill chicken and remove fat hardened on top. Melt margarine in very large pot, add vermicelli and cook, stirring constantly, until dark brown. Add
rice and stir to coat with margarine. Add chicken, salt,
pepper, cinnamon and reserved defatted chicken stock.
Bring to boil on high heat and stir well. Lower heat to low-
est setting, cover and cook for 30 minutes. Fluff with fork
and serve as a main dish.

Moonlee Karam

	Cal	Fat(g)	% Fat Cal	Sat Fat(g)	Chol(mg)	Sod(mg)
Per Serving	277	4.9	16	1.2	34	278

Fettuccine *with Ham, Shrimp and Mushrooms*
Yield: 6 servings

1 medium onion, chopped
1/2 bell pepper, chopped
1 clove garlic, minced
1/2 cup chopped celery
1 tablespoon olive oil
1 tablespoon margarine
4 ounces sliced mushrooms
1 cup lean ham, cut in bite-sized cubes
1/2 pound peeled shrimp
One 10 3/4-ounce can light cream of mushroom soup
1/4 cup skim milk
1/3 cup white wine
1/4 teaspoon pepper
1/8 teaspoon each red and white pepper
8 ounces dry fettuccine
6 tablespoons freshly grated Parmesan cheese

Sauté onion, pepper, garlic and celery in margarine and
olive oil until transparent; add mushrooms and ham. Cook
about 5 minutes. Lower heat and stir in shrimp, soup, milk,
wine and seasonings. Continue cooking until well heated
but do not boil. Cook fettuccine separately until al dente;
drain well. Combine sauce, fettuccine and cheese and toss
lightly. May substitute crawfish for the shrimp.

Mary Elizabeth Cash

	Cal	Fat(g)	% Fat Cal	Sat Fat(g)	Chol(mg)	Sod(mg)
Per Serving	340	10.4	28	3.6	79	796

Pasta *with Sun Dried Tomatoes*
Yield: 14 servings

2 tablespoons olive oil
1 large onion, finely chopped
4 ribs celery, finely chopped
1 bunch green onions, finely chopped
1 bunch parsley, finely chopped
1 large bell pepper, finely chopped
2 toes garlic, finely chopped
Two 15-ounce cans tomato sauce, less salt
One 10-ounce can tomato soup, less salt
One 6-ounce can tomato paste, no salt added
1 tablespoon chopped fresh basil, OR 1 teaspoon
    dried basil
1 teaspoon black pepper
2 bay leaves
1 pound thin spaghetti, cooked
1 cup oil-packed sun dried tomatoes, rinsed, drained
    and chopped
1 cup freshly grated Parmesan cheese

Sauté onion, celery, green onion, parsley, bell pepper, and garlic in olive oil until soft. Add tomato sauce, soup, paste, basil, black pepper and bay leaves. Bring to a boil. Cover and simmer at least 2 hours; more is even better. In a 9x13-inch casserole, add the cooked pasta. Spoon the sauce over the top and mix carefully. Cover the top with the sun dried tomatoes and sprinkle with the cheese. Heat in a 350-degree oven for 10 minutes or until cheese is melted and casserole is very hot. This may all be done ahead and simply heated to serve.

Carol Anne Blitzer

	Cal	Fat(g)	% Fat Cal	Sat Fat(g)	Chol(mg)	Sod(mg)
Per Serving	277	6	20	2	6	268

Nutrition Nibble

When available, using fresh herbs instead of dried herbs can often improve or enhance the flavor of a dish.

Crabmeat Angel Hair Pasta

Yield: 8 servings

2 tablespoons tub margarine
1 cup chopped green onions
1 cup chopped fresh parsley
8 ounces sliced fresh mushrooms
One 8-ounce can water chestnuts, rinsed and coarsely
    chopped
1 tablespoon cornstarch
One 12-ounce can evaporated skim milk, divided
4 ounces light cream cheese, cut in small pieces
1 pound peeled shrimp
1 pound claw crabmeat
1 pound blanched fresh asparagus, diced
1/3 cup white wine
1/4 teaspoon salt
1/4 teaspoon red pepper
4 dashes Tabasco sauce
1/2 pound angel hair pasta, cooked
1/2 cup freshly grated Parmesan cheese

In a nonstick skillet, sauté the onions, parsley, mushrooms
and water chestnuts in the margarine for 5 minutes. Blend
the cornstarch with 1/2 cup of the evaporated milk until
smooth. Add this and the cream cheese to the skillet, stir
until it is melted. Add the remaining evaporated milk gradually. Add the shrimp and cook 5 minutes more. Add the
remaining ingredients and pour into a 9x13-inch baking
dish. Sprinkle the Parmesan cheese on top and bake 20
minutes at 350 degrees.

Anne K. Rabenhorst

	Cal	Fat(g)	% Fat Cal	Sat Fat(g)	Chol(mg)	Sod(mg)
Per Serving	353	8.8	22	3.6	127	581

Nutrition Nibble

Use nonstick skillets
and pans to help cut
back the fat called for
in a recipe.

One Step Further

**Crabmeat Angel
Hair Pasta**

Save a little over 2gm
fat per serving by omit-
ting the margarine and
sautéing the vegetables
in low fat chicken or
seafood broth, or wine.
Omit the salt and save
67mg sodium in each
serving.

Meats
& Game

1970s

As an outgrowth of the Junior League Museum project, originally an exhibit of historical dolls, the Junior League formed and developed the Baton Rouge Arts and Science Center. In 1963, the Louisiana legislature gave the Baton Rouge Arts and Science Center a permanent home — the Old Governor's Mansion on North Boulevard. As the American space program seized the imaginations of children and adults everywhere, a planetarium was added to the Arts and Science Center so that children could learn more about the universe outside their own backyards.

Beef Stew à la Ruth
Yield: 6 servings

6 tablespoons fat-free roux
1 1/2 large onions, chopped
1 1/2 cups chopped bell pepper
5 1/2 ribs celery, chopped
3 cloves garlic, chopped
1 tablespoon oil
1 1/2 pound boneless beef sirloin, well trimmed, cubed
3 tablespoons catsup
2 teaspoons sugar
1/2 teaspoon cinnamon
1/4 teaspoon white pepper
1/2 teaspoon black pepper
Two 14.5-ounce cans defatted beef broth, less salt, divided
3/4 can water or red wine
1 1/2 cups cooked rice
1/4 cup freshly chopped parsley

Preheat oven to 400 degrees. Prepare fat-free roux from the "Something Extra" section. Meanwhile, sauté onions, bell pepper, celery and garlic in oil in a nonstick skillet. Add beef cubes and smother till vegetables are soft. Add some of the beef broth if items start to stick. Drain meat and vegetables then place in soup pot. Add catsup, sugar, cinnamon and peppers. Gradually blend 3/4 cup of the beef broth into the 6 tablespoons roux to form a smooth paste. Set aside. Add remaining beef broth and water or wine to soup pot. Let simmer for a few minutes. Slowly stir in broth and roux mixture. Stir until well blended. Cook slowly for 2 hours, stirring occasionally to scrape bottom of pot. Serve over fluffy rice, garnishing with parsley.

Dawn W. Abbott

	Cal	Fat(g)	%Fat Cal	Sat Fat(g)	Chol(mg)	Sod(mg)
Per Serving	291	9.1	28	2.9	83	558

Beer Soaked Flank Steak
Yield: 8 servings of 3 3/4 ounces each

1 1/2 cups beer
1 bunch green onions, sliced
2 tablespoons olive oil
1/3 cup reduced sodium soy sauce
2 tablespoons honey or molasses
1 tablespoon grated ginger root
2 large garlic cloves, minced
1/2 teaspoon Tabasco sauce
2 1/2 pounds flank steak, well trimmed

Combine all ingredients except steak. Add steak and marinate several hours or overnight in the refrigerator. Drain and pat dry. Grill over hot coals 3 to 4 minutes on each side for medium rare. Cut across the grain on the diagonal into thin slices.

Ashley Hamilton Higginbotham

	Cal	Fat(g)	% Fat Cal	Sat Fat(g)	Chol(mg)	Sod(mg)
Per Serving	260	10.8	37	4.4	62	330

Garlic Laced Pork Tenderloin *in Wine*
Yield: 12 servings of 3 ounces each

3-pound pork tenderloin, well trimmed
3 pods garlic, slivered
1/4 teaspoon salt
1 1/2 teaspoons salt-free lemon-pepper
1/4 teaspoon sage
1/4 teaspoon nutmeg
1 teaspoon oil
1/4 cup chopped parsley
1/2 cup chopped onion
1 cup wine (red or white)
1/2 cup beef broth

Stuff garlic in pork and rub with dry ingredients. Heat oil in a heavy skillet and brown tenderloin. Put in baking dish

Nutrition Note

Beer Soaked Flank Steak

Nutrition information is based on at least 1/2 of the marinade drained off and discarded.

148

with parsley, onion, and wine. Cook uncovered for 1 hour at 350 degrees or until meat thermometer reaches 160 degrees. Turn twice. Add broth last 10 minutes.

Mary Terrell Joseph

	Cal	Fat(g)	% Fat Cal	Sat Fat(g)	Chol(mg)	Sod(mg)
Per Serving	168	5	27	1.5	81	180

Venison Tenderloin
Yield: 2 servings

One 8-ounce venison backstrap tenderloin, well trimmed
1 teaspoon olive oil
2 tablespoons coarse black pepper
1 tablespoon thyme
1 teaspoon oregano
1/4 teaspoon salt
1/4 teaspoon red pepper
1 teaspoon white pepper
1 teaspoon garlic powder

Rub tenderloin with olive oil. Mix remaining ingredients together then rub tenderloin with seasonings. Marinate in refrigerator 8 hours, covered. Bake on rack in 500 degree oven for 5 minutes, then bake at 350 degrees for 12 to 20 minutes. Slice and serve with natural gravy.

Debbie Brown

	Cal	Fat(g)	% Fat Cal	Sat Fat(g)	Chol(mg)	Sod(mg)
Per Serving	174	4.6	35	2.9	93	330

Nutrition Nibble

Using a meat thermometer will help avoid overcooking leaner meats. Skinless chicken, lean beef and lean pork cuts often require 20 to 25% less cooking time. Overcooking will dry out and toughen these meats. To prevent drying out lean meats and skinless chicken, cover the pan with foil for about 3/4 of the cooking time. Remove foil at the end to brown meat. To produce a crispy outside, broil the meat for the last 2 to 4 minutes.

Apple Glazed Pork
Yield: 6 servings of 3 ounces each

1 tablespoon flour
1/2 teaspoon salt
1 1/2 teaspoons dry mustard
1/8 teaspoon red pepper
1/4 teaspoon black pepper
1 1/2 pounds pork tenderloin, well trimmed
2 cups unsweetened applesauce
1/3 cup brown sugar
3/4 teaspoon cinnamon
1/4 teaspoon powdered cloves

Heat oven to 325 degrees. Mix flour, salt, mustard and peppers. Rub pork with this mixture. Roast 35 to 45 minutes, or until internal temperature reaches 160 degrees. Mix applesauce, brown sugar, cinnamon and cloves. Thirty minutes before meat is done, spread the fruit mixture over the top and return to the oven. Baste occasionally. This may be prepared with a 3- to 4-pound pork roast. Simply roast to 175 degrees (25 to 30 minutes per pound).

Libby Kaul Clark

	Cal	Fat(g)	% Fat Cal	Sat Fat(g)	Chol(mg)	Sod(mg)
Per Serving	232	4.4	17	1.5	81	242

Spicy Creole Roast
Yield: 8 servings of 3 ounces each

2 1/4-pound round tip roast, well trimmed
1 tablespoon light Creole seasoning
2 teaspoons salt-free lemon-pepper
1 onion, finely chopped
1/4 cup Worcestershire
1 tablespoon steak sauce
2 tablespoons parsley
2 cups water

Rub roast with Creole seasoning and lemon-pepper. Brown on top of stove in large pot with lid. Add onions and brown for 2 to 3 minutes. Pour Worcestershire, steak sauce, parsley and water around roast. Turn stove on

Nutrition Nibble

The leanest cuts of beef include: top round, eye round, round tip, top sirloin, top loin and tenderloin. These average only 24mg cholesterol per cooked ounce and 25 to 43% of their calories from fat. It is essential to trim all visible fat.

medium-low heat for 30 minutes (it will boil). Turn down to low heat for 1 1/2 hours. If you want a thicker gravy, blend 3 tablespoons flour with a little water and add to gravy, stirring well.

Lisa Town

	Cal	Fat(g)	% Fat Cal	Sat Fat(g)	Chol(mg)	Sod(mg)
Per Serving	183	6.8	34	2.4	68	322

Honey and Sesame Seed Pork Tenderloin
Yield: 4 servings of 3 ounces each

1-pound whole pork tenderloin, well trimmed
1/2 cup reduced sodium soy sauce
2 cloves garlic, minced
1 tablespoon grated fresh ginger or 1 teaspoon dry ginger
1 tablespoon sesame oil
1/4 cup honey
2 tablespoons brown sugar
4 tablespoons sesame seeds, lightly toasted

Combine soy, garlic, ginger and sesame oil. Place tenderloin in heavy zippered plastic bag and pour soy mixture over to coat. Let marinate overnight in refrigerator. Remove pork and pat dry. Mix together honey and brown sugar in shallow plate. Place sesame seeds in separate plate. Roll pork in honey, then roll in seeds. Roast in pan for 20 to 30 minutes at 375 degrees or until thermometer reads 160 degrees.

Michele Bienvenu

	Cal	Fat(g)	% Fat Cal	Sat Fat(g)	Chol(mg)	Sod(mg)
Per Serving	318	10.7	30	2.4	81	590

Nutrition Nibble

Old recommendations for cooking pork include cooking to higher internal temperature. Leaner cuts of pork will turn out dry, leathery and less flavorful if overcooked. New recommendations suggest using a meat thermometer and cooking to an internal temperature of 160 degrees. The center should be juicy with just a trace of pink.

Nutrition Note

Honey and Sesame Seed Pork Tenderloin
Nutrition information is based on at least 1/2 of the marinade drained off and discarded before cooking.

Rosemary Grilled Pork Tenderloin

Yield: 6 servings of 3 ounces each

2 tablespoons olive oil
2 tablespoons balsamic, white wine or flavored vinegar
2 tablespoons lemon juice
Zest of 1 lemon
2 cloves garlic, crushed
1 tablespoon chopped fresh rosemary OR 2 teaspoons
    dried rosemary
1 tablespoon honey
1 teaspoon freshly ground pepper or lemon-pepper, salt
    free
Two 3-4 pound pork tenderloins, well trimmed

Combine all ingredients except pork in a 12x8x2-inch
dish; stir well. Add tenderloins and turn to coat in marinade. Cover and chill for 1 to 3 hours or longer. Grill tenderloins over hot coals for 20 minutes or longer, covered,
until done. Slice to serve. If desired, microwave the marinade for 30 seconds to 1 minute and then brush pork
slices. Serve hot or room temperature.

Ashley Hamilton Higginbotham

	Cal	Fat(g)	% Fat Cal	Sat Fat(g)	Chol(mg)	Sod(mg)
Per Serving	201	8.5	38	2.1	80	87

Jalapeño Pork Tenderloin

Yield: 6 servings of 3 ounces each

2 pork tenderloins, about 3/4 pound each
1 inch piece of fresh ginger, peeled and minced
1 jalepeño pepper, seeded and minced
1/4 teaspoon crushed red pepper flakes
1/3 cup honey
3 tablespoons reduced sodium soy sauce
1 tablespoon sesame oil
1 tablespoon vinegar (rice vinegar is preferable)

Trim tenderloins of excess fat. Make a marinade of remaining ingredients. Place in shallow dish or in a zippered
plastic bag and cover with marinade. Cover and refrigerate several hours or overnight, turning several times.

Remove from marinade, saving liquid for basting. Grill over medium hot coals for 10 to 15 minutes with pit cover down, turning once. Do not overcook! Using a meat thermometer, internal temperature should reach 160 degrees. Serve hot in 3/4-inch slices.

Mrs. James E. Toups, Jr.

	Cal	Fat(g)	% Fat Cal	Sat Fat(g)	Chol(mg)	Sod(mg)
Per Serving	228	6.5	26	1.8	81	393

Sweet and Sour Brisket
Yield: 22 servings of 3 ounces each

One 6-pound brisket, flat half, trimmed well
12 ounces tomato sauce, no salt added
1/2 cup red wine vinegar
2 tablespoons brown sugar
3 tablespoons liquid smoke
1/2 cup reduced sodium soy sauce
2 tablespoons Worcestershire sauce
2 tablespoons steak sauce
2 tablespoons lemon juice
1 tablespoon white wine Worcestershire sauce
1/2 cup barbecue sauce
1 tablespoon tarragon vinegar
Tabasco sauce to taste
1/2 cup corn syrup
1 tablespoon garlic powder
1 tablespoon dry mustard
6 ounces lemon-lime soft drink

Trim brisket of all visible fat. Place brisket into crockpot. In mixing bowl, combine all of the above ingredients, mixing well. Pour over brisket. Cook in crockpot on high heat for 2 hours or until sauce is bubbly. Turn heat to low and cook for 7 hours or until done.

Kathleen L. Howell

	Cal	Fat(g)	% Fat Cal	Sat Fat(g)	Chol(mg)	Sod(mg)
Per Serving	231	9.4	37	3.4	67	374

Nutrition Note

Sweet and Sour Brisket
Untrimmed, whole briskets generally have more than 75% of their calories from fat. The leanest part of the brisket is the flat half. The point half tends to have a higher fat content. To obtain this leaner version, it is essential to use the flat half and trim it of all visible fat before placing it in the crockpot.

Cinnamon Pork Tenderloin
Yield: 4 servings of 3 ounces each

One 1-pound whole pork tenderloin, well trimmed
1/4 cup reduced sodium soy sauce
1 tablespoon vinegar
2 tablespoons dry red wine
1 tablespoon brown sugar
1 tablespoon honey
1/2 tablespoon ground cinnamon
1 clove garlic, crushed
1 green onion, cut in 1-inch pieces then split in half

Mix all ingredients except pork. Add pork, turning to coat. Cover and let marinate overnight in the refrigerator. Bake at 350 degrees for 30 minutes basting every 10 minutes.

Elaine O. Dupuy

	Cal	Fat(g)	% Fat Cal	Sat Fat(g)	Chol(mg)	Sod(mg)
Per Serving	190	4.2	20	1.4	81	590

Venison Enchiladas
Yield: 8 servings

1 pound ground venison, well trimmed
1/2 cup chopped onion
8 corn tortillas
1/2 cup shredded Monterey Jack cheese plus 1/2 cup
     part skim mozzarella cheese
1/2 cup taco sauce
4 tablespoons cornstarch
One 14 1/2-ounce can defatted chicken broth, less salt
1/4 cup water, less salt
1/2 cup light sour cream
1/4 cup green chilies
1/2 cup nonfat plain yogurt

Nutrition Nibble

The leanest pork cuts are largely from the loin. Trimmed pork tenderloin is comparable to skinless chicken. Trimmed center loin and rump roast are comparable to lean beef.

Cook meat and onions. Drain off fat. Steam tortillas in microwave briefly until just soft. Spoon equal portions of meat on each. Top with 1 tablespoon each of cheese and taco sauce. Roll up. Place seam side down in baking dish. Blend cornstarch and 1/2 cup of the broth until smooth paste is formed. Warm the rest of the broth with the water.

Slowly stir in cornstarch "paste" and blend. Continue to heat and stir till thick. Remove from heat. Add sour cream, chilies and yogurt. Pour over tortillas and top with remaining cheese. Bake at 400 degrees for 15 minutes.

Rosemary Campbell

	Cal	Fat(g)	% Fat Cal	Sat Fat(g)	Chol(mg)	Sod(mg)
Per Serving	234	7.8	30	4.6	66	398

Stuffed Bell Peppers
Yield: 6 servings

3/4 pound extra lean ground beef
1 onion, chopped
1 small bell pepper, chopped
2 stalks celery, chopped
1 clove garlic, minced, optional
8 sprigs parsley, chopped
5-6 pieces toast
1/4 teaspoon salt
Pepper to taste
3 bell peppers, halved

In a nonstick skillet, sauté meat with onion, bell pepper, celery, garlic and parsley. Drain off fat. Blot meat with paper towels. Wipe pan. Return mixture to pan. Wet toast in a colander and break up. Put in skillet. Salt and pepper mixture. Mix well. Put seeded halves of bell pepper into pot of water and cook until soft. Stuff peppers with mixture and put into shallow baking dish with small amount of water. Bake in oven at 350 degrees for 20 minutes. These freeze well! **Variation:** Can substitute 1 cup of lean ham, shrimp or lean ground round. May top with a tomato sauce.

Mrs. Rivers Wall, Jr.
River Road Recipes II, page 104

Original Recipe

	Cal	Fat(g)	% Fat Cal	Sat Fat(g)	Chol(mg)	Sod(mg)
Per Serving	291	18.3	56	7.2	50	338

Lightened Recipe

	Cal	Fat(g)	% Fat Cal	Sat Fat(g)	Chol(mg)	Sod(mg)
Per Serving	204	8.0	35	2.9	36	241

You will often find locals at Romano's Blue Ribbon store. They take a number from the ticket dispenser and stand patiently in line for a chance to point through the glass front of the steam table at heaping containers of stuffed bell peppers, turnip greens, smothered pork chops, crowder peas, peach cobbler, and corn bread. Three ladies with hair nets and quick smiles follow the pointing fingers with big stainless steel spoons, filling styrofoam cartons with a little bit of heaven.

One Step Further

Stuffed Bell Peppers
To trim off over 3.5gm more fat per serving, try well-trimmed lean ground round in place of the ground beef.

Blackberry and Port Venison

Yield: 4 servings of 3 ounces each

1 pound backstrap or venison tenderloin
1/4 teaspoon red pepper
1/4 teaspoon black pepper
1/2 teaspoon garlic powder
1 tablespoon light Creole seasoning
1/3 cup flour
1 tablespoon oil
1/2 cup ruby port
1/2 cup blackberry jam

Season and flour meat and sauté in oil. Set aside and keep warm. Do not overcook! Blot pan with paper towels to remove most of the grease. Deglaze pan with port and sauté for 2 minutes. Add jam and cook until thickened. Pour over venison. Duck breast can be substituted.

Peggy Barton

	Cal	Fat(g)	% Fat Cal	Sat Fat(g)	Chol(mg)	Sod(mg)
Per Serving	336	5.4	14	2.9	93	391

Curried Sausage

Yield: 10 servings

1 pound light bulk sausage
1 cup ground skinless turkey
1 cup chopped green pepper
1 cup sliced mushrooms
2 tablespoons tub margarine
2 tablespoons flour
2 teaspoons curry powder
1 1/2 cups skim milk
Freshly ground pepper to taste
Bread crumbs
4 tablespoons freshly grated Parmesan cheese

Nutrition Note

Curried Sausage
Although this is still somewhat high in fat, it has less than 1/2 the fat of the original.

Crumble sausage and turkey in skillet, cook until brown, separating with fork. Drain off and discard fat. Drain meat on paper towels and blot off fat. In a nonstick skillet, sauté green pepper and mushrooms in margarine. Mix well. Blend in flour and curry powder, gradually add milk. Stir until thickened. Add pepper to taste. Add turkey and sausage and spoon into shallow 8x12-inch baking dish. Sprinkle with bread crumbs and Parmesan cheese. Bake 30 minutes at 350 degrees.

Ann Champagne Solanas

	Cal	Fat(g)	% Fat Cal	Sat Fat(g)	Chol(mg)	Sod(mg)
Per Serving	**188**	**11.1**	**53**	**3.5**	**49**	**385**

Dutch Oven Doves
Yield: 4 servings

8 doves, cleaned and dressed
1/4 teaspoon salt
Freshly ground pepper to taste
1/4 cup flour
1 tablespoon vegetable oil
1 tablespoon finely chopped parsley
1/4 teaspoon thyme
1/4 teaspoon rosemary
1/2 cup finely chopped onion
One 4-ounce can button mushrooms, drained and lightly
    rinsed
1 cup white wine

Salt and pepper doves. Dredge in flour. Spray a nonstick Dutch oven with vegetable oil cooking spray and heat oil. Brown doves. Sprinkle with parsley, thyme and rosemary. Cover and cook slowly for 15 minutes. Add onions, mushrooms and white wine. Cover and simmer for 1 hour or until tender.

Mrs. John G. Blanche
River Road Recipes II, page 161

Original Recipe
	Cal	Fat(g)	% Fat Cal	Sat Fat(g)	Chol(mg)	Sod(mg)
Per Serving	**311**	**10.6**	**32**	**5.8**	**114**	**380**

Lightened Recipe
	Cal	Fat(g)	% Fat Cal	Sat Fat(g)	Chol(mg)	Sod(mg)
Per Serving	**262**	**6.2**	**22**	**1**	**91**	**253**

My husband hunted all his life, growing up in Tensas Parish and later in Baton Rouge, after he was graduated from the Naval Academy and was teaching at LSU. He loved to cook the game he hunted, but I never ate it myself! He would entertain his luncheon club, a group of men, and serve this recipe.

Mrs. John G. Blanche

Medallions of Pork *with Fresh Mint*
Yield: 6 servings

Six 4-ounce pork loin center fillet chops, 1-inch thick
5 tablespoons Worcestershire sauce
1 tablespoon vinegar
1/2 teaspoon red pepper
2 teaspoons garlic powder
1/3 cup dijon mustard
1/2 cup honey
1/4 cup mint leaves

Marinate well-trimmed pork in Worcestershire sauce, vinegar and seasonings for 2 hours or longer. Baste with mustard and honey. Place mint leaf on top of each chop and place pork onto barbecue grill. Grill for approximately 22 minutes or 11 minutes per side.

A. Hays Town, III

	Cal	Fat(g)	% Fat Cal	Sat Fat(g)	Chol(mg)	Sod(mg)
Per Serving	303	8.9	27	2.8	58	460

Rack of Lamb
Yield: 6 servings

One rack of lamb
1/4 teaspoon paprika
1/4 teaspoon salt
1 teaspoon white ground pepper
1 tablespoon olive oil
2-3 tablespoons Herbes de Provence*
2 cloves garlic, mashed
2 tablespoons reduced sodium soy sauce
1/4 cup dijon mustard
1 tablespoon cider vinegar
1/4 teaspoon ginger

Trim all visible fat from the rack of lamb. Mix paprika, salt and pepper. Rub mixture into meat. Heat a nonstick skillet on high and add olive oil. Sear the rack on both sides and place in roasting pan. Make herb-mustard coating with rest of ingredients and spread on meat side of rack. Place in a 450-degree oven and roast 15 to 20 minutes. Meat should

Nutrition Note

Rack of Lamb
This has close to only 1/3 the fat of the original, yet can be even lighter if leaner cuts are used, such as well trimmed leg of lamb or loin chops. These can save over 5gm fat per serving.

One Step Further

Medallions of Pork with Fresh Mint
To save over 180mg of sodium per serving, reduce the dijon mustard to 2 tablespoons and add 1 tablespoon dry mustard and 3 tablespoons white wine to the honey.

remain pink on the inside. Let rest 5 minutes before carving into chops. *An herb blend of thyme, basil, savory, fennel, lavender.

Dr. John R. Romero, III

	Cal	Fat(g)	% Fat Cal	Sat Fat(g)	Chol(mg)	Sod(mg)
Per Serving	273	16.2	53	5	86	584

Fig Glazed Pork
Yield: 12 servings of 3 ounces each

3 pounds pork loin roast, well trimmed
1 tablespoon reduced salt seasoning
1 tablespoon cinnamon
2 pods garlic, chopped
1/2 teaspoon chopped fresh ginger
1/4 cup reduced sodium soy sauce
1/2 cup honey
1 1/2 cups white wine

Sprinkle pork with seasoning and cinnamon and rub in. Stuff roast with garlic pieces. Marinate in ginger, soy sauce and honey mixture overnight. Sear pork on top of stove in nonstick pan. Place roast in Dutch oven and add wine. Bake in oven at 350 degrees for 45 minutes.

Glaze
1 cup fig preserves
1/4 cup balsamic vinegar
1-2 onions, quartered
1 1/2 cups white wine
1 pound whole mushrooms
1 cinnamon stick

Mix the above ingredients, place on top of roast and bake 30 more minutes or until meat thermometer reaches 160 to 170 degrees.

Theresa Prendergast

	Cal	Fat(g)	% Fat Cal	Sat Fat(g)	Chol(mg)	Sod(mg)
Per Serving	286	10.4	34	3.5	78	255

Nutrition Note

Fig Glazed Pork
Nutritional information is based on at least 1/2 of the marinade drained off and discarded.

Marinated Raspberry Pork Chops
Yield: 4 servings of 3 ounces each

Four 4-ounce boneless center cut loin pork chops, well
    trimmed
1/4 cup raspberry vinegar from "Something Extra"
3 tablespoons Worcestershire sauce
1 1/2 teaspoons light Creole seasoning

Pound flat and marinate the pork chops in the seasonings
for 1 to 3 hours. Grill for 5 to 8 minutes per side, being
careful not to overcook. This may also be "pan fried" in a
nonstick skillet, sprayed with cooking spray, for about 5
minutes per side.

Josephine Gomez

	Cal	Fat(g)	% Fat Cal	Sat Fat(g)	Chol(mg)	Sod(mg)
Per Serving	**219**	**11.1**	**46**	**3.8**	**60**	**385**

New Orleans Grillades
Yield: 6 servings

1 1/2 pounds lean round steak, 1/2 inch thick
2-3 tablespoons beef or chicken broth or wine
1 tablespoon oil
2 tablespoons flour
2 onions, chopped
3 cloves garlic, minced
1 bell pepper, chopped
1 large stalk celery, chopped
One 16-ounce can whole peeled tomatoes, chopped,
    liquid reserved
Hot water plus reserved tomato liquid to equal 1 1/2 cups
2 bay leaves, crumbled
1/4 teaspoon thyme
2 tablespoons chopped parsley
1/4 teaspoon salt
1/4 teaspoon celery seed

Pound steak with meat mallet and flatten to 1/4 inch thickness, trim fat and cut into 6 squares. Brown meat in a nonstick skillet. Add broth or wine as needed to prevent sticking. Remove meat, drain on paper towels. Blot pan with

Nutrition Nibble

Some red meat may be
used by health con-
scious individuals inter-
ested in lowering cho-
lesterol. Look for cuts
with the least amount of
marbled fat and then
trim them well. A serv-
ing portion is about
1/4 of a pound well-
trimmed raw meat or 3
ounces cooked lean
meat.

paper towel to remove fat. Add oil, blend in flour and stir until brown. Add onion, garlic, bell pepper and celery, stirring frequently until vegetables soften. Add a little tomato liquid or broth if needed. Put in crockpot at this point and add remaining ingredients. Stir until well mixed. Add browned steak and slow cook all day or cook on stove until meat falls apart. Serve with Garlic Cheese Grits.

Karen Gulotta

	Cal	Fat(g)	% Fat Cal	Sat Fat(g)	Chol(mg)	Sod(mg)
Per Serving	235	7.5	29	2.1	69	267

Venison Chili
Yield: 10 servings

2 tablespoons vegetable oil
1 large onion, chopped
1 green pepper, chopped
2 large garlic cloves, minced
2 1/2 tablespoons chili powder
1 1/2 pounds well-trimmed venison, cubed
3/4 pound well-trimmed venison, ground
One 28-ounce can crushed tomatoes
3 tablespoons red wine vinegar
2 tablespoons ground cumin
2 tablespoons Worcestershire sauce
1/2 teaspoon red pepper
1/2 teaspoon salt, optional
1 teaspoon black pepper

Heat oil in large skillet. Stir in onion, green pepper, garlic and chili powder. Sauté until tender. Add meat. Stir with wooden spoon 4 or 5 minutes, brown well until no longer red. Drain off fat and pat skillet with paper towel to remove oil. Add other ingredients. Bring to a boil. Reduce heat, continue cooking uncovered for 30 minutes or longer to thicken. If too thin, add 3 tablespoons fine corn meal. Freezes well.

Dr. Judy Fishbein

	Cal	Fat(g)	% Fat Cal	Sat Fat(g)	Chol(mg)	Sod(mg)
Per Serving	178	5.3	26	2.6	84	348

Lasagna
Yield: 12 servings

1 pound lean ground round
1 white onion, chopped
3 cloves garlic, chopped
One 28-ounce can tomato puree, no salt added
One 6-ounce can tomato paste, no salt added
One 16-ounce can stewed tomatoes with liquid
1/4 cup red wine
1 stalk celery, chopped
1 carrot, finely chopped
1 tablespoon dried oregano
1/4 teaspoon salt
Black pepper to taste
24 ounces light cottage cheese
1/2 cup freshly grated Parmesan cheese
One 10-ounce package frozen, chopped spinach, cooked
     and well drained
2 egg whites, OR 1/4 cup egg substitute OR 1 egg
One 16-ounce package lasagna noodles, cooked
1 3/4 cups shredded part skim mozzarella cheese

Brown meat and onions; drain meat on paper towels to remove excess fat. Wipe out skillet. Return meat to pan and add garlic, all tomatoes and red wine. Add celery, carrots, oregano, salt and pepper. Cook uncovered for 1/2 hour on simmer. Sauce will be very dry. Mix the next four ingredients. To assemble lasagna, spray 11x13-inch glass baking dish with cooking spray. Place 1 cup of the sauce in bottom. Layer 1/2 of the lasagna noodles. Cover with spinach mixture. Layer remaining noodles. Cover with remaining sauce. Sprinkle with mozzarella cheese. Cover with foil and cook in a 350-degree oven for 45 minutes.

Machita Eyre

	Cal	Fat(g)	% Fat Cal	Sat Fat(g)	Chol(mg)	Sod(mg)
Per Serving	384	9.5	22	4.7	77	4452

Mushroom Meatloaf *with Dijon-Horseradish Sauce*
Yield: 6 servings

2 tablespoons defatted chicken broth, less salt
1 cup sliced mushrooms
1 cup chopped onions
1 clove garlic, minced
1/2 cup low fat ricotta cheese
1/2 teaspoon black pepper
1/2 teaspoon salt
3 egg whites or 1/2 cup egg substitute
1/2 cup skim milk
1 1/2 pounds of lean ground round
3/4 cup bread crumbs
1 tablespoon Worcestershire sauce
2 tablespoons dijon mustard

Sauté in chicken broth the mushrooms, onions and garlic. Cream ricotta cheese and add to mixture. Set aside. Combine rest of ingredients in another bowl. Put 1/2 of meat mixture into a 9x5x3-inch pan. Make a shallow trough down the center of meat. Spoon ricotta cheese-mushroom mixture in the trough. Shape the rest of the meat over the filling making sure all of the filling is covered. Seal meat well around edges. Place loaf on a baking rack in a pan and bake at 350 degrees for 1 hour and 15 minutes. Drain off grease and discard. Let stand 14 minutes before slicing.

Sauce
2 teaspoons flour
1/2 cup nonfat plain yogurt
1/2 cup light sour cream
2 teaspoons dijon mustard
1 tablespoon horseradish
1/4 teaspoon salt
1/8 teaspoon nutmeg
Dash red pepper
1/8 teaspoon white pepper

Blend flour into yogurt. Stir all ingredients over low heat. Serve over meatloaf slices.

Betty D. Backstrom

	Cal	Fat(g)	% Fat Cal	Sat Fat(g)	Chol(mg)	Sod(mg)
Per Serving	307	8.9	27	3.7	80	701

One Step Further

Mushroom Meatloaf

Another 260mg per serving of sodium can be trimmed off if you omit the salt in this recipe.

In south Louisiana, cooking is as much a part of male culture as it is female. In fact, some cooking tasks – like the roasting of the milk-fed pig – have been elevated to the status of tribal ritual. The cochon de lait, *as it's called in French, requires that the men build a special outdoor roasting pit, around which they huddle throughout the entire night before the pig is to be eaten. Drinking and telling stories and "male-bonding," a century before pop psychiatrists ever coined that phrase.*

Smoked Pork l'Orange

Yield: 20 servings of 3 ounces each

3/4 cup cider vinegar
1 large navel orange, quartered, unpeeled
3 lemons, quartered, unpeeled
1/4 cup orange juice concentrate
2 tablespoons Worcestershire sauce
1 teaspoon salt
2 tablespoons dark corn syrup
1 teaspoon dried mint leaves
1 teaspoon allspice
1 teaspoon dry mustard
1/4 teaspoon paprika
2 teaspoons Tabasco sauce
1/4 teaspoon pepper
1 beef bouillon cube, less salt
1/4 cup catsup
1 teaspoon dried basil
1/2 cup water
One 6-pound whole boneless pork loin, well trimmed
Salt and pepper to taste

Puree vinegar, oranges and lemons in food processor. Add all other ingredients except pork, salt and pepper. Transfer to saucepan. Bring to boil, stirring constantly, being careful not to burn. Reduce heat and cook uncovered 10 minutes. Salt and pepper pork. Place in large, heavy duty plastic bag and add sauce. Marinate 24 hours. Remove meat from sauce, reserving marinade. Place on smoker that has a water bath. Cook 4 to 6 hours, basting with sauce. (Note: This may be cooked conventionally; be careful about rapid browning. I suggest a fail test. Cook until interior temperature is 160 to 170 degrees.) Remove from grill and wrap in foil. Bring marinade to a gentle boil and simmer for 5 to 10 minutes. Slice pork and place in bottom of a skillet. Pour reheated marinade down center of pork and barely reheat. Serve.

Helen W. Whitley

	Cal	Fat(g)	% Fat Cal	Sat Fat(g)	Chol(mg)	Sod(mg)
Per Serving	209	10.7	44	3.6	52	258

Rabbit Hasenpfeffer

Yield: 6 servings of 3 ounces each

One 2 1/2-pound skinned wild rabbit
1/4 cup oil, divided
One 18-ounce can tomatoes
1 tablespoon sugar
1 cup vinegar
1 cup water

Marinade
2 large onions, sliced
3 stalks celery, cut
6 sprigs parsley, chopped
2 cloves garlic
1/2 teaspoon cloves
1/2 teaspoon allspice
2 bay leaves
1/4 teaspoon red pepper
1/2 teaspoon salt
Vinegar to cover rabbit

Wash rabbit and cut into pieces; put into large bowl that can be covered. Pour the above marinade over rabbit and cover. Place in refrigerator overnight. When ready to cook, drain rabbit and vegetables. Spray a nonstick skillet and heat 1/2 of the oil. Brown the rabbit pieces on all sides. Remove rabbit and drain on paper towels. Add the remaining oil to the skillet and sauté the drained vegetables well. To this add the tomatoes and sugar. Cook about 15 minutes to cook down tomatoes. Add the vinegar and water. Bring to a boil and add rabbit. Cook slowly for 1 1/2 hours.

Mrs. J. R. Black
River Road Recipes, *page 143*

Original Recipe

	Cal	Fat(g)	% Fat Cal	Sat Fat(g)	Chol(mg)	Sod(mg)
Per Serving	295	12.5	37	2.1	104	730

Lightened Recipe

	Cal	Fat(g)	% Fat Cal	Sat Fat(g)	Chol(mg)	Sod(mg)
Per Serving	241	6.3	24	1.3	104	375

Nutrition Note

Rabbit Hasenpfeffer

Nutrition information is based on wild rabbit, which is leaner than domestic raised rabbit. This is true of most game. If domestic rabbit is used, fat content would increase by over 4gm per portion.

Sweet and Sour Pork
Yield: 6 servings

First step
1 pound loin of pork
1 tablespoon Chinese or Japanese wine or sherry
2 tablespoons reduced sodium soy sauce
2 tablespoons flour
1 tablespoon cornstarch
1 tablespoon vegetable oil

Second step
3 green peppers, quartered
1 onion, quartered
1 carrot, cut into small wedges and boiled for 8 minutes
One 4-ounce can bamboo shoots, cut into small wedges
2 slices juice packed pineapple, quartered, liquid reserved
1 tablespoon oil

Third step
1 tablespoon sugar
4 tablespoons reduced sodium soy sauce
1 tablespoon wine
2 tablespoons wine vinegar
4 tablespoons tomato sauce, no salt added
1 tablespoon cornstarch, mixed with 1/2 cup pineapple
    juice

Cut pork into 1-inch cubes, trimming all visible fat. Mix well with other "first step" ingredients, except oil. Sauté pork in oil heated in nonstick skillet until crisp and golden. If oil is completely absorbed before completed, add pineapple juice to finishing sautéing. Set pork aside. Wipe out skillet. Heat from "second step" oil and sauté those ingredients. Once again add pineapple juice if needed. Mix "third step" ingredients (excluding cornstarch mixture) in bowl and add to "second step" ingredients. Bring mixture to a boil and add cornstarch mixture. Allow to boil until cornstarch mixture is well blended, stirring constantly. Add pork cubes and mix well. Serve hot. Good over a bed of rice.

Doris LaRoche

One Step Further

Sweet and Sour Pork

Use lean, well-trimmed pork tenderloin to trim back another 1.5gm fat per serving.

	Cal	Fat(g)	% Fat Cal	Sat Fat(g)	Chol(mg)	Sod(mg)
Per Serving	238	9.8	36	2.3	48	566

Seafood

1980s

In 1964, the League donated $4000 to hire a director for the activity center at the Baton Rouge Association for Retarded Children. In 1968, the League published *Baton Rouge: A Guide for the Handicapped,* a guidebook providing useful information to handicapped citizens about access to public buildings. The book received a citation from the President's Commission for the Handicapped and predated today's concern for the handicapped by 25 years. During the 1960s, League members also volunteered at the Louisiana State School for the Visually Impaired.

We learned that we could make a difference in combatting prejudice and that our efforts could contribute to more productive lives for the physically challenged.

Crawfish Pie

Yield: 6 servings

2/3 cup defatted chicken broth, less salt, divided
3 tablespoons diet margarine
1 large onion, chopped
1/2 green pepper, chopped
1/2 cup sliced celery
2 tablespoons all-purpose flour
1 pound crawfish tails, lightly rinsed and drained
6 ounces shredded low-fat mozzarella cheese (1 1/2
     cups)
1/2 cup plain bread crumbs
1/3 cup sliced green onions
1/4 teaspoon salt
Pepper to taste
1 egg white
2 light pie crusts

In large skillet, heat 1/3 cup of broth and margarine.
Sauté onions, bell pepper and celery. Add flour; mix well.
Add remaining 1/3 cup of broth and stir until well blended
(this is a very thick mixture). Add crawfish tails and stir
over medium heat about 5 minutes. Add cheese, bread
crumbs, green onions and salt and pepper. Mix well and
remove from heat. Prepare pie crust following recipe found
in "Something Extra" section. Place 1/2 crust mixture into
a deep 9-inch pie plate. Place the remaining crust
wrapped in plastic in the refrigerator. Pour the crawfish
mixture into the unbaked prepared pie shell. Roll out the
remaining crust, as per noted recipe, between wax paper.
Peel off one sheet of wax paper, place shell over pie and
remove other wax paper. Pinch edges together, trimming
pie shell as needed. Cut several slits in pie shell and brush
with beaten egg white. Bake at 350 degrees for 35 minutes.

Joan Love

	Cal	Fat(g)	% Fat Cal	Sat Fat(g)	Chol(mg)	Sod(mg)
Per Serving	338	15.4	41	3.8	90	353

One of the most essential social skills in South Louisiana is the ability to peel crawfish. Swiftly and adeptly. Here this skill is acquired about the age of six along with bicycle rid-ing. First we pluck a crawfish from the steaming pile. We rip the head away, then deftly search for the precise spot at the base of the tail. A sharp pinch . . . and voila. One perfect, succulent piece of crawfish meat will slide effortlessly out of its shell and into your mouth.

Summertime Crab Quiche
Yield: 8 servings

Two 10-inch soft flour tortillas
Two 1-ounce slices no fat Swiss cheese
1/2 cup chopped onion
6 ounces crabmeat
1/2 of a 14-ounce can chopped artichoke hearts
1/4 teaspoon salt
1/2 teaspoon crushed red pepper flakes
One 8-ounce carton egg substitute
One 8-ounce can evaporated skim milk

Line a 9-inch pie pan with tortillas. Cover with the cheese slices. Add the chopped onion, crabmeat, artichoke hearts, salt, and crushed red pepper. Mix the egg substitute and evaporated milk and pour into the pie pan. Bake for 40 minutes at 350 degrees.

Shelley Brunson

	Cal	Fat(g)	% Fat Cal	Sat Fat(g)	Chol(mg)	Sod(mg)
Per Serving	140	2.4	15	0.7	25	317

Mom's Oyster Dressing
Yield: 10 servings

2 tablespoons oil
3 cups chopped celery
2 cups chopped green onions
1 cup chopped white onions
2 cloves garlic, chopped
1/2 cup chopped green pepper
1 cup chopped parsley
5 dozen oysters and oyster water
1 turkey neck and gizzard, cooked in water
1 cup grated french bread
1/4 teaspoon salt
Pepper to taste
4 egg whites, beaten or 1/2 cup egg substitute
Marjoram, bay leaf, chervil, optional

Clean and chop all vegetables. Heat oil in a large pot and sauté celery until soft. Then add white onions, green peppers, green onions, and garlic. If more liquid is needed to sauté, add 2 to 3 tablespoons of oyster water or white wine. Steam with cover on low heat. Add parsley. When sautéed, add oysters. Cool turkey neck and gizzard in water in separate pot. Pull meat off turkey necks and chop gizzard. Add this to oyster dressing. Add a little oyster water to dressing. Stir french bread into dressing. Add pepper to taste and salt if needed. When cool, add beaten eggs. Stuff turkey with dressing. If not stuffed into turkey, dressing can be put in a covered ovenproof dish and heated in oven for 30 to 45 minutes at 300 degrees. Remove cover last 15 minutes to brown.

Kathleen L. Howell

	Cal	Fat(g)	% Fat Cal	Sat Fat(g)	Chol(mg)	Sod(mg)
Per Serving	209	7.3	24	1.5	84	294

Seafood Eggplant Casserole
Yield: 8 servings

One 1 1/2-2 pound eggplant
4 tablespoons flour
2 tablespoons canola oil
1 cup skim milk
1 cup chopped cooked shrimp
1 pound lump crabmeat
1 cup bread crumbs
1 bunch green onions, chopped
1/2 teaspoon each basil, oregano, thyme, paprika
1 teaspoon minced garlic
2 tablespoons parsley
1/2 teaspoon salt
1/4 teaspoon pepper
1/4 teaspoon red pepper

Peel and cube eggplant. Boil in water until tender, drain. Make a roux with the oil and flour. Add milk and stir until thickened. Fold in the eggplant and remaining ingredients. Place in 2-quart baking dish sprayed with vegetable oil cooking spray and bake for 30 minutes at 350 degrees.

Susan Giglio

	Cal	Fat(g)	% Fat Cal	Sat Fat(g)	Chol(mg)	Sod(mg)
Per Serving	196	5.3	24	0.6	96	441

Nutrition Note

Seafood Eggplant Casserole

For a more robust flavor and to decrease nutrient loss, roast the eggplant instead of boiling. Slice in half lengthwise and crisscross the flesh with a knife. Place cut side down on a baking sheet sprayed with cooking spray. Roast in 400-degree oven until flesh is very soft. Scoop out flesh and leave the skin behind. Continue with recipe.

One Step Further

Seafood Eggplant Casserole

Omit the oil and use the fat-free roux recipe in "Something Extra," saving 3.4gm fat and 30 calories per serving. Omitting the salt will cut 133mg sodium for each serving.

Crabmeat Au Gratin
Yield: 6 servings

2 tablespoons flour
1 1/2 tablespoons margarine
1 cup evaporated skim milk
1/2 cup dry white wine
1 bunch green onions, chopped
Pinch of nutmeg, optional
1 cup shredded reduced fat sharp cheddar cheese
1 pound lump crabmeat
1/2 cup bread crumbs

Make a white sauce by combining the flour and margarine in a saucepan. Cook on medium heat for a few minutes, then slowly add the milk. Stir and cook until thickened, then add the wine, green onions, nutmeg, cheese, and crabmeat. Pour into a 2-quart glass casserole. Sprinkle with bread crumbs. Bake for 15 minutes at 350 degrees, or until the top is nicely browned.

Michelle Bienvenu

	Cal	Fat(g)	% Fat Cal	Sat Fat(g)	Chol(mg)	Sod(mg)
Per Serving	240	7.8	29	2.8	87	481

Spinach Crabmeat Loaf
Yield: 6 servings

4 green onions, finely chopped
1 pound fresh spinach, washed and well drained
1 pound crabmeat
2 cups fresh bread crumbs
1/2 cup skim milk
1 whole egg plus 2 egg whites
Juice of 1 lemon
1/4 teaspoon salt
1/4 teaspoon freshly ground black pepper
1/4 teaspoon white pepper
1/8 teaspoon nutmeg
1/4 cup freshly grated Parmesan cheese

Preheat oven to 375 degrees. Mix everything together. Let the mixture sit for 5 minutes. Place in a loaf pan sprayed with butter-flavored vegetable oil cooking spray and then

One Step Further

Crabmeat Au Gratin

To reduce the sodium content, use a low fat and reduced sodium cheese.

spray the top lightly. Bake for 40 to 50 minutes. Let cool for 10 minutes before inverting onto a serving dish. May also be prepared with quality pink salmon (one 1-pound can) in place of crabmeat.

Mary Aycock

	Cal	Fat(g)	% Fat Cal	Sat Fat(g)	Chol(mg)	Sod(mg)
Per Serving	186	5.2	25	1.5	111	534

Grilled Marinated Fish

Yield: 8 servings

1/2 inch fresh ginger root
1 clove garlic
6 mint leaves
4 sprigs parsley
1/8 teaspoon black pepper
1/8 teaspoon salt
1/8 teaspoon cayenne pepper
2 dashes Tabasco sauce
1 1/2 teaspoons bottled stir fry sauce
1/2 teaspoon reduced sodium soy sauce
1/4 cup dry sherry
1 tablespoon lemon juice
1/3 cup defatted chicken broth, less salt
2 tablespoons olive salad oil
Eight 5-ounce fish fillets (salmon, mahi-mahi, grouper)

Place first 10 ingredients in food processor and finely chop. Add sherry and lemon juice. Process. Slowly add chicken broth, then oil with blade "on" until smooth. Wash and pat dry fillets. Place in glass dish and cover with marinade. Refrigerate for 1 hour. Place marinated fish on grill. Turn and brush frequently. Test for doneness with fork. Reduced sodium soy sauce with a dash of vinegar and sugar may be used in place of the stir fry sauce for similar results.

Ann Champagne Solanas

	Cal	Fat(g)	% Fat Cal	Sat Fat(g)	Chol(mg)	Sod(mg)
Per Serving	254	12	44	2.1	56	188

One Step Further

Spinach Crabmeat Loaf

Trim off another 35mg cholesterol if the whole egg is omitted and 3 egg whites or 1/2 cup egg substitute is used. More sodium can be trimmed by omitting the salt (88mg saved per serving) and the Parmesan cheese (75mg saved per serving).

Sunk Boat Trout

Yield: 6 servings

1/3 cup grated Parmesan cheese
1/3 cup all-purpose flour
1/4 teaspoon salt
1/2 teaspoon pepper
1 1/2 teaspoons paprika
1/4 cup skim milk
1 egg white, beaten
Six 6-ounce trout or catfish fillets
3 tablespoons sliced almonds

Combine cheese, flour, salt, pepper, and paprika. Set aside. Combine milk and beaten egg. Dip fillets in egg-milk mixture and dredge in flour mixture. Arrange in a 9x13-inch baking dish. Spray each fillet with vegetable oil cooking spray and sprinkle with almonds. Bake, covered, at 350 degrees for 35 to 40 minutes.

Allen Benitez
Mrs. Mark W. Heroman

	Cal	Fat(g)	% Fat Cal	Sat Fat(g)	Chol(mg)	Sod(mg)
Per Serving	340	15.7	42	3.3	103	295

Crawfish Jambalaya

Yield: 8 servings

2 ribs celery, chopped
1 large onion, chopped
1 bell pepper, chopped
1/4 cup chopped parsley
One 8-ounce package fresh mushrooms, sliced
1 tablespoon vegetable oil
1 tablespoon tub margarine
1 can cream of shrimp soup
1 cube reduced-sodium beef bouillon
1 1/4 cups boiling water
1 can Rotel tomatoes, chopped
1 1/2 cups raw rice
1 to 1 1/2 pounds crawfish tails, lightly rinsed

Sauté celery, onion, bell pepper, parsley and mushrooms in oil and margarine until soft. Add soup, bouillon dis-

Nutrition Nibble

Crawfish fat is generally found in the crawfish heads and in bags of peeled crawfish tails. This yellowish fat is high in saturated fat and should be rinsed from the crawfish tails and heads before using.

One Step Further

Crawfish Jambalaya
Reduce sodium further by omitting the shrimp soup and using your choice of the reduced salt cream soups available.

solved in boiling water, tomatoes, rice and crawfish. Mix well, cover and bake at 350 degrees for an hour and 10 minutes, stirring well after 15 minutes.

Adrienne M. Percy

	Cal	Fat(g)	% Fat Cal	Sat Fat(g)	Chol(mg)	Sod(mg)
Per Serving	263	5.5	19	1.6	83	598

Lime Shrimp in Tortillas
Yield: 8 servings

1/4 cup fresh lemon or lime juice
1 tablespoon olive oil
2 tablespoons defatted chicken broth OR seafood stock, less salt
1 teaspoon each garlic powder
1 teaspoon pepper
1/4 teaspoon salt
1 teaspoon parsley flakes or cilantro
1 pound fresh peeled and deveined medium shrimp
1 small onion, sliced into rings
1/2 green bell pepper, sliced
2 teaspoons olive oil
8 warm 6- to 8-inch flour tortillas
Optional toppings: salsa, shredded reduced fat cheese, light sour cream or yogurt.

Combine lemon or lime juice, 1 tablespoon olive oil, chicken broth, garlic, pepper, salt, and parsley flakes in zippered plastic bag. Add shrimp and marinate 15 to 30 minutes. In a nonstick skillet, sauté onion and green pepper in 2 teaspoons olive oil for 3 to 5 minutes. Drain and discard marinade from shrimp. Add shrimp to skillet and cook 5 to 8 minutes until done. Serve with tortillas and desired toppings. **Variation:** To make this a Shrimp Fajitas Dish add 2 teaspoons chili powder and 1/8 teaspoon ground cumin to the marinade and proceed with recipe as above.

Cindy Stewart
Joan M. Surso

	Cal	Fat(g)	% Fat Cal	Sat Fat(g)	Chol(mg)	Sod(mg)
Per Serving	193	5.6	27	1.2	87	275

Nutrition Nibble

Shrimp can be used by heart conscious chefs. They are higher in cholesterol than most meats and seafood, yet are low in fat content, especially low in saturated fat; therefore, they do not affect your blood cholesterol level as much, when eaten in moderate portions. Recommended serving size is a 3- to 4-ounce cooked portion.

Oysters Impromptu
Yield: 6 servings

1 tablespoon olive oil
1 bunch green onions, chopped
1/2 bunch parsley, chopped
2 pints raw oysters
1 tablespoon lemon juice
1/2 teaspoon Tabasco sauce
3 tablespoons Parmesan cheese
1/4 teaspoon black and white pepper
1/2 teaspoon basil
1/2 teaspoon oregano
1/4 teaspoon paprika
1/2 teaspoon garlic
1 1/2 cups plain bread crumbs

Heat oil and sauté onions and parsley until limp. Add oysters straight from jar. If too watery, pour off liquid. Add seasonings when oysters curl slightly. Add bread crumbs, stir, and serve.

Dawn W. Abbott

	Cal	Fat(g)	% Fat Cal	Sat Fat(g)	Chol(mg)	Sod(mg)
Per Serving	246	8.3	30	2.1	85	419

Grouper Spectacular
Yield: 8 servings

3 pounds grouper fillets, or any mild fish
1/3 cup lemon juice
1 medium onion, diced
1 medium bell pepper, diced
1 tablespoon vegetable or olive oil
2 medium tomatoes, diced
1/8 teaspoon salt
Pepper to taste
1 1/2 cups shredded mozzarella cheese
One 2.25-ounce can sliced black olives

Place fish fillets in a shallow container. Pour lemon juice over fish and refrigerate 2 hours. Sauté onions and bell pepper in oil for 5 minutes. Add tomatoes and cook for 2 more minutes. Remove from heat and set aside. Remove fish from lemon juice, place skin side down in a lightly greased 13x9x2-inch dish. Sprinkle with salt and pepper. Bake, uncovered, at 350 degrees for 30 minutes. Spoon vegetable mixture over fish. Sprinkle with cheese. Bake at 350 degrees for an additional 15 minutes or until fish flakes easily when tested with a fork. Sprinkle with black olives.

Karen Deumite

	Cal	Fat(g)	% Fat Cal	Sat Fat(g)	Chol(mg)	Sod(mg)
Per Serving	258	7.8	27	2.9	74	275

Shrimp Fiesta
Yield: 6 servings

1 pound deveined shrimp
2 tablespoons tub margarine
3 tablespoons flour
1 tablespoon chili powder
1/2 bell pepper, chopped
1 medium onion, chopped
One 16-ounce can no-added-salt tomatoes
One 16-ounce package frozen whole kernel corn
1/2 cup water or defatted chicken broth, less salt
One 2.5-ounce can ripe olives, chopped
2 bay leaves
1/4 teaspoon Tabasco sauce
1/8 teaspoon salt
Pepper to taste

Boil shrimp for 4 to 5 minutes; drain and cool. In a non-stick skillet melt margarine, stir flour and chili powder in until smooth. Add bell pepper and onion and sauté lightly. Add tomatoes in liquid and corn and cook until slightly thickened, stirring occasionally. Add chicken broth. Add shrimp, olives, bay leaves, Tabasco sauce, salt, and pepper. Cover and simmer 15 minutes. Serve over rice.

Anita Spaht (Mrs. H. Dale)

	Cal	Fat(g)	% Fat Cal	Sat Fat(g)	Chol(mg)	Sod(mg)
Per Serving	200	5.2	23	1.0	116	345

One Step Further

Shrimp Fiesta
Save 3gm more fat and close to 27 calories each serving by omitting the margarine and using 3 tablespoons of fat-free roux (see "Something Extra" section).

Stuffed Crabs

Yield: 8 servings

1 1/4 cups finely chopped onion
2/3 cup finely chopped celery
1 tablespoon margarine
1/2 cup plus 3 tablespoons defatted chicken broth or seafood stock, less salt, divided
1/8 teaspoon sage, optional
1/8 teaspoon thyme, optional
Two 5-ounce cans evaporated skim milk
2 cups cornflakes
2 pounds crabmeat OR 1 pound each lump and claw
1 tablespoon lemon juice
1/2 teaspoon garlic powder, optional
1/4 teaspoon pepper
1 teaspoon Worcestershire sauce
2 tablespoons dry sherry
20 saltine crackers, no salt tops, crumbled

Sauté onions and celery in margarine until onions are wilted, adding chicken broth or seafood stock as needed. Add the remaining 1/2 cup of chicken or seafood stock, sage, thyme, and evaporated milk and let boil. Crumble cornflakes and mix with crabmeat. Add and let heat. Mix well and add lemon juice, garlic powder, pepper, Worcestershire sauce and dry sherry. Sprinkle the crumbled saltines with the 3 tablespoons of stock and toss lightly. Set aside. Spray individual crab shells with vegetable oil cooking spray and put mixture in them. Sprinkle with crackers and spray lightly with vegetable oil cooking spray. Bake 20 minutes at 375 degrees. This recipe lends itself well as an appetizer. There are 16 appetizer servings per recipe.

Susan Marcus Dampf

	Cal	Fat(g)	% Fat Cal	Sat Fat(g)	Chol(mg)	Sod(mg)
Per Serving	233	5.6	22	0.7	110	542

Crawfish Cornbread Dressing

Yield: 12 servings

1 cup chopped onion
1 toe garlic, chopped
1/4 cup chopped green onion tops
1/4 cup chopped fresh parsley
1 tablespoon margarine
1 teaspoon corn oil
1 pound crawfish tails, lightly rinsed and drained
1/3 cup water
1/3 cup white wine
Two 8-ounce packages cornbread mix
1 egg
2 egg whites
2/3 cup low fat OR skim milk
One 14-ounce can defatted chicken broth, less salt
1 large chopped onion
1 cup chopped celery
1 green bell pepper, chopped
2 toes garlic, minced
2 tablespoons poultry seasoning
1/4 cup water

Sauté onion, garlic, onion tops, and parsley on low heat in margarine and oil until oleo rises to the top (about 30 minutes). DO NOT BURN. Add crawfish. Add water and wine to the pot. Bring mixture to a boil and then simmer for 10 minutes. Prepare cornbread similar to the package, but use only a total of 1 egg and replace other eggs with 2 egg whites (egg substitute may also be used), and use low fat or skim milk. Cool and crumble into a large bowl. Use 1/4 to 1/3 cup of the chicken broth to sauté the remaining vegetables. Add to cornbread, plus the rest of ingredients, reserving the crawfish mixture. Put in a 9x13-inch pan. Lightly mix 1/2 of crawfish mixture into cornbread mixture. Cover with foil. Bake 30 minutes at 350 degrees. Use rest of crawfish mixture as a sauce.

Mary R. Aycock

	Cal	Fat(g)	% Fat Cal	Sat Fat(g)	Chol(mg)	Sod(mg)
Per Serving	249	7.3	26	0.7	72	787

At first glance the table looks like it would anywhere in the country. A big brown turkey, stuffed with dressing. Only this stuffing will be cornbread. Or if it is white bread, full of plump oysters. The iced tea will automatically be sweet. And what looks like pumpkin pie, might just as likely be sweet potato. But the gratitude in the hearts of those around the table is the same as everywhere on this day that we set aside to be thankful for all that God has bestowed upon our nation. Made even richer by the wonderful diversity of its people.

Nutrition Note

Crawfish Cornbread Dressing

To reduce the sodium content further make a low sodium homemade cornbread. Conveniene products, as mixes, tend to be higher in sodium.

179

It's an old family recipe which has evolved and changed over the years, and always a special treat for out-of-town guests during crawfish season. In fact, they expect it! I can make it in large quantities when crawfish are a good buy, and freeze it for future occasions.

– Mrs. Wray Edward Robinson

Crawfish Etouffée or Pie Filling
Yield: 12 servings

1/4 cup margarine
1/4 cup oil
1 cup flour
2 bunches green onions
3 bell peppers
1 stalk celery
One 16-ounce can tomatoes
3 teaspoons garlic powder
2 teaspoons salt
1 tablespoon lemon juice
1 tablespoon black pepper
1 teaspoon cayenne pepper
1/4 cup fresh chopped parsley
3 tablespoons Worcestershire sauce
6 cups water (or homemade seafood stock)
3 pounds peeled crawfish tails, lightly rinsed and drained
3 cups uncooked rice

Heat oil and margarine preferably in an iron Dutch oven that has been sprayed with nonstick spray. Add flour and brown lightly. Chop green onions and reserve tops. In food processor or blender chop the vegetables and tomatoes. Add to the roux. Add seasonings, cover and cook about 15 to 20 minutes, stirring frequently. Add water and cook slowly for at least an hour. Add crawfish tails and chopped onion tops and cook about 15 minutes. For etouffée, cook rice. Serve crawfish over rice. For pies, use three 9-inch unbaked pie crusts. Pour filling over bottom crust and cover with top crusts. Cut slits in top. Bake on cookie sheet at 350 degrees for 15 minutes. Reduce heat to 300 degrees and bake for 15 minutes until golden brown. Pies will be considerably higher in fat content.

Mrs. Wray Edward Robinson
River Roads Recipes II, *Page 127*

One Step Further

Crawfish Etouffée or Pie Filling

If you use 1 cup of fat-free roux and omit the oil and margarine you can save over 60 calories and over 7gm fat for each serving, making the etouffée with only 5% of its calories from fat. The vegetables can simmer in broth or the juice from the canned tomatoes.

Original Recipe

	Cal	Fat(g)	% Fat Cal	Sat Fat(g)	Chol(mg)	Sod(mg)
Per Serving	681	33	44	6.5	259	2174

Lightened Recipe

	Cal	Fat(g)	% Fat Cal	Sat Fat(g)	Chol(mg)	Sod(mg)
Per Serving	409	9.3	21	1.5	155	583

Oyster Dressing for Turkey

Yield: 24 servings

1 pound light bulk turkey sausage
2 tablespoons vegetable oil
4 onions, chopped
2 bunches shallots, chopped
2 bunches parsley, chopped
2 stalks celery, chopped
1/4 cup defatted turkey broth OR oyster juice
One 8-ounce package cornbread mix
One 8-ounce package herb seasoned stuffing mix
1 loaf stale french bread, grated
5 dozen oysters and liquid (four 10-ounce containers)
2 egg whites
1/2 teaspoon sage
2 tablespoons lemon juice
1 teaspoon poultry seasoning
1/4 teaspoon pepper

Fry sausage until browned. Remove from skillet and drain on paper towels. Wipe skillet with paper towels. Heat oil and sauté the chopped seasonings until soft. Add broth or oyster juice as needed while sautéing the vegetables. Set aside. Meanwhile cook cornbread mix according to package directions (using skim milk) and when cooled, crumble it in a large mixing bowl. Add to this the sausage, cooked greens, herb seasoned stuffing mix and grated french bread. Add oysters and their liquid and combine this well. If oysters are extremely large, they can be cut in half. Add 2 egg whites and blend together again. Season to taste with sage, lemon juice, poultry seasoning and pepper. If too dry, add more oyster water, gradually. This makes enough dressing to stuff a 24-pound turkey and have enough left to fill a large casserole dish.

Katherine Melius

	Cal	Fat(g)	% Fat Cal	Sat Fat(g)	Chol(mg)	Sod(mg)
Per Serving	219	6.4	46	1.3	41	640

One Step Further

Oyster Dressing for Turkey

Trim off more than 120mg sodium from each serving by omitting the herb stuffing mix and using 10 slices of toasted whole wheat bread. Increase the spices.

Fresh Herb Shrimp

Yield: 6 servings

2 tablespoons tub margarine
1 1/2 pounds fresh jumbo shrimp, peeled, tails left on
1 tablespoon finely chipped fresh basil
1 tablespoon finely chopped fresh thyme
1 tablespoon finely chopped fresh chives
1 garlic clove, crushed
1/4 cup defatted chicken broth, less salt OR seafood
    stock
1 tablespoon cornstarch
1/2 cup dry white wine
Pepper, freshly ground
Herbed Grits
Fresh rosemary, for garnish

In large nonstick saucepan over medium heat, melt the margarine. Add the shrimp, basil, thyme, chives, and garlic. Sauté for 2 to 3 minutes, then add the broth. Meanwhile, in a small bowl mix the cornstarch with the wine. When the shrimp begin to turn pink, stir the wine mixture into the shrimp. Continue to cook until the shrimp are just done, another minute. Do not overcook. Season to taste with pepper and serve immediately over grits. Garnish with rosemary.

Herbed Grits

3 cups water
1/4 teaspoon salt
1 cup quick-cooking grits
One 12-ounce can evaporated skim milk
2 tablespoons tub margarine
1 clove garlic, minced
3 ounces light cream cheese, cubed and softened
1/4 cup chopped fresh parsley
2 tablespoons chopped fresh chives
Pepper, freshly ground

In a large saucepan, bring water and salt to a boil. Slowly add the grits then blend in the evaporated milk. Cook for ten minutes, stirring frequently. Add the margarine, garlic and cream cheese. When they are melted, add the parsley and chives, and stir to blend thoroughly. Season to taste with black pepper.

Margo Bouanchaud, Unique Cuisine

	Cal	Fat(g)	% Fat Cal	Sat Fat(g)	Chol(mg)	Sod(mg)
Per Serving	310	9.5	28	3.1	124	503

Crawfish Fettuccine
Yield: 16 servings

1/4 cup vegetable oil
3 medium onions, chopped
3 stalks celery, chopped
2 bell peppers, chopped
1/4 cup flour
8 ounces fresh mushrooms, sliced
Three 12-ounce cans evaporated skim milk less 1/2 cup
1/2 pound jalapeño Velveeta cheese
4 cloves garlic, minced
1 tablespoon light Creole seasoning
1 teaspoon pepper
1 pound fettuccine noodles, cooked
3 pounds crawfish tails, lightly rinsed
1/2 pound freshly grated Parmesan cheese
4 tablespoons parsley
1/2 teaspoon paprika

In a 5-gallon pot heat oil. Then add chopped vegetables and sauté until soft. Add flour and mushrooms to this mixture and cook for 20 minutes. Stir. Add milk, jalapeño cheese, garlic, Creole seasoning and pepper. Cook covered on low heat 20 minutes. Use a separate pot and cook fettuccine noodles according to directions on package. Drain and add noodles to sauce. Add crawfish, mix in Parmesan cheese. Put into 2 large casserole dishes, sprinkle with parsley and paprika, and bake at 350 degrees for 45 minutes.

Rosalyn Cordell
Lynn Gildersleeve Michelli

	Cal	Fat(g)	% Fat Cal	Sat Fat(g)	Chol(mg)	Sod(mg)
Per Serving	393	11.8	27	5.1	137	452

Great with Sensation Salad and french bread. May be prepared ahead of time and baked at the last minute. Can be halved. Also freezes well.

Rosalyn Cordell & Lynn Michelli

Crabmeat Casserole
Yield: 6 servings

One 14-ounce can artichoke hearts
1 pound crabmeat
1/4 cup defatted chicken broth, less salt
1/2 pound fresh mushrooms
1/2 pound red peppers, sliced
1/2 cup chopped green onions
2 tablespoons vegetable oil
2 1/2 tablespoons flour
1 cup evaporated skim milk
1/2 teaspoon seasoned salt
1 teaspoon Worcestershire sauce
1/4 cup medium-dry sherry
Paprika, black and red pepper to taste
1/4 cup grated Parmesan cheese

Slice artichokes and place on bottom of a 9x12-inch dish. Sprinkle crabmeat on top. Heat chicken broth, sauté mushrooms, red peppers and green onions until wilted and place over crabmeat. Heat oil, stir in flour and make a paste. Cook until bubbly. Stir in milk and remaining ingredients except cheese. Cook until thickened. Pour over crab and sprinkle with cheese. Cook at 375 degrees for 30 minutes or until it bubbles in the middle.

Bryan Clark

	Cal	Fat(g)	% Fat Cal	Sat Fat(g)	Chol(mg)	Sod(mg)
Per Serving	220	7.1	29	1.8	77	520

Grilled Redfish
Yield: 4 servings

Four 6-ounce redfish fillets with skin
4 tablespoons tub margarine
1/3 cup white wine
1 tablespoon Worcestershire sauce
1 tablespoon garlic powder
1 tablespoon light Creole seasoning
2 lemons

Fillet fish leaving skin on each half. Melt margarine and add white wine, Worcestershire sauce, and garlic pow-

Nutrition Nibble

Chicken, seafood or other broths can be used in recipes to replace or decrease the amount of oil used to sauté ingredients and for other purposes.

der. Pour half of liquid over redfish (with skin side down). Generously sprinkle Creole seasoning over redfish. Slice 1 lemon and place slices on redfish. Place redfish directly on medium grill. Cook for 20 to 25 minutes, basting occasionally with butter liquid. After cooking, squeeze fresh lemon on top and serve.

Buck Gladden

	Cal	Fat(g)	% Fat Cal	Sat Fat(g)	Chol(mg)	Sod(mg)
Per Serving	248	8.8	32	1.8	60	480

Fancy Fillets
Yield: 6 servings

2 pounds catfish fillets or other fresh fish
1 tablespoon oil
1 small onion, chopped
1 clove garlic, minced
1/2 cup sliced mushrooms
1/2 cup dry white wine
1 teaspoon flour
1/4 cup nonfat plain yogurt
1/4 teaspoon thyme
1/4 teaspoon salt
1/2 teaspoon pepper
1/8 teaspoon cayenne pepper
1/4 cup light sour cream

Line a 9x13x2-inch pan with heavy-duty foil. Spray foil lightly with vegetable oil cooking spray to prevent sticking. Arrange fillets in single layer. Heat oil over low heat; add onion and garlic and sauté until transparent. Add mushrooms and wine, cooking until done. Blend flour into yogurt, add spices and sour cream. Add this mixture to the onion and mushroom mixture and then stir until warm. Pour sauce over fillets and seal foil over fish. Bake in preheated oven at 350 degrees for 20 to 25 minutes. Fish should flake easily when tested with a fork.

Mary Elizabeth Cash

	Cal	Fat(g)	% Fat Cal	Sat Fat(g)	Chol(mg)	Sod(mg)
Per Serving	233	10	39	2.5	91	197

Just as Louisiana adapts cooking styles from all over to our local tastes, Louisiana cooking is adapted to fit local preferences in other parts of the country, sometimes with unexpected results. When a restaurant in Virginia decided to apply Chef Paul Prudhomme's famous technique for "blackening" fish to its locally available seafood, the resulting menu entry read "Fish of the Day: Blackened Bluefish."

One Step Further
Fancy Fillets
Save over 2gm more fat per serving by omitting the oil and sauté all the vegetables in the wine.

Crustless Crawfish Quiche

Yield: 6 servings

1 tablespoon diet margarine OR 1 1/2 teaspoons oil
1 clove garlic, crushed
1/4 cup or more green onions
8 ounces crawfish tails, lightly rinsed
1/8 teaspoon seasoned salt OR 1/4 teaspoon light
    Creole seasoning
1 cup grated sharp reduced fat cheddar cheese
1 cup cholesterol free egg substitute
1 cup evaporated skimmed milk
1/2 teaspoon dry mustard
1/8 teaspoon pepper
Paprika

In skillet, melt margarine. Sauté garlic and onions briefly. Add crawfish. Remove from heat, cool slightly. Sprinkle mixture with seasoned salt. (If using boiled crawfish instead of packaged ones, you may not need the seasoned salt.) Mixture should be lukewarm. Stir in cheese. It may melt slightly but should not melt much at this point. Put mixture in the bottom of a pie plate that has been sprayed with vegetable oil cooking spray. Mix egg substitute, milk, mustard, and pepper. Pour over mixture in pie pan. Sprinkle with paprika. Bake at 400 degrees for 30 minutes or until set. Crabmeat or shrimp may be substituted for the crawfish.

Nell W. McAnelly (Mrs. Robert)

	Cal	Fat(g)	% Fat Cal	Sat Fat(g)	Chol(mg)	Sod(mg)
Per Serving	176	6.4	33	2.6	83	316

Nutrition Note

Crustless Crawfish Quiche

If you do not use egg substitute, similar results can be achieved with 2 whole eggs and 3 egg whites. Nutritional information will be similar, except cholesterol content raises to 153mg per serving.

Shrimp Creole

Yield: 4 servings

2 tablespoons all purpose flour
1 1/2 tablespoons oil
1 large onion, chopped
1/2 bell pepper, chopped
1/2 cup sliced celery
5 ounces diced Rotel tomatoes (1/2 of a 10-ounce can)
One 8-ounce can no-salt-added tomato sauce
1 bay leaf
1/2 cup water
1 pound peeled and deveined shrimp
1/3 cup sliced green onions
1/2 teaspoon black pepper
1 teaspoon lemon juice
Parsley, to garnish
1 cup cooked brown rice

In a heavy skillet, make roux with flour and oil, stirring constantly until medium brown. Add onions, bell pepper and celery and sauté until tender crisp. Add tomatoes, tomato sauce, bay leaf, and water. Cook on medium heat until thickened, about 10 minutes. Add shrimp and green onions, cook until shrimp are done, about 7 minutes. Season as needed with pepper and lemon, and garnish with parsley. Serve over cooked rice. This is a new twist to an old standby since the amount of roux is so small. If you really like "spicy," use the whole can of Rotel tomatoes.

Peggy Love (Mrs. Glen S.)

	Cal	Fat(g)	% Fat Cal	Sat Fat(g)	Chol(mg)	Sod(mg)
Per Serving	**286**	**7.8**	**25**	**1.2**	**175**	**367**

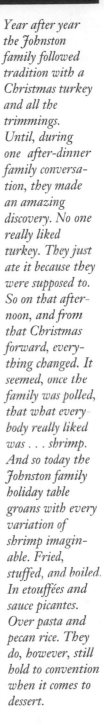

Year after year the Johnston family followed tradition with a Christmas turkey and all the trimmings. Until, during one after-dinner family conversation, they made an amazing discovery. No one really liked turkey. They just ate it because they were supposed to. So on that afternoon, and from that Christmas forward, everything changed. It seemed, once the family was polled, that what everybody really liked was . . . shrimp. And so today the Johnston family holiday table groans with every variation of shrimp imaginable. Fried, stuffed, and boiled. In etouffées and sauce picantes. Over pasta and pecan rice. They do, however, still hold to convention when it comes to dessert.

Shrimp St. Jacques

Yield: 8 servings

1 pound shrimp, peeled and deveined
1 onion, chopped
1 1/2 teaspoons vegetable oil
2 tablespoons flour
1 cup evaporated skim milk OR low fat OR skim milk
1 teaspoon dry mustard
1/2 teaspoon Tabasco sauce
2 tablespoons white wine
1 cup grated cheese (2 ounces each Havarti and
      reduced fat sharp cheddar)
1 teaspoon grated onion
1/4 cup chopped parsley
1/8 teaspoon salt
1/4 teaspoon pepper
1 pound lump crabmeat

Boil shrimp in water seasoned with chopped onion until tender. Make a white sauce with oil, flour, and milk. Add mustard, Tabasco sauce, wine, cheese, onion, and parsley. Add salt and pepper. Fold in crabmeat and shrimp. Pour into a greased casserole. If desired, sprinkle with bread crumbs. Bake until brown.

Carolyn B. Landry
Jan L. Bienvenu

	Cal	Fat(g)	% Fat Cal	Sat Fat(g)	Chol(mg)	Sod(mg)
Per Serving	204	7.6	34	3.1	155	427

One Step Further

Shrimp St. Jacques
Save another 1.5gm fat per serving by replacing the Havarti cheese with reduced fat cheddar, mozzarella or Swiss cheese. Omit the oil, use fat-free roux (see "Something Extra") and save over 2gm fat per serving.

Poultry

1980s

The Louisiana Arts and Science Guild was established to help recruit volunteers and to raise funds in the community for LASC. The Junior League has continued its involvement with the commitment of financial contributions and volunteer hours toward the restoration of the Oval Room in the Old Governor's Mansion, the reconstruction of a riverboat pilot house at LASC-Riverside, Discovery Depot and the new Science Center at LASC-Riverside to help children experience science and art in a fresh and exciting way.

Chicken Tetrazzini
Yield: 6 servings

1 tablespoon flour
1 tablespoon margarine
1 cup skim milk
1/4 teaspoon salt
1/4 teaspoon pepper
1/4 teaspoon paprika
1/4 teaspoon dry mustard
3 drops onion juice
1 teaspoon lemon juice
1/2 cup chopped mushrooms
1 1/2 cups skinless cooked chicken
3/4 cup cooked spaghetti
1/2 cup grated fresh Parmesan cheese OR reduced fat
    sharp cheddar cheese
1/2 cup bread crumbs

Make a medium white sauce of flour, margarine, milk and salt. Add pepper, paprika, dry mustard, onion and lemon juices, and mushrooms to white sauce and heat to boiling point. Add chicken and spaghetti. Spray individual casseroles or one large casserole with vegetable cooking spray and fill with mixture and top with cheese and bread crumbs. Bake in 425-degree oven about 15 minutes until the crumbs are very brown and ingredients are bubbly. Turkey or veal also work well in this recipe.

Mrs. C. Lenton Sartain (Peggy)
River Road Recipes, *Page 131*

Original Recipe

	Cal	Fat(g)	% Fat Cal	Sat Fat(g)	Chol(mg)	Sod(mg)
Per Serving	315	16.7	48	8.4	71	623

Lightened Recipe

	Cal	Fat(g)	% Fat Cal	Sat Fat(g)	Chol(mg)	Sod(mg)
Per Serving	215	7	30	2.7	40	412

Nutrition Nibble

To reduce fat use less cheeses and the low fat alternatives. Use those richest in flavor, such as freshly grated Parmesan and Romano, or sharp reduced fat cheddar.

Chicken Teriyaki
Yield: 8 servings

1 cup saki
3/4 cup reduced sodium soy sauce
8 tablespoons brown sugar
2 cloves garlic, crushed
2 onions, sliced
4 skinless chicken breasts

Combine first 5 ingredients for marinade. Cut whole chicken breasts into halves. Marinate overnight if possible, turning occasionally. Drain marinade and grill chicken and baste occasionally, or bake at 350 degrees for 1 hour, basting occasionally. May substitute steaks for chicken.

Mrs. Eric Reimsnyder

	Cal	Fat(g)	% Fat Cal	Sat Fat(g)	Chol(mg)	Sod(mg)
Per Serving	180	3.1	15	0.9	73	460

White Chili
Yield: 8 servings

1 pound bag dried navy beans
2 cups chopped onions
2 cloves garlic
One 10-ounce can Rotel tomatoes with green chilies
1/2 teaspoon salt
2 teaspoons chili powder
4 tablespoons ground cumin
1/2 teaspoon pepper
1/4 teaspoon cayenne
Two 14.5-ounce cans defatted chicken broth, less salt
4 skinless chicken breast halves
1 tablespoon lemon juice
1/2 teaspoon pepper
1 onion, chopped
2 cloves garlic
1 stalk celery
1/4 cup parsley sprigs

Put first 10 ingredients in large pot and bring to a boil adding water as necessary to cover beans. Lower heat to

Nutrition Note

Chicken Teriyaki

Nutrient analysis based on 1/2 the marinade absorbed or used and 1/2 drained off and discarded.

One Step Further

White Chili

Try omitting the salt or only adding after cooked and tasted. If omitted, the dish is reduced by over 130mg sodium per serving.

simmer and cook until beans are tender. Rub lemon juice and pepper into chicken and boil in water seasoned with onion, garlic, celery and parsley sprigs. Reserve stock. Debone and cut into large pieces. Add cut-up chicken and enough reserved chicken stock to eat as a "bean soup." You may prefer to eat over rice in South Louisiana!

Maretta Creveling

	Cal	Fat(g)	% Fat Cal	Sat Fat(g)	Chol(mg)	Sod(mg)
Per Serving	312	3.8	11	0.9	42	616

Lone Star Game Hens
Yield: 8 servings of 1/2 hen each

4 cornish game hens, approximately 1 1/2 pounds each

Seasoning

1/4 teaspoon salt
1 teaspoon garlic powder
2 teaspoons chili powder

Sauce

1/2 cup apple or pepper jelly
1/2 cup chili sauce
2 tablespoons cider vinegar
1 teaspoon chili powder

Split hens in half, remove skin and underlying fat. Rub inside and out with seasoning and, if time allows, cover and refrigerate for several hours. Spray grill rack with vegetable oil spray and then spray hens lightly with spray. Place on grill and cover with grill lid. Prepare sauce by melting jelly in a small saucepan; add chili sauce, vinegar and chili powder. Stir. After 20 minutes of grilling, brush hens with sauce. Continue grilling and basting for 30 minutes or until hens are browned and tender. This sauce may also be used on skinless chicken breasts for a very low fat entree. A simple and delicious way to prepare game hens so that no one misses the fattening dressings and gravies!

Ashley Hamilton Higginbotham

	Cal	Fat(g)	% Fat Cal	Sat Fat(g)	Chol(mg)	Sod(mg)
Per Serving	313	10.6	31	2.9	79	369

For a smokey flavor with Lone Star Game Hens, add 1 cup pecan shells soaked in water to hot coals before putting hens on grill.

Ashley H.
Higginbotham

Lime Chicken *with Apricots*
Yield: 4 servings

4 boneless, skinless chicken breast halves
2 limes
1/2 cup reduced sugar or no-sugar-added apricot
    preserves
2 tablespoons peeled and minced fresh ginger
1 tablespoon reduced sodium soy sauce

Heat oven to 450 degrees. Place chicken in a baking pan. Grate peel from one lime and squeeze the juice. In a small bowl combine preserves, ginger, soy sauce, lime peel and juice. Pour over chicken and bake 12 to 15 minutes or until fork tender. If possible, baste with sauce in pan every 5 minutes. Serve with remaining lime cut into wedges.

Cristina M. Ball

	Cal	Fat(g)	% Fat Cal	Sat Fat(g)	Chol(mg)	Sod(mg)
Per Serving	203	3.2	14	0.9	73	230

Curried Chicken and Linguine
Yield: 8 servings

Nutrition Nibble

Although stick margarine has essentially the same number of fat grams and calories as butter, butter has more than three times the saturated fat content. Margarine is cholesterol free, butter has more than 30mg per tablespoon.

One Step Further

Curried Chicken and Linguine

To further reduce sodium content, omit salt and use fresh mushrooms to save 120mg per serving. To save over 50mg cholesterol per serving, use an egg-free noodle.

3 tablespoons all-purpose flour
1 tablespoon curry powder
1/4 teaspoon salt
Pepper to taste
2 tablespoons diet margarine OR 1 tablespoon vegetable
    oil
6 skinless, boneless chicken breast halves
1 large onion, sliced
1 cup diagonally sliced celery
2 medium carrots, diagonally sliced
One 4-ounce can sliced mushrooms
One 8-ounce can water chestnuts, drained and sliced
3 cups defatted chicken broth, less salt
1 pound medium linguine

Combine flour, curry powder, salt and pepper. Set aside. Melt margarine or warm oil in large skillet. Cut chicken into bite-size pieces and coat with flour mixture and brown lightly in melted margarine. Add onions, celery, carrots, mushrooms and water chestnuts to chicken. Add chicken broth and bring to boil. Reduce heat and simmer about 20 minutes, stirring occasionally. Cook noodles as directed on package; drain. Serve chicken mixture over noodles. To make ahead you may mix chicken mixture with noodles and bake in a 350-degree oven for 30 minutes.

Mrs. Glen S. Love

	Cal	Fat(g)	% Fat Cal	Sat Fat(g)	Chol(mg)	Sod(mg)
Per Serving	391	6.9	16	1.6	113	465

Chicken Stew
Yield: 6 servings

3 pounds skinless chicken pieces
1/2 teaspoon salt
1/4 teaspoon black pepper
1/4 teaspoon red pepper
One 10-ounce bag frozen seasoning vegetables OR
    1 cup chopped onion
    2 stalks celery, chopped
    1/2 red bell pepper, chopped
    1/2 green bell pepper, chopped
    2 tablespoons chopped parsley
1-2 cups water
1 tablespoon bottled browning sauce
2 tablespoons gravy flour

Season chicken pieces with salt and both peppers. Place frozen vegetables or chopped fresh vegetables in large skillet or Dutch oven. Add 1/4 cup water and boil until vegetables are softened. Place chicken pieces into pan. Add 1 cup water and browning sauce. Reduce heat to simmer and cover pan. Let cook one hour, turning pieces occasionally. Dissolve flour in 1/2 cup water. Add to pan juices and cook on high heat until gravy is thickened. Add water as needed. Correct seasonings. Serve over rice.

Helen House Boyer

	Cal	Fat(g)	% Fat Cal	Sat Fat(g)	Chol(mg)	Sod(mg)
Per Serving	212	6.9	29	1.9	84	289

One Step Further

Chicken Stew
Reduce salt to 1/4 teaspoon and cut almost 90mg sodium for each serving; omit salt altogether and save 178mg sodium for every serving.

Bourbon Chicken

Yield: 6 servings

6 skinless, boneless chicken breasts
1/2 teaspoon pepper
1 teaspoon garlic powder
1/4 cup bourbon whiskey
1/4 cup reduced sodium soy sauce
One 8-ounce can crushed pineapple, in juice

Season chicken breasts to taste with pepper and garlic powder. Marinate for several hours in bourbon and soy sauce. Place chicken pieces and marinade in 9x12-inch glass baking dish. Top with crushed pineapple, including the juice. Bake in 325 degree oven for about 45 minutes or until chicken is well done. Baste several times during baking.

Janie S. Braud (Mrs. Charles H.)

	Cal	Fat(g)	% Fat Cal	Sat Fat(g)	Chol(mg)	Sod(mg)
Per Serving	184	3.1	15	0.9	73	416

Pollo de Mexicana

Yield: 4 servings

3/4 cup raw brown rice
2 1/2 cups defatted chicken broth, less salt
2 whole chicken breasts
2 cloves garlic, minced
1 onion, chopped
1 red bell pepper, sliced OR 1/2 cup chopped pimento
1/2 cup canned green chilies, chopped
2 tomatoes peeled and chopped
1/2 teaspoon red pepper
4 ounces reduced fat sharp cheddar cheese, grated
1/4 cup chopped cilantro OR fresh coriander

Cook rice in broth until rice is slightly underdone. Divide whole chicken breasts into halves; remove skin and bone; brown lightly in nonstick skillet. Add garlic and onion and cook until golden brown. Add red bell pepper, green chilies, tomatoes and red pepper. Cover and simmer 10 minutes. Arrange chicken in baking dish, saving vegetables. Mix these with rice and pour over chicken. Sprinkle with cheese. Bake 25 minutes at 350 degrees. Sprinkle with cilantro before serving, if desired.

Debbie Row

	Cal	Fat(g)	% Fat Cal	Sat Fat(g)	Chol(mg)	Sod(mg)
Per Serving	414	10.2	22	4.5	99	683

Chicken *with Artichoke Hearts*
Yield: 8 servings

8 skinless chicken breast halves
1/8 teaspoon salt
1/2 teaspoon pepper
1/2 teaspoon paprika
2 tablespoons margarine
One 1-pound can artichokes hearts, drained
2 teaspoons olive or vegetable oil
2 tablespoons flour
4 tablespoons chopped onions
6 ounces sliced mushrooms
2/3 cup defatted chicken broth, less salt
1/4 cup dry white wine
1/4 cup dry sherry
1 teaspoon fresh rosemary

Sprinkle chicken with salt, pepper, and paprika to season. In a nonstick skillet brown chicken pieces on all sides in the margarine; transfer to 3-quart covered casserole. Arrange artichoke hearts among chicken pieces. Add olive oil to the skillet over medium heat. Sprinkle with flour and stir. Add onions and mushrooms and sauté just until tender. If they begin to stick, add some of the chicken broth. Add the remaining chicken broth, wine, sherry, and rosemary. Cook, stirring for a few minutes until liquid is blended and slightly thickened. Pour over chicken. Cover and bake in a moderate oven at 375 degrees for 1 hour or until chicken is tender.

Julie Hubbell

	Cal	Fat(g)	% Fat Cal	Sat Fat(g)	Chol(mg)	Sod(mg)
Per Serving	214	7.2	30	1.7	74	221

Nutrition Nibble

Defat fresh or canned broths by placing in the refrigerator for 20 to 30 minutes or freezer for 2 to 5 minutes. Remove hardened fat on top and discard.

One Step Further

Chicken with Artichoke Hearts
To save 3gm fat per serving, omit the olive oil and 1 tablespoon of margarine by sautéing the chicken, mushrooms and onions in chicken broth. Then make cream sauce with 1 tablespoon of margarine and the 2 tablespoons of flour in a nonstick skillet.

197

Garlic-Lemon Chicken
Yield: 4 servings

4 skinless, boneless chicken breast halves
1/2 teaspoon salt
1/2 teaspoon pepper
2 teaspoons extra virgin olive oil
1 teaspoon tub margarine
4 cloves garlic, pressed
1/2 to 1 lemon (at least 3 tablespoons juice)

Pound breasts with mallet and season with salt and pepper. Heat oil and margarine in heavy skillet on medium until hot. Add breasts to skillet and sprinkle with garlic. Cook 7 minutes. Turn, squeeze lemon over breasts and cook an additional 7 minutes. Try the same method with fish, using a little dill weed.

Claire G. Gowdy

	Cal	Fat(g)	% Fat Cal	Sat Fat(g)	Chol(mg)	Sod(mg)
Per Serving	179	6.3	32	1.4	73	340

Chicken Breasts *with Provincial Sauce*
Yield: 6 servings

1/2 cup defatted chicken broth, less salt
1/2 bell pepper, chopped
2 stalks of celery, chopped
1/2 medium yellow onion, chopped
1/4 cup tomato paste, no salt added
One 15-ounce can of stewed, sliced tomatoes
8 ounces fresh sliced mushrooms
1 clove of garlic
1-2 teaspoons basil
1/2 cup dry white wine
1/2 teaspoon celery seed
6 skinless, boneless chicken breast halves
1/2 teaspoon light Creole seasoning
1 cup part skim milk mozzarella cheese

In a medium saucepan, bring the chicken broth to a boil. Stir in bell pepper, celery and onion and cook uncovered approximately 5 minutes until vegetables are wilted. Add

One Step Further

Garlic-Lemon Chicken

To trim fat another 3gm per serving, omit oil and margarine and sauté breasts in defatted reduced salt chicken broth. To reduce sodium over 130mg per serving, cut salt to 1/4 teaspoon.

the tomato paste, stewed tomatoes, mushrooms, garlic and basil and cook another 5 minutes. Stir in wine and celery seed. Arrange the chicken breasts in a single layer in a glass baking dish and sprinkle with Creole seasoning. Spoon sauce over them and bake covered 25 minutes at 350 degrees. Remove cover and sprinkle with mozzarella and bake an additional 10 minutes. Serve over rice or angel hair pasta.

Michelle Odom Nesbit

	Cal	Fat(g)	% Fat Cal	Sat Fat(g)	Chol(mg)	Sod(mg)
Per Serving	261	6.7	23	2.9	85	445

Barbecue Chicken Cordon Bleu
Yield: 6 servings

Barbecue Sauce
1/2 cup bottled barbecue sauce
1 tablespoon brown sugar
1/2 tablespoon honey

6 skinless, boneless chicken breast halves
1/2 tablespoon vegetable oil
1 tablespoon liquid smoke
Six 1-ounce slices honey-cured lean ham
1/2 cup mozzarella cheese
1/2 cup reduced fat sharp cheddar cheese
1 fresh tomato, cubed

Mix first 3 ingredients in a small bowl. In large, ovenproof nonstick skillet, brown chicken breasts in vegetable oil and liquid smoke on medium heat about 10 minutes or until brown. Reduce heat and continue cooking for about 8 minutes, basting breasts with barbecue sauce every 2 to 3 minutes. Lay sliced ham on top of each breast, sprinkle with mozzarella and cheddar cheese. Cover and simmer about 10 minutes. Add cubed tomato and broil in oven until nearly brown.

Cindy Buie Maughan

	Cal	Fat(g)	% Fat Cal	Sat Fat(g)	Chol(mg)	Sod(mg)
Per Serving	277	9.8	32	3.2	85	628

One Step Further

Barbecue Chicken Cordon Bleu

This recipe is still moderately high in sodium, with the ham and barbecue sauce contributing the largest amounts. By omitting the ham you save 250 to 300mg sodium and more than 1gm fat per serving. Try a low sodium barbecue sauce to further reduce sodium.

Brown Bag Chicken

Yield: 6 servings of 3 1/2 ounces each

One 3-pound fryer or baking hen
3 tablespoons Worcestershire sauce
1 teaspoon seasoned salt
1 onion, quartered
1 medium-sized brown paper bag

Heat oven to 350 degrees. Remove skin from chicken. Wash chicken thoroughly and dry inside and out with dish towels. Thoroughly coat entire front, back and inside cavity with "wooster," then spray lightly with vegetable oil cooking spray. Then sprinkle entire outside and inside of cavity with seasoned salt. Insert onion into chicken cavity. Gently put chicken into brown paper bag and fold over end. Place on baking sheet and put into oven. Do not let any part of bag touch any part of oven. Bake 80 minutes in 350-degree oven.

Madelene Hubbs Riché

	Cal	Fat(g)	% Fat Cal	Sat Fat(g)	Chol(mg)	Sod(mg)
Per Serving	**195**	**6.9**	**32**	**1.8**	**78**	**304**

One Step Further

Brown Bag Chicken
Save another 160mg sodium per serving by omitting the seasoned salt and using one of your favorite seasoning blends with no salt.

Lemon Chicken
To reduce more fat, omit the oil and margarine and sauté the chicken strips in chicken broth—a savings of over 3gm more fat per serving. To save more sodium, omit the salt in the flour, add a favorite salt free seasoning, then use only 8 ounces of chicken broth concentrate with 8 ounces of water—saving more than 120mg sodium per serving.

Lemon Chicken

Yield: 8 servings

6 skinless, boneless chicken breast halves
1 tablespoon tub margarine
1 tablespoon vegetable oil
2 cups defatted chicken broth, less salt
2 tablespoons lemon juice
4 tablespoons white wine
1/8 cup fresh chopped parsley

Seasoned flour

1/2 cup flour
1/8 teaspoon salt
Pepper to taste

Cut chicken in strips. Shake in seasoned flour. Heat margarine and oil in a nonstick skillet and brown chicken strips and remove; drain on paper towels. (If the chicken strips begin to stick while browning, add some of the chicken broth.) In the same skillet, boil chicken broth, lemon juice, and wine. Reduce heat and cook for 5 minutes. Put chicken back in skillet and cook for 10 minutes. Add parsley and serve over rice.

Mrs. Frederic T. Billings III

	Cal	Fat(g)	% Fat Cal	Sat Fat(g)	Chol(mg)	Sod(mg)
Per Serving	172	5.7	30	1.3	57	238

Chicken Santa Fe
Yield: 4 servings

4 skinless chicken breast halves
1 tablespoon olive oil
2 cloves garlic, minced
1 onion, chopped
1 red bell pepper, julienned
1 green bell pepper, julienned
1 fresh or canned jalapeño pepper, minced
1 1/2 cups defatted chicken broth, less salt
1 cup raisins
1/4 cup tomato paste, no salt added
1 1/4 teaspoons ground coriander or cilantro
1/8 teaspoon red pepper
1/4 teaspoon pepper
1/4 teaspoon salt, optional

In a large skillet brown chicken in oil, turning once. Add garlic, onion, and red, green, and jalapeño peppers; sauté 2 minutes. Drain off fat, pat skillet with paper towel to remove oil. Mix in broth, raisins, tomato paste, and coriander. Bring to a boil, reduce heat, cover and simmer 10 minutes. Uncover and cook 10 minutes longer or until chicken is tender and sauce is slightly reduced. Stir in red and black pepper. Taste. If needed, add the salt.

Ashley Hamilton Higginbotham

	Cal	Fat(g)	% Fat Cal	Sat Fat(g)	Chol(mg)	Sod(mg)
Per Serving	337	7.4	19	1.6	77	372

Nutrition Nibble

To prevent drying out skinless chicken, cover pan with foil for about 3/4 of cooking time. Remove foil at end to brown.

 201

Chicken Cacciatore
Yield: 6 servings

3 skinless chicken breast halves
3 skinless leg quarters
1 teaspoon garlic powder, divided
1/4 teaspoon salt, divided
1/2 teaspoon pepper, divided
1/2 teaspoon paprika, divided
1 1/2 tablespoons olive oil, divided
2 large onions sliced and separated into rings
2 green bell peppers, julienned
1 clove garlic, minced
One 16-ounce can stewed tomatoes
1 teaspoon oregano
3/4 cup red wine
4 ounces sliced fresh mushrooms
1/2 tablespoon tub margarine
1 tablespoon fresh chopped parsley
1 tablespoon freshly grated Parmesan cheese

Season chicken well with 1/2 each of the garlic powder, paprika, salt and pepper. Heat 1 tablespoon of olive oil in a nonstick skillet and brown chicken pieces. Remove to large deep pot. Sauté onion, bell pepper and minced garlic in remaining oil in skillet. Add juice from tomatoes if needed to complete. Add tomatoes and remaining juice, oregano, and wine. Simmer slowly. Sauté mushrooms in margarine on the side. Add mushrooms to sauce and pour over chicken. Season sauce with remaining garlic, paprika, salt, pepper. Cover and cook slowly until chicken is tender. Serve alone or over noodles. Before serving sprinkle with parsley and Parmesan cheese.

Diane Crona
Cary Kearney

	Cal	Fat(g)	% Fat Cal	Sat Fat(g)	Chol(mg)	Sod(mg)
Per Serving	300	10.8	32	2.5	82	399

Darlin's Chicken

Yields: 6 servings of 4 ounces each

One 3-pound chicken, cut up and skinned
1/4 teaspoon salt
2 teaspoons pepper
1/2 cup evaporated skim milk
1 egg white
1 tablespoon baking powder
1 tablespoon white vinegar
3/4 cup flour
Paprika

Season chicken with salt and pepper. In large bowl, beat egg white and milk. Add baking powder and vinegar. Stir. Place chicken in milk and egg mixture. Then flour generously. Place roasting rack over a pan sprayed with vegetable oil cooking spray. Place chicken on rack and sprinkle with paprika. Put a small amount of water in pan, covering the bottom of the pan, but not deep enough to touch the rack or chicken. Cover tightly with foil. Bake at 375 degrees for 35 minutes. Remove foil cover, turn heat up to 450 degrees and roast until crispy on outside and done throughout. This recipe is spicier if the chicken is seasoned and refrigerated the day before.

Beulah Bijeaux Bezet

	Cal	Fat(g)	% Fat Cal	Sat Fat(g)	Chol(mg)	Sod(mg)
Per Serving	269	8.1	28	2.1	86	350

I married a Yankee. And I still remember the day he had his first REAL southern fried chicken. We were visiting my Aunt Maddie's farm just outside of Many. While we cooked, the menfolk visited. He told me later that much of the conversation that morning focused on the best way to cook 'possum. And tips like how you boil the meat first to get out the smell. Now I understand his concerned expression when we sat down to dinner. He wasn't real sure just what that meat was under Aunt Maddie's perfect golden crust.

Delta Oriental Chicken
Yield: 4 servings

1 1/2 pounds skinless, boneless chicken breasts
2 tablespoons corn oil
1/3 cup reduced sodium soy sauce
1 large onion, sliced diagonally
2 stalks celery, sliced diagonally
1 bell pepper, sliced diagonally
4-5 green onions, chopped
1 pound fresh mushrooms, cleaned and left whole with
    stems removed
Fresh broccoli florets from one large bunch
Pepper to taste
1/4 cup dry white wine

Cut chicken into bite-size pieces and sauté in corn oil until slightly brown, about 10 minutes. Add soy sauce and all other ingredients. Cover and sauté about 5 to 10 minutes. Serve over hot rice or oriental noodles.

Sue Spaht (Mrs. Homer)

	Cal	Fat(g)	% Fat Cal	Sat Fat(g)	Chol(mg)	Sod(mg)
Per Serving	318	10.7	29	1.8	69	810

Nutrition Note

Delta Oriental Chicken
Still high in sodium, but less than 1/2 the sodium content of the original.

One Step Further

Paulie's Poulet Dijonaise
To save over 450mg more sodium per serving, omit the dijon mustard and use 2 1/2 tablespoons of dry mustard and 1/3 cup white wine. Save 50 calories and over 5 1/2gm fat per serving by omitting the margarine and using defatted chicken broth to sauté chicken.

Paulie's Poulet Dijonaise
Yield: 4 servings

4 skinless, boneless chicken breast halves
1/2 teaspoon ground black pepper
2 tablespoons tub margarine
1/3 cup dijon mustard
1 tablespoon cornstarch
1 teaspoon mustard powder
One 12-ounce can evaporated skim milk
1/3 cup skim milk
1/4 cup white wine

Cut chicken into 1-inch strips and sprinkle with pepper. Sauté chicken in the margarine over medium heat for about 5 minutes or until brown. Transfer chicken to platter. Stir dijon mustard into the remaining margarine and juices in the pan, scraping up the bits. Blend cornstarch and mustard powder together. Slowly add 2 to 4 tablespoons of evaporated milk to the cornstarch, stirring until a smooth paste is formed. Continue to slowly blend in remaining milk. Then whisk milk mixture into margarine in pan. Stir wine into mixture, reduce heat and cook the sauce until it is reduced by 1/4. Stir or whisk frequently. It should be thick and velvety. Adjust seasonings and add chicken back to sauce. Serve over spinach fettucine or linguini.

Paula Merritt

	Cal	Fat(g)	% Fat Cal	Sat Fat(g)	Chol(mg)	Sod(mg)
Per Serving	319	10.6	30	2	77	735

Crunchy Oven Fried Chicken

Yield: 8 servings

8 skinless chicken breast halves
1/2 teaspoon light Creole seasoning
1/2 teaspoon pepper
1 cup Italian seasoned bread crumbs
1/2 teaspoon garlic powder
1/2 cup skim milk
2 tablespoons margarine, melted

Lightly season chicken breasts with Creole seasoning and pepper. Place bread crumbs and garlic in a large plastic bag. Place milk in a medium-sized bowl. Dip chicken in milk then bread crumbs (may repeat if needed). Place in single layer in casserole baking dish well sprayed with vegetable oil cooking spray (pieces should not touch). Drizzle with melted margarine. Bake at 350 degrees for about 45 minutes or until chicken is tender.

James D. Surso, M.D.

	Cal	Fat(g)	% Fat Cal	Sat Fat(g)	Chol(mg)	Sod(mg)
Per Serving	217	6.4	27	1.6	74	443

One Step Further

Crunchy Oven Fried Chicken

To reduce sodium content further, omit the seasoned bread crumbs and use plain bread crumbs with 1 teaspoon each of basil, oregano and marjoram, saving over 200mg sodium each serving. To cut over 2 1/2gm more fat per serving, omit melted margarine and spray each breast lightly with vegetable oil spray. Try recipe with other pieces of skinless chicken; nutritional content will vary.

Chicken *with Basil Salsa*
Yield: 4 servings

4 skinless chicken breasts

Marinade

2 tablespoons lemon juice
2 tablespoons olive oil
2 tablespoons defatted chicken broth, less salt
1 clove garlic, pressed
1 tablespoon chopped fresh rosemary OR
1/2 tablespoon dried rosemary

Salsa

1 tomato, peeled, seeded and chopped
2 tablespoons chopped fresh basil
1 tablespoon balsamic vinegar
1 teaspoon capers

Coat chicken breasts with marinade and refrigerate for 4 hours or overnight. Grill until desired doneness. Top with salsa made by combining all salsa ingredients.

Martha R. Singer

	Cal	Fat	% Fat Cal	Sat Fat	Chol	Sod
Per Serving	185	6.7	33	1.4	73	132

Nutrition Nibble

Marinades should not be used to baste meat at the end of grilling or roasting unless the marinade is first brought to a boil. Raw meat, fish and poultry harbor bacteria which will be transferred to the marinade liquid. Thus, the marinade is unsafe unless first boiled on the stovetop or in the microwave.

Nutrition Note

Chicken with Basil Salsa
Nutritional information based on 1/2 of the marinade drained off and discarded.

Cajun Cabbage Casserole
Yield: 6 servings

One 8-ounce package chopped cabbage or cole slaw
1 pound ground turkey or extra lean ground beef
2 medium onions, chopped
2 cloves garlic, minced
One 10 3/4-ounce can light cream of mushroom soup
1 1/2 cups cooked rice
1/4 cup chopped green onion tops
1/2 teaspoon light Creole seasoning
1 teaspoon Worcestershire sauce
1/4 cup bread crumbs

Cook cabbage until tender; drain and reserve one cup liquid. In a heavy cast-iron skillet or nonstick skillet brown meat, onions and minced garlic. Mix cabbage, soup, rice and green onions with the above and season with light Creole seasoning and Worcestershire sauce. Top with bread crumbs and bake at 350 degrees for 30 minutes in a baking dish sprayed with vegetable oil cooking spray.

Mrs. Richard D. Clanton

	Cal	Fat(g)	% Fat Cal	Sat Fat(g)	Chol(mg)	Sod(mg)
Per Serving	232	7	27	2.9	30	308

Pineapple Chicken *with Dijon Mustard*
Yield: 4 servings

One 20-ounce can pineapple chunks in juice
4 skinless chicken breast halves
2 cloves garlic, pressed
1 tablespoon olive oil OR vegetable oil
1 teaspoon saltless lemon-herb seasoning
1 large onion, quartered
1 green bell pepper, cored, seeded and julienned
3 tablespoons dijon mustard
2 tablespoons Worcestershire sauce
1 teaspoon crumbled marjoram
1/2 teaspoon freshly ground pepper

Drain pineapple; reserve juice. Brown chicken with garlic in oil. Sprinkle lemon-herb seasoning over chicken. Add onion and bell pepper to skillet; sauté until soft. Drain excess fat from skillet. Add reserved juice to skillet. Stir in dijon mustard, Worcestershire sauce, marjoram and pepper. Spoon over chicken. Cover and simmer 25 minutes. Add pineapple; heat through. Serve with brown rice.

Ashley Hamilton Higginbotham

	Cal	Fat(g)	% Fat Cal	Sat Fat(g)	Chol(mg)	Sod(mg)
Per Serving	312	7.4	21	1.4	73	409

Light Chicken Enchiladas
Yield: 6 servings of 2 enchiladas each

One 16-ounce can no-salt-added stewed tomatoes
1 1/2 cups picante sauce, divided
3 cups skinless cooked chicken, shredded or diced
1 red bell pepper, chopped
1/4 cup coarsely chopped slivered toasted almonds
1/4 teaspoon cinnamon
1 clove garlic, minced
Twelve 7- to 8-inch flour tortillas
1/2 cup shredded Monterey Jack cheese
1/2 cup shredded part skim mozzarella cheese

Optional garnishes
Lettuce, ripe olive slices, chopped tomatoes, nonfat yogurt or reduced fat sour cream.

Combine tomatoes, 3/4 cup of picante sauce, chicken, red pepper, almonds, cinnamon, and garlic in 10-inch skillet. Bring to a boil, reduce heat and simmer uncovered 10 minutes or until most of liquid is absorbed. Spoon 1/3 cup chicken mixture down center of each tortilla. Roll up; place seam side down in a 13x9x2-inch baking dish sprayed with vegetable oil cooking spray. Spoon remaining 3/4 cup picante sauce evenly over tortillas. Cover with foil. Bake at 350 degrees for 20 minutes or until heated through. Sprinkle with cheese; let stand for 5 minutes. Garnish as desired and serve with additional picante sauce.

Pat McCarty Scheffy

	Cal	Fat(g)	% Fat Cal	Sat Fat(g)	Chol(mg)	Sod(mg)
Per Serving	443	16.3	33	5.4	71	817

One Step Further

Light Chicken Enchiladas
The sodium content is still moderately high in this entree. A low sodium picante sauce would trim back the sodium content further. To further reduce the fat content, omit the Monterey Jack cheese and use all mozzarella, saving almost 1 1/2gm more per serving. Omit the almonds for a savings of 2.5gm fat per serving.

Cabbage Rolls

Yield: 4 servings

1/2 onion, chopped
1 stalk celery, chopped
1/2 green bell pepper, chopped
1 clove garlic, chopped
2 teaspoons olive oil
1/2 pound ground turkey
1/2 cup raw rice
1/2 can tomato paste, no salt added
1/2 teaspoon salt
1/2 teaspoon pepper
3/4 teaspoon ground cinnamon
1 1/2 teaspoons lemon juice
1 medium head cabbage
1/4 can tomato paste, no salt added

Sauce
One 11-ounce can tomatoes, no salt added
One 8-ounce can tomato sauce, no salt added
1/4 can tomato paste, no salt added
1 3/4 cups water
Juice of 1 lemon
3 tablespoons brown sugar

Sauté first 4 ingredients in oil. Drain and blot off any remaining oil. In large bowl, combine sautéed vegetables and the next 7 ingredients. Core cabbage and boil leaves until al dente. Drain and separate leaves. Put 1 tablespoon mixture on single leaf and roll, sealing sides by folding. Put rolls in pot 1 layer deep. Cover with mixture of water and 1/4 can of tomato paste to just cover rolls. Cook on simmer 1 hour or more. Meanwhile, boil sauce ingredients until reduced and thickened. Serve over cabbage rolls.

Sari Turner

	Cal	Fat(g)	% Fat Cal	Sat Fat(g)	Chol(mg)	Sod(mg)
Per Serving	344	7.3	19	1.6	42	401

One step further

Cabbage Rolls
For further fat savings, precook the turkey and blot off any fat before adding to the mixture. Add 1 to 2 tablespoons of water, wine or defatted broth.

Chicken Tom

Yield: 4 servings

4 skinless, boneless chicken breast halves
1/4 teaspoon light Creole seasoning
1 tablespoon margarine
1 tablespoon olive oil
One 6-ounce can mushrooms in butter
2 tablespoons chopped green onions, optional
1 tablespoon Worcestershire sauce
1 tablespoon white wine Worcestershire sauce
1 1/2 cups cooked rice

Season chicken with Creole seasoning to taste. Lightly brown in melted margarine and olive oil over medium-high heat. Add mushrooms with liquid, green onions, if desired, and Worcestershire sauces. Simmer covered 10 minutes or until chicken is done. Serve over a bed of rice with steamed fresh asparagus as a side dish. Also good served over pasta.

Tom Holliday

	Cal	Fat(g)	% Fat Cal	Sat Fat(g)	Chol(mg)	Sod(mg)
Per Serving	285	7.7	25	1.6	73	343

Fourth Friday Turkey Salad

Yield: 6 servings

One 3-ounce package oriental noodle soup
1 tablespoon peanut oil
1 clove garlic, minced
1 onion, chopped
1 teaspoon peeled and minced fresh ginger
1 red bell pepper, julienned
1 green bell pepper, julienned
One 8-ounce package mushrooms, sliced
2 cups fresh smoked, skinless turkey breast, cubed
1 teaspoon sesame oil
2 teaspoons reduced sodium soy sauce
2 teaspoons sesame seeds

Break soup noodles in half, cook as directed, and drain. Sauté garlic, onion and ginger in peanut oil for 5 minutes.

Nutrition Note

Fourth Friday Turkey Salad

This nutritional information reflects the sodium content if home smoked turkey is used; commercially smoked turkey will increase the sodium content. To further reduce the sodium content, omit the oriental soup flavor package, saving over 150mg per serving.

Add peppers and mushrooms, and cook 2 more minutes. Toss in turkey, noodles, sesame oil, and soy sauce. Stir well. Toast sesame seeds on high for 2 to 3 minutes in microwave and use to garnish.

Sharon Randall Lanius

	Cal	Fat(g)	% Fat Cal	Sat Fat(g)	Chol(mg)	Sod(mg)
Per Serving	191	6.8	31	1.7	42	398

Camp Meetin' Chicken *and Wild Rice*
Yield: 8 servings

4 skinless chicken breast halves
1 onion, chopped
One 4-ounce can mushrooms, chopped
2 ribs celery, diced
2 tablespoons margarine, melted
2 boxes wild rice (1 1/2 cups raw)
1/4 teaspoon salt
1 can of cream of mushroom soup, less salt/low fat
1 cup light sour cream
1/2 cup grated cheese (1 ounce reduced fat sharp cheddar and 1 ounce skim mozzarella) OR 1/4 cup sliced almonds

Boil chicken breasts in enough water to reserve 5 cups of broth. Debone and chop chicken. Chill broth until fat hardens on top, remove and discard fat. Sauté onion, mushrooms, and celery in margarine. Cook wild rice in 4 2/3 cups of reserved defatted broth and 1/4 teaspoon salt. Mix rice, chicken, onion, mushrooms, celery, cream of mushroom soup, sour cream and 1/3 cup reserved broth. Place in casserole and top with grated cheese or sliced almonds. Bake at 350 degrees until hot and bubbly.

Mrs. John Hutchinson (Kay)

	Cal	Fat(g)	% Fat Cal	Sat Fat(g)	Chol(mg)	Sod(mg)
Per Serving	300	10.3	31	4.4	55	318

Nutrition Nibble

Freeze leftover defatted canned or homemade broth in ice trays. Once frozen, place in freezer bags. These cubes are now ready to use as needed, in small or larger quantities.

Twenty-Five Minute Turkey Dinner
Yield: 4 servings

1 large sweet potato
10 ounces fresh or frozen brussels sprouts
2 tablespoons tub margarine, divided
1/2 teaspoon salt, divided
1/2 cup fresh or frozen cranberries OR blueberries
1/4 cup port wine OR cranberry juice
1 tablespoon all-purpose flour
1/4 teaspoon sage
1 pound skinless turkey cutlets, pounded to 1/4-inch thick
1 tablespoon vegetable oil
2 slices white bread, crumbled
2 tablespoons chopped Italian parsley, plus extra sprigs for
    garnish
1/4 teaspoon each black pepper and white pepper

Peel and cut potato into 1-inch chunks. Bring brussels sprouts and potato to a boil in enough water to cover. Reduce heat, cover, and simmer until vegetables are tender. Drain, and toss with 1 tablespoon margarine and 1/4 teaspoon salt. Meanwhile, in 1-quart saucepan, bring berries and port (or cranberry juice) to a boil; reduce heat and simmer, uncovered, until liquid is absorbed and berries are tender. In small dish, combine flour, sage, and 1/4 teaspoon salt; coat cutlets with mixture. Heat vegetable oil in 12-inch nonstick skillet over medium heat and sauté cutlets until lightly browned and cooked through, about 4 minutes. Remove and cover with foil to keep warm. In same skillet, heat 1 tablespoon margarine. Add bread crumbs and cook until golden and crisp, stirring occasionally. Add berries, parsley, and pepper; toss. Top turkey with mixture. Serve with vegetables and garnish with parsley sprigs.

Joan W. Chastain

	Cal	Fat(g)	% Fat Cal	Sat Fat(g)	Chol(mg)	Sod(mg)
Per Serving	333	9.3	25	1.7	66	462

Nutrition Nibble

Flavors can be enhanced with defatted broths, wine, lemon juice and other fruit juices.

Grilled Chicken Breasts *with Vegetables*
Yield: 6 servings

3 whole skinless, boneless chicken breasts, split

For the marinade
1/3 cup lemon juice (or half wine vinegar)
3/4 cup olive oil
2 teaspoons Worcestershire sauce
2-3 cloves garlic, minced
1 teaspoon sugar
1/4 cup wine

Any or all of the following vegetables
3 zucchini, sliced lengthwise about 1/2-inch thick
2 sweet red peppers, cored and quartered
1 large red onion, sliced into 1/2-inch-thick rounds
6 shiitake or large button mushrooms, trimmed
3 small sweet potatoes
2 small eggplants, sliced lengthwise 1/2-inch thick

Optional marinade flavorings
1 teaspoon grated fresh ginger, OR
1/4 cup pesto, OR
1/2 teaspoon Tabasco sauce

Arrange the chicken breast halves in a large, flat dish, pour over half the marinade, cover and refrigerate for 2 hours. If using eggplant, salt the slices and drain under a weight to extract bitter juices (this will increase the sodium content). Pat dry. If using sweet potatoes, bake in a 400-degree oven for 15 minutes until partially done. Peel and slice into rounds. Arrange the vegetables in a large, flat dish, pour over the remaining marinade and let marinate for 1 hour. Drain the chicken and vegetables. Grill them for about 5 minutes each side or until lightly browned but not overcooked.

Laura Field

	Cal	Fat(g)	% Fat Cal	Sat Fat(g)	Chol(mg)	Sod(mg)
Per Serving	360	12.6	31	2.2	73	85

Nutrition Note

Grilled Chicken Breasts with Vegetables
Nutritional analysis based on 1/3 of marinade absorbed or used, 2/3 drained off and discarded.

213

Chicken à la Roma

Yield: 6 servings of 3 1/4 ounces each

2 teaspoons olive oil
3/4 cup thinly sliced green onions
2 teaspoons minced garlic
1/2 pound fresh mushrooms, sliced
1/2 of a 6-ounce can tomato paste, no salt added
One 8-ounce can tomato sauce, no salt added
1/2 cup dry white wine
1 tablespoon instant chicken bouillon granules
1 teaspoon sugar
1 1/2 teaspoons dried basil
1 tablespoon dried oregano
1/3 cup ripe olives
1/4 teaspoon white pepper
1/4 teaspoon paprika
1/2 teaspoon black pepper
2 1/2-3 pound skinless chicken, cut up
1/4 cup grated Parmesan cheese
6 ounces marinated artichoke hearts, lightly rinsed and
    well drained

In a 10-inch ceramic or glass dish place oil, onion, garlic and mushrooms. Cover and microwave on high 4 to 6 minutes. May be drained. Stir in tomato paste, tomato sauce, wine, bouillon, sugar and seasonings. Add chicken pieces. Spoon sauce over top making sure all pieces are covered with sauce. Microwave on high 10 minutes. Rotate dish 1/2 turn and microwave on medium high (70% power) 16 minutes. Rearrange chicken and sprinkle with cheese. Cover and microwave at medium high 16 to 19 minutes. Arrange artichoke hearts around chicken pieces. Cover. Microwave on high for 5 minutes. Let stand covered 5 minutes.

Helen Whitley
(Mrs. John B.)

One Step Further

Chicken à la Roma
To save close to 200mg more sodium per serving, use reduced salt bouillon granules.

	Cal	Fat(g)	% Fat Cal	Sat Fat(g)	Chol(mg)	Sod(mg)
Per Serving	271	11.5	38	3	76	705

Desserts

1980s

1987
➤ Capitol Complex Visitor's Center
➤ Media Literacy
➤ Teen Pregnancy Prevention

1988
➤ Education! The Key to Success
➤ Volunteer Connection
➤ State Archives Volunteer Project
➤ Opportunity Knocks
➤ Magnolia Mound Weekend Cooks

1989
➤ Greater Baton Rouge Food Bank Volunteer Management
➤ Kidd Town
➤ Master Plan – Juvenile Detention Center

The overwhelming success generated by the River Road Recipes cookbooks gave rise to the first Million Dollar Committee. To aid the visually impaired and the elderly, the original *River Road Recipes* was published in large print.

We wanted to make the arts part of everyone's daily life, and undertook projects like Symphony at Twilight, City Arts and Cultural Resources and the Fine Arts Series to bring music, visual art, and dance to everyone.

Maw Maw's Fruit Pizza Tart

Yield: 16 servings

Crust

2 1/2 cups cake flour
2 tablespoons baking powder
1/4 teaspoon salt
1 1/4 cups confectioners' sugar
2 teaspoons vanilla extract
2/3 cup low fat ricotta cheese
1/4 cup margarine
1 egg white
2 tablespoons skim milk

Topping

4 ounces light cream cheese
1/2 cup low fat ricotta cheese
1 teaspoon vanilla extract
1/4 cup sugar

Glaze

1 cup orange juice
1/3 cup sugar
2 tablespoons cornstarch

Garnish

3 kiwis
1 can mandarin oranges, well drained
1/2 bag frozen blueberries OR 8 ounces fresh
1/2 bag frozen strawberries OR 8 ounces fresh
(nectarines and peaches may also be used)

Mix all dry ingredients for crust in a food processor. Add the remaining crust ingredients. Pulse on and off just until the dough is mixed and forms a ball. Shape into ball, cover with plastic wrap and refrigerate for at least 2 hours. Spread in bottom of large aluminum pizza pan. Bake at 375 degrees for 10 to 12 minutes until golden and done. Mix together topping ingredients until very smooth and spread over cooled dough. Cook orange juice, sugar and cornstarch over medium heat, stirring to avoid lumps, until thickened. Cool. Slice and arrange garnish on pizza and topping. Pour the cooled glaze on top of fruit.

Mrs. Ed Bradley

	Cal	Fat(g)	% Fat Cal	Sat Fat(g)	Chol(mg)	Sod(mg)
Per Serving	225	5	20	1.7	5	234

Nutrition Nibble

Our primary goal with the desserts was to cut the fat. Whenever possible, we also moderately cut the sugar content. You may wish to experiment with reducing the sugar content further. Start slowly. Remember, even low fat desserts should be eaten as a treat in smaller portions.

Most of America's bananas enter this country through ports on the Gulf coast. And before they've gotten very far inland at all, Louisiana's chefs have already grabbed them and made them our own.

Baked Bananas

Yield: 9 servings

6 bananas
1/3 cup brown sugar
1 teaspoon orange peel
1 1/2 teaspoons cinnamon
1/4 teaspoon nutmeg
1 tablespoon liquid margarine or melted tub margarine
2 tablespoons rum

Slice bananas lengthwise in thirds. Place in a 9x13-inch glass baking dish sprayed with vegetable oil cooking spray. Mix the remaining ingredients together and pour over the bananas. Bake at 325 degrees for 30 minutes.

Augusta Waggenspack

	Cal	Fat(g)	% Fat Cal	Sat Fat(g)	Chol(mg)	Sod(mg)
Per Serving	117	1.4	10	0.4	0	19

Espresso Ice Cream

Yield: 1 quart, 8 servings of 1/2 cup

2/3 cup sugar
1 1/2 cups skim milk
1 envelope of plain gelatin
1 egg white
2 1/4 cups evaporated skim milk
1/2 cup very strong espresso, cooled
1 tablespoon vanilla
1/2 cup (about 3 ounces) coarsely crushed
    chocolate-covered espresso beans

Mix sugar and skim milk together; sprinkle gelatin over mixture and let sit 1 minute. Place over medium heat, stirring constantly until dissolved. Add a small amount of this mixture slowly to the egg white, stirring all the time, then gradually stir back into the milk mixture. Cook for about 2 minutes, then remove from heat and cool. Stir in evaporated milk, espresso and vanilla. Stir well, cover and refrigerate for 4 hours, or until very cold. In an electric mixer on medium speed, beat the chilled espresso milk 6 to 8 minutes until it is thick and custardlike. Pour the mixture into an

One Step Further

Baked Bananas
Sugar-free "brown sugar" substitutes are available. If used, they will trim off over 7gm sugar and over 25 calories per serving.

ice cream maker and freeze until partially frozen according to the manufacturer's instructions. Stop the machine and quickly stir in the crushed chocolate-covered espresso beans. Continue churning until the ice cream is frozen. Do not over-churn. Pack with ice and rock salt and let stand approximately 1 hour before serving.

Susan Saurage-Altenloh

	Cal	Fat(g)	%Fat Cal	Sat Fat(g)	Chol(mg)	Sod(mg)
Per Serving	180	1.2	6	0.8	4	123

Poached Bosc Pears
Yield: 6 servings

2 cups water
1 tablespoon lemon juice
6 medium ripe, firm pears
2 cups dry red wine
1/2 cup sugar
1 small cinnamon stick
1 strip lemon rind, 2x2 1/2 inches long
2 tablespoons cognac

Combine 2 cups water with lemon juice in a large bowl. Peel pears and immerse in mixture. Bring wine, sugar, cinnamon stick and lemon rind to a boil in saucepan. Add drained pears and bring to a boil. Reduce heat and simmer, turning pears every 5 minutes, just until tender, for 10 to 15 minutes. Remove with a slotted spoon and place upright in serving dish. Increase heat to high and boil liquid until syrupy and reduced by half; about 5 to 7 minutes. Remove from heat and add cognac. Discard cinnamon stick and lemon peel. Pour sauce over pears. Cover and cool, then refrigerate at least 2 hours. Serve well chilled with a dollop of nonfat vanilla yogurt or light sour cream, if desired. This makes a light but elegant finale to any meal.

Charlotte Breard Hamilton

	Cal	Fat(g)	% Fat Cal	Sat Fat(g)	Chol(mg)	Sod(mg)
Per Serving	207	0.7	3	trace	0	51

This is an easy no-cook ice cream with real flavor and texture appeal. Chocolate-covered espresso beans are available at candy and specialty shops. If you can't find them, your ice cream will still be wonderful. Do not substitute coffee bean-shaped candies, coffee-flavored chocolates or chocolate chips; they are much too sweet for a real espresso ice cream.

Susan Saurage-Altenloh

Cool and Citrus Ice Cream Pie
Yield: 16 slices

1/2 gallon sugar-free, fat-free vanilla frozen dairy dessert
One 6-ounce can frozen orange juice concentrate, thawed
1/2 small tub of sugar-free lemonade crystals
2 graham cracker pie crusts

Soften frozen dairy dessert. Stir in orange juice concentrate. Mix well. Add lemonade crystals. Mix well. Pour into two graham cracker crusts. Freeze. Serve frozen.

Bunny Epps

	Cal	Fat(g)	% Fat Cal	Sat Fat(g)	Chol(mg)	Sod(mg)
Per Serving with above crust	199	4.3	20	0.9	0	195

Pralines de Louisiane
Yield: 75 pralines, 1 per serving

1 cup white sugar
3/4 cup brown sugar
1/2 cup evaporated skim milk
3 tablespoons margarine
1 1/2 cups chopped pecans
1/2 teaspoon vanilla extract
Waxed paper (chill in refrigerator)

Be prepared to work quickly. Assemble your ingredients ahead of time. Mix sugars and milk in a large saucepan. On medium heat bring to a rolling boil, stirring constantly to prevent sticking. Add margarine. Immediately after margarine melts, add pecans and vanilla. Beat by hand until smooth. Drop teaspoon size patties of the mixture onto sheets of cold waxed paper, as quickly as possible. If the mixture crystallizes, add a small amount of milk and bring to a boil. Let cool and enjoy!

Cindy Buie Maughan

	Cal	Fat(g)	% Fat Cal	Sat Fat(g)	Chol(mg)	Sod(mg)
Per Serving	38	1.9	44	0.2	trace	8

One Step Further

Cool and Citrus Ice Cream Pie
Most of the fat and sugar in this recipe come from the store-bought pie crust. Trim off more than 3gm fat and 55 calories in each serving by making your own crust.

Crust
2 cups graham cracker crumbs
1/4 cup sugar OR 6 packages sweetener
6 tablespoons tub margarine, melted
2 1/2 tablespoons water

Stir graham cracker crumbs and sugar together. With a fork gently blend in melted margarine; once thoroughly mixed, blend in water. Press into bottom and sides of two pie pans. Bake at 350 degrees for 10 minutes, or till lightly browned. Cool and pour in filling.

Pralines de Louisiane
To reduce fat and calories further, try replacing 1/3 to 1/2 of the pecans with Grapenuts cereal. Remember they are still high in sugar, moderation is the key!

Amaretto Brownies
Yield: 32 squares, 1 per serving

One 20-ounce box light brownie mix

Icing
3 tablespoons tub margarine
4 ounces light cream cheese, room temperature
3 cups confectioners' sugar
1 teaspoon almond extract
1-2 tablespoons milk

Topping
1 square (1 ounce) semi-sweet chocolate
2 teaspoons tub margarine
6 tablespoons cocoa powder
1 tablespoon sugar
1 tablespoon cornstarch
1/4 cup corn syrup
1 tablespoon skim milk
1 tablespoon Amaretto

Prepare brownie mix according to directions. Bake in a 9x13-inch pan. Cream margarine and cream cheese together, adding confectioners' sugar and almond extract. Add just enough milk to make smooth and spreadable. Spread over cooled brownies. Melt chocolate square and margarine. Mix cocoa powder, sugar and cornstarch. Stir corn syrup and milk into cocoa mixture gradually. Add to melted chocolate and continue cooking, stirring until well mixed and smooth. Remove from heat. Mix in Amaretto. Cool slightly. Spread over icing. Refrigerate until firm. Cut into small squares.

Mrs. Wray E. Robinson

	Cal	Fat(g)	% Fat Cal	Sat Fat(g)	Chol(mg)	Sod(mg)
Per Serving	148	3.6	22	1.6	9	99

My friend Annette from Boston insists on calling them PRAY-leens and each time I gently correct her. In Louisiana we call these miraculous confections of butter and brown sugar and pecans . . . PRAW-leens. And I send her another couple dozen from the latest variation on the recipe I'm trying. Something tells me she's not as slow to catch on as I think.

World's Fastest Strawberry Mousse
Yield: 4 servings

One 10-ounce package frozen unsweetened strawberries
1 cup plain nonfat yogurt
1/3 cup sugar
1 tablespoon vanilla
1 teaspoon lemon juice

Mix all ingredients in blender and freeze. Serve in sherbet glasses. **Variations:** Replace the strawberries with your favorite fresh or frozen fruit—raspberries, blueberries, etc.

Mrs. T. O. Perry, Jr.
River Road Recipes II, *page 186*

Original Recipe

	Cal	Fat(g)	% Fat Cal	Sat Fat(g)	Chol(mg)	Sod(mg)
Per Serving	292	12.1	37	7.5	26	33

Lightened Recipe

	Cal	Fat(g)	% Fat Cal	Sat Fat(g)	Chol(mg)	Sod(mg)
Per Serving	125	trace	<1	1	1	42

Banana Nut Torte
Yield: 1 bundt cake or 2 loaves, 20 slices total

1/2 stick margarine
1 1/2 cups sugar
1/2 cup vegetable oil
2 eggs plus 3 egg whites, or 1 cup egg substitute
3 cups flour
1 teaspoon salt
1 teaspoon cloves
1 teaspoon allspice
2 teaspoons cinnamon
2 teaspoons baking soda
7 large or 9 small bananas
1 1/2 cups raisins
3/4 cup nuts, chopped (preferably pecans)

One Step Further

World's Fastest Strawberry Mousse
This can be readily converted to a sugar-free dessert by using an artificial sweetener. Omitting the sugar will save close to 60 calories per serving. It will be a little coarser in texture.

Preheat oven to 300 degrees. Beat margarine, sugar, and oil in mixer for about 10 minutes until creamy. Add eggs to mixture. In separate bowl, sift the dry ingredients together. Add this to the batter. Mash bananas with fork and add to batter along with raisins and nuts. Stir well and pour into a lightly greased bundt pan. Bake for 1 1/2 to 1 3/4 hours or until a toothpick inserted comes out clean. Can also be baked in two 5 1/2 x 9-inch loaf pans.

Cindy Buie Maughan

	Cal	Fat(g)	% Fat Cal	Sat Fat(g)	Chol(mg)	Sod(mg)
Per Serving	304	11.5	34	1.64	21	232

Black Forest Cake
Yield: 16 servings

Cake
3/4 cup egg substitute OR 1 egg and 3 egg whites
1 teaspoon almond flavoring
1 box light chocolate cake mix, preferably devil's food or fudge
One 18-ounce can reduced sugar cherry pie filling OR cherries packed in light syrup

Glaze
1/2 cup cocoa powder
1/2 cup granulated sugar
2 teaspoons cornstarch
1/3 cup skim OR low fat milk
1 tablespoon margarine
2 teaspoons vanilla extract

Beat eggs by hand. Add flavoring. Stir in cake and blend well; batter will be thick. Fold in pie filling. Pour into greased bundt pan and bake at 350 degrees for 45 to 50 minutes. Cool and remove from pan. **Glaze:** In a saucepan, mix cocoa, sugar and cornstarch together until well blended. Place over medium heat and gradually whisk in milk. Bring to a boil, stirring frequently. Cook for about 2 minutes until thickened; continue stirring. Remove from heat and whisk in margarine and vanilla. Stir until smooth. Drizzle over cake. This cake travels well.

Nell W. McAnelly (Mrs. Robert V.)

	Cal	Fat(g)	% Fat Cal	Sat Fat(g)	Chol(mg)	Sod(mg)
Per Serving	214	3.8	16	1.1	trace	288

Claire's Chewy Chocolate Cookies
Yield: 7 1/2 dozen cookies

2/3 cup vegetable oil
1 1/2 cups sugar
2 eggs OR 1/2 cup egg substitute
2 teaspoons vanilla extract
2 cups flour
3/4 cup cocoa powder
1 teaspoon soda
1/2 teaspoon salt
1 1/4 cups broken pecan pieces

Cream oil and sugar. Add eggs and vanilla. Blend well. Combine flour, cocoa, soda and salt and add to creamed mixture. Stir in pecans. Drop by teaspoonfuls on ungreased cookie sheet. Bake in a 350-degree oven for 8 to 10 minutes, being careful not to overbake.

Robin R. Coerver

	Cal	Fat(g)	% Fat Cal	Sat Fat(g)	Chol(mg)	Sod(mg)
Per Cookie	52	2.9	49	.4	5	23

Chocolate Walnut Tart *with Bourbon and Maple*
Yield: 30 servings, 1 slice per serving

3 light pastry pie crust shells
6 eggs plus 10 egg whites
2 cups brown sugar
1 cup sugar
1/2 cup boiling water
1 cup cocoa powder
3 tablespoons tub margarine
1/2 cup bourbon
1 1/2 cups light corn syrup
1/3 cup plus 1 tablespoon maple syrup
1 1/2 tablespoons vanilla
1 cup "mini" chocolate chips
1 1/2 cups chopped walnuts

Prepare pie crusts from "Something Extra" section. Then beat eggs and egg whites with the 2 sugars. Slowly stir 1/2 cup boiling water into cocoa powder and stir until

Nutrition Note

Chocolate Walnut Tart with Bourbon and Maple

This is still a very rich dessert yet has 130 less calories and only 1/2 the fat and cholesterol per serving of the original. Replacing some of the chocolate chips with cocoa saved fat calories, especially saturated fat.

One Step Further

Claire's Chewy Chocolate Cookies

If 1/2 cup egg substitute or egg whites are used, the cookies will be cholesterol free. If nuts are omitted, 1gm fat per serving is saved.

Chocolate Walnut Tart with Bourbon and Maple

Make cholesterol free by omitting eggs and egg whites and using 3 cups cholesterol-free egg substitute.

smooth. Add margarine, stir until melted and mixed. Add bourbon. Add this mixture to the eggs and sugar along with the syrups and vanilla, beat. Divide chocolate chips and walnuts among the 3 shells. Pour in filling. Bake at 300 degrees for 1 1/2 hours or until filling has set like gelatin. Cool. Cut into small slices. If desired, serve with nonfat yogurt flavored with 4 tablespoons powdered sugar and 1 teaspoon bourbon. The tarts freeze well. This recipe is easily divided to make one pie at a time. Very decadent!

Elaine Renée Aycock

	Cal	Fat(g)	% Fat Cal	Sat Fat(g)	Chol(mg)	Sod(mg)
Per Serving	321	12	33	2.6	43	85

Praline Cake
Yield: 12 servings

1/2 cup graham cracker crumbs
3/4 cup brown sugar
3 tablespoons melted margarine
2/3 cup chopped pecans
1 package yellow cake mix
3/4 cup water
3 tablespoons cooking oil
1/4 cup praline liqueur
3/4 cup egg substitute or egg whites

Icing
1 can vanilla frosting, reduced fat
8 ounces light whipped topping
2 tablespoons praline liqueur

Prepare 3 round 9-inch metal pans by mixing the first 4 ingredients and putting 1/3 of the mixture in each pan. Mix the last 5 ingredients and pour 1/3 of the mixture over each of the crusts. Bake 25 to 35 minutes in a 350-degree oven. Cool completely. Stir icing ingredients together and frost between each layer, sides and top.

Gail Goings Brooks, (Mrs. K. Cleve)

	Cal	Fat(g)	% Fat Cal	Sat Fat(g)	Chol(mg)	Sod(mg)
Per Serving	560	19.7	31	5.5	1	456

Every year we go to Mama's house in Mamou for our Christmas visit. And every year the presents for the "men-folk" are always exactly the same. A dollar to buy a pair of socks. A jar of fig preserves. And a bag of pecans. Pecans from the yard of an 80-year-old lady who stoops to pick them as effortlessly as she did 50 years ago. They go into a paper bag that has been used so many times it now has the look and texture of chamois. And each bag is tightly tied with a sliver of an old slip that had finally become too worn to wear.

Nutrition Note

Praline Cake
Although this has moderate high fat content it has less than 1/2 the fat and saturated fat of the original.

225

Iced Fruit
Yield: 8 servings

1 cup water
1/2 cup granulated sugar
3/4 cup light corn syrup
1 pineapple, shredded
2 bananas, mashed
1 cup strawberries
1 tablespoon lemon juice

Boil water and sugar together for about 2 minutes. Add corn syrup to hot liquid. Stir to mix. Add fruits and lemon juice. Mix and freeze. Remove from freezer before hard frozen, or allow to thaw partially. Whip with electric hand mixer until smooth and then refreeze. Scoop onto plates and garnish with a fresh strawberry or a fresh sprig of mint.

Alice Witcher

	Cal	Fat(g)	% Fat Cal	Sat Fat(g)	Chol(mg)	Sod(mg)
Per Serving	142	0.4	3	trace	0	11

Pecan Pie
Yield: 10 servings

One 10-inch deep dish pie crust
3/4 cup egg substitute
1/2 cup sugar
1 cup light corn syrup
2 tablespoons flour
1/2 teaspoon cinnamon
1 tablespoon corn oil margarine
1 teaspoon vanilla extract
3/4 cup chopped pecans

Prepare pie crust using the Light Pie Crust recipe found in the "Something Extra" section. Set aside one unbaked crust for this recipe. Preheat oven to 350 degrees. Combine all ingredients above except pecans. Pour into the unbaked pie shell. Pat in the pecans. Place pie on a cookie sheet and bake for 10 minutes or until crust is brown. Turn oven heat

Nutritional Note

Iced Fruit

The sugar and calorie content of the original recipe was reduced by almost 1/2 in this modified version. This dish is practically fat and sodium free.

One Step Further

Pecan Pie

Reduce the fat content by 3gm more per serving by reducing the pecans to 1/3 cup and adding 1/2 cup Grapenuts cereal. Mix the Grapenuts into the pie filling, then press the pecans on the top. This will reduce the fat from calories to 27%.

down to 250 degrees and bake for 30 to 40 minutes more. Pie will feel firm to the touch when done.

Helen Lamont Worthen (Mrs. Mark S.)
Ruth Floyd Lamont (Mrs. Neil)

	Cal	Fat(g)	% Fat Cal	Sat Fat(g)	Chol(mg)	Sod(mg)
Per Serving	300	12	35	1.4	0.2	92

Chocolate Pecan Tart *with Whipped Topping*
Yield: 10 servings

10 saltine crackers, unsalted
3/4 cup sugar
1 teaspoon vanilla extract
1/2 cup lightly toasted chopped pecans, divided
2 stiffly beaten egg whites
1 large box chocolate fudge pudding, sugar free
2 cups skim milk
One 8-ounce package light whipped topping
1-2 tablespoons cocoa powder

Roll crackers into fine crumbs. Mix in sugar, vanilla, and 1/4 cup pecans. Gently fold in the beaten egg whites. Spread this mixture into a 10-inch pie pan sprayed with vegetable oil cooking spray. Bake for 25 minutes at 350 degrees. Let cool and place in the refrigerator. Make the chocolate pudding as directed for pie filling using the skim milk. Pour into the pie shell and cover with whipped topping. Garnish lightly with sprinkles of cocoa powder and the remaining 1/4 cup of pecans. Chill until serving time.

Michelle Bienvenu

	Cal	Fat(g)	% Fat Cal	Sat Fat(g)	Chol(mg)	Sod(mg)
Per Serving	194	7.2	32	2.9	1	134

We once drove fifty miles out of our way to buy a pie. Well, it wasn't just any pie. It was a pecan pie from Lea's. While this family-owned diner may be physically non-descript, it has a reputation for its pies that is a hundred times larger than the tiny town of LeCompte in which it resides. And now a new Interstate carries travelers almost within smelling range of Lea's pies. You had best stop early in the day for the best selection.

Meringue Shells
Yield: 8 servings

3 egg whites
1/2 teaspoon baking powder
3/4 cup granulated sugar
1 teaspoon water
1 teaspoon white vinegar
1 teaspoon vanilla extract
Pinch of salt

Beat egg whites until stiff. Add dry ingredients and liquid, alternating about 1 teaspoon at a time. Spoon into 8 or more mounds on a cookie sheet sprayed with vegetable oil cooking spray. Spread each mound from the center with a spoon into a nest shape. Bake 1 hour at 250 degrees. Delicious served with a scoop of ice milk or frozen yogurt and fresh fruit. Drizzle with berry puree such as strawberry or raspberry.

Nancy Crawford

	Cal	Fat(g)	% Fat Cal	Sat Fat(g)	Chol(mg)	Sod(mg)
Per Serving	76	0	0	0	0	72

Sour Cream Pound Cake - *A Better Way*
Yield: 16 servings

2 sticks light margarine OR 2/3 cup tub margarine
2 1/4 cups sugar
3 cups flour
3/4 teaspoon baking powder
1/4 teaspoon soda
1/2 teaspoon salt
1 1/2 cups egg substitute or 12 egg whites
1 cup nonfat plain yogurt
2 teaspoons vanilla extract
1 teaspoon almond extract

Cream margarine and sugar. Sift flour with other dry ingredients. Add to creamed mixture, alternating with egg substitute. Beat after each addition. Add yogurt and extracts;

Nutrition Note

Meringue Shells
This can also be used as an excellent fat-free crust alternative for any no-bake pies. Line pie shell with meringue mixture—bake as above—cool—fill.

Sour Cream Pound Cake
The submitter lightened this recipe. This revised recipe lowers fat and cholesterol as the original used butter, eggs, and sour cream. The savings over the traditional recipe were close to 100 calories per slice, over 9gm fat and a savings of 100mg cholesterol per serving.

fold in gently. Pour into a tube pan sprayed with vegetable oil cooking spray. Very delicious and may be frozen.

Glenda McCarty

	Cal	Fat(g)	% Fat Cal	Sat Fat(g)	Chol(mg)	Sod(mg)
Per Serving	266	7	23	1.2	<1	195

This is an old family recipe that was a favorite of my Cajun grand- mother.

Gary Bezet

Date Nut Praline Roll
Yield: 12 servings

1/2 cup pecans
1 1/2 cups granulated sugar
3/4 cup evaporated skim milk
2 tablespoons dark corn syrup
2 tablespoons tub margarine
1 tablespoon vanilla extract
1/8 teaspoon salt
1 cup dried chopped dates

Toast pecans briefly in 325-degree oven for 5 to 10 minutes. Be sure to avoid scorching. Chop and set aside. Combine sugar, milk and corn syrup in heavy pot. Cook on medium high heat; bring to a boil and cook until the soft ball stage (120 degrees on a candy thermometer). This takes about 10 to 15 minutes; the mixture will have a toffee-brown color. Remove from heat. Add margarine, vanilla and salt. Mix until melted. Add dates and pecans. Let cool for approximately 10 minutes. Roll up like a sausage in waxed paper. Let cool until set. Cut into 1-inch slices and serve.

Gary A. Bezet

	Cal	Fat(g)	% Fat Cal	Sat Fat(g)	Chol(mg)	Sod(mg)
Per Serving	201	5	21	0.6	trace	69

Nutrition Nibble

1 cup evaporated skim milk = 0.5gm fat, 199 calories

1 cup half-and-half = 27.8gm fat, 315 calories

1 cup of heavy cream = 88 gm fat, 820 calories

Oatmeal Cookies
Yield: 4 dozen cookies

1/2 cup chopped pecans
3 tablespoons vegetable oil
1/4 cup tub margarine
3/4 cup brown sugar
1/2 cup granulated sugar
1 egg plus 1 egg white
4 tablespoons water
3/4 teaspoon salt
1 cup flour
1/2 teaspoon baking soda
1 teaspoon vanilla
3 1/2 cups quick oats

Place pecans in 350-degree oven 5 to 10 minutes, until toasted slightly. Watch carefully. Set aside to cool. Mix remaining ingredients in a mixer, except oats and pecans. Fold pecans and oats in by hand. Place dough by table-spoons onto greased cookie sheet. Bake 10 to 12 minutes at 350 degrees.

Michele Bienvenu

	Cal	Fat(g)	% Fat Cal	Sat Fat(g)	Chol(mg)	Sod(mg)
Per Serving	76	2.8	33	0.4	4	58

One Step Further

Oatmeal Cookies
Substitute 1 cup of raisins for the pecans and save almost 1gm fat per serving. To make almost cholesterol free omit the eggs and use 1/2 cup egg substitute or egg whites.

Nutrition Note

"No Bake" Cheese Cake
This recipe has almost 1/2 the fat and saturated fat of the same size portion of classic cheese cake.

"No Bake" Cheese Cake
Yield: 35 squares, 1 per serving

1 small box sugar-free lemon-flavored gelatin dessert
1 cup hot water
1 cup lemon wafer cookies, crushed
3 tablespoons plus 2 teaspoons margarine, melted
1 1/2 tablespoons water
8 ounces light cream cheese
3/4 cup sugar
1/2 cup nonfat vanilla yogurt
One 8-ounce package light whipped topping
1 teaspoon vanilla extract

Mix gelatin in hot water and set aside to cool. Combine crumbs and margarine and mix well. Lightly mix in 1 1/2 tablespoons of water and press firmly on bottom of 9x13-inch glass container or 2 square cake-size dishes. May reserve some crumbs to decorate the top. Cream the cheese and sugar; add gelatin mixture to this. Add yogurt, then whipped topping and vanilla. Spoon into crumb crust. Chill and sprinkle with crumbs.

Elizabeth Hutchison

	Cal	Fat(g)	% Fat Cal	Sat Fat(g)	Chol(mg)	Sod(mg)
Per Serving	73	3.6	44	1.8	4	72

Low-Cal Bread Pudding
Yield: 12 servings

8 slices thin light white bread
1 stick light margarine, melted
1 cup egg substitute
1 1/2 cups granulated sugar
1 cup skim milk
Two 12-ounce cans evaporated skim milk
1 teaspoon cinnamon
1/2 teaspoon nutmeg
1/2 cup raisins
1 tablespoon vanilla extract

Toast bread on both sides and crumble into small pieces. Put crumbled bread into 9x13-inch glass baking dish. Pour margarine over crumbs. Beat together egg substitute and sugar; add milk and spices. Pour milk mixture over crumbs; let stand until crumbs absorb some of liquid. Stir in raisins and extract. Bake 350 degrees for 1 hour or until light brown and set in middle. Serve warm with scoop of light whipped topping or top with a scoop of vanilla yogurt.

Mrs. Jerry R. Bowman

	Cal	Fat(g)	% Fat Cal	Sat Fat(g)	Chol(mg)	Sod(mg)
Per Serving	249	5.3	18	1	3	218

Nutrition Nibble

Although stick margarine has essentially the same number of fat grams and calories as butter, butter has more than three times the saturated fat content.

Blackberry Mint Sorbet

Yield: 1 1/2 quarts, 12 servings of 1/2 cup each

3/4 cup sugar
1 cup water
1 cup tightly packed fresh mint leaves
4 cups blackberries or dewberries
1 cup red burgundy wine
Lemon juice, optional
Additional berries, for garnish

In a medium saucepan, combine the sugar, water, and mint. Bring to a boil, then simmer over medium heat, stirring occasionally, for about 5 minutes to make a mint-flavored simple syrup. Strain, discarding mint leaves, and cool. In a food processor, coarsely puree the berries. Turn into a bowl and stir in the wine and the mint syrup. Taste and add lemon juice if you prefer a tarter flavor. Pour the liquid into an ice cream maker and freeze until firm according to manufacturer's directions. Garnish with additional berries.

Margo Bouanchaud, Unique Cuisine

	Cal	Fat(g)	% Fat Cal	Sat Fat(g)	Chol(mg)	Sod(mg)
Per Serving	86	0.2	2	trace	0	14

Pineapple Cream Cheese *in Phyllo*
Yield: 8 servings

1/3 cup sugar
1 tablespoon cornstarch
One 8-ounce can crushed pineapple, drained
4 ounces light cream cheese, softened
1/2 cup drained nonfat cottage cheese
1/2 cup sugar
1/4 teaspoon salt
2 egg whites plus one whole egg OR 1/2 cup egg
 substitute
1/4 cup skim milk
1 1/2 teaspoons vanilla extract
12 sheets phyllo pastry
2 egg whites
4 tablespoons oil
1/8 teaspoon salt
1/4 cup lightly toasted chopped pecans

Place 1/3 cup sugar, cornstarch and pineapple in a saucepan over medium heat. Cook until thickened and clear. Remove and cool. Beat cream cheese and cottage cheese with an electric mixer or food processor until smooth. Add 1/2 cup sugar, 1/4 teaspoon salt, 2 egg whites, 1 egg, milk and vanilla. Mix until combined. Preheat oven to 350 degrees. Whisk 2 egg whites, oil and salt together. Spray a 9-inch pie pan with vegetable oil cooking spray and place 1 sheet of phyllo dough inside pan, letting excess hang over sides. Brush lightly with egg white/oil mixture and repeat with 5 more sheets, brushing with egg white mixture between each sheet. Pour pineapple mixture into pan, top with cream cheese mixture and sprinkle with chopped pecans. Cover with 6 more sheets of phyllo, brushing with egg white/oil mixture between each sheet and on top. Trim excess dough to fit to the edge of the pie pan. Bake for 30 minutes until golden brown. Cool and refrigerate until firm before cutting.

Kay Ewing's Everyday Gourmet Cooking School

	Cal	Fat(g)	% Fat Cal	Sat Fat(g)	Chol(mg)	Sod(mg)
Per Serving	**315**	**12.7**	**35**	**3**	**32**	**377**

Nutrition Nibble

Toasted nuts: Spread nuts in single layer on a cookie sheet. Bake at 300 to 325 degrees for 5 to 10 minutes, until aromatic. Check and shake half way through; be sure not to burn. Cool and chop. This procedure enhances the flavor; less will taste like more.

One Step Further

Pineapple Cream Cheese in Phyllo

In the pie filling, omit the 2 egg whites and whole egg and use 1/2 cup egg substitute or 4 egg whites and save 27mg cholesterol per serving.

233

Growing up, it was a family birthday tradition to make meringue cups filled with raspberry or fruit filling. We would enjoy these along with a yummy angel food birthday cake. I took these two traditions and combined them into this scrumptious dessert.

Adele Aycock

Raspberry Meringue Angel Cake
Yield: 12 servings

Meringue
1/2 teaspoon cream of tartar
4 egg whites
1 1/4 cups granulated sugar
2 teaspoons almond flavoring

In an electric mixer, beat egg whites and cream of tartar until stiff. Add sugar slowly with mixer still on. Fold in almond flavoring. Draw two 10-inch circles on a piece of parchment. Using a pastry bag, squeeze meringue to line the circle, filling it in with a coil-like design. Bake in a 200-degree oven for 1 hour or until firm. Or place in 350-degree oven overnight turning off the oven when the meringues are placed in it.

Filling
One 12-ounce package raspberries with sugar
1/3 cup granulated sugar
2 tablespoons cornstarch
1-2 tablespoons Framboise (raspberry liqueur or Kirsch)

Cook raspberries with sugar and cornstarch until slightly thickened. Add Framboise. Remove from heat and cool in the refrigerator.

Topping
One 24-ounce carton light whipped topping
2 tablespoons Framboise

One 10-inch (16 ounce) angel food cake

To whipped topping, fold in Framboise. Slice angel food cake into two layers. Place one layer on a platter, top with half of raspberry filling. Place meringue on top and one cup of the whipped topping. Repeat cake, filling, and meringue and cover entire cake with remaining whipped topping. Refrigerate overnight.

Adele Claire Aycock

	Cal	Fat(g)	% Fat Cal	Sat Fat(g)	Chol(mg)	Sod(mg)
Per Serving	375	7.5	18	6.5	0	161

Chefs'
Recipes

1990s

As we slipped from the '70s into the '80s, a new phrase loomed on the horizon . . . the "me" generation . . . but the Junior League of Baton Rouge remained, as always, firmly committed to "us."

The organization of the Parenting Center, where courses were taught daily to improve parenting skills in Baton Rouge, reflected the League's deep concern for the future of our children.

The League's involvement in the Battered Women's Program stemmed from our growing consciousness of a woman's right to be treated with respect, and the understanding that physical and emotional health for all citizens is critical to a thriving community.

Seafood Paella
Yield: 12 servings

2 tablespoons olive oil
1 cup chopped onions
1 cup chopped celery
1 cup diced red bell pepper
1 cup diced tomato
1 tablespoon diced garlic
1 cup frozen peas
1/3 cup diced andouille sausage (1/4 pound)
4 1/2 cups fish stock, fresh
3 cups raw rice
1 teaspoon salt
Cracked black pepper and red pepper to taste
2 tablespoons minced fresh parsley
1 teaspoon cumin
1 1/2 teaspoons chili powder
1/2 cup sliced green onions
1 cup, 170-190 count shrimp, peeled and deveined
      (6 ounces)
1 cup crawfish tails, rinsed and drained (6 ounces)
1 cup crabmeat

Preheat oven to 350 degrees. Using a vegetable oil cooking spray, spray a paella pan or other ovenproof baking dish, then heat olive oil over medium high heat. Sauté onions, celery, bell pepper, tomato, garlic until vegetables are wilted, approximately 3 to 5 minutes. Add frozen peas and blend well. In a separate nonstick skillet, sauté andouille sausage until light brown, 3 to 5 minutes. Remove to paper towels and blot off surface fat. Add sausage to paella pan. Add fish stock, bring to a rolling boil and reduce to simmer. Add rice and season to taste using salt, peppers, parsley, cumin and chili powder. Blend in sliced green onions, shrimp, crawfish and crabmeat. Cover pan with aluminum foil and bake 45 minutes to 1 hour. Remove from oven, stir and allow to set 30 minutes before serving. Tasty, easy entrée. May make seafood stock by simmering the shrimp and crab peelings and the lightly rinsed crawfish peelings in water for 20 minutes or more. Then strain and discard the peelings. Chill and skim off any fat.

Chef John Folse

	Cal	Fat(g)	% Fat Cal	Sat Fat(g)	Chol(mg)	Sod(mg)
Per Serving	292	6	19	1.4	58	361

Nutrition Nibble

Crawfish tails and shrimp can be used by heart conscious chefs. They are higher in cholesterol than most meats and seafood, yet are low in fat content, especially low in saturated fat; therefore, they do not affect your blood cholesterol level as much when eaten in moderate portions. Recommended serving size is a 3- to 4-ounce cooked portion.

Venison Parola

Yield: 8 servings

Marinade
3-4 pounds of venison ribs
4 stalks celery, divided
4 onions, divided
4 carrots, divided
4 tomatoes, cut in cubes
2 bay leaves
2 cloves
5 whole black peppercorns
5 garlic cloves, crushed
3/4 cup burgundy wine
3/4 cup brandy

Soup
1 1/2 quarts water
1/4 cup vegetable oil
1/3 cup flour
1/2 teaspoon salt
Pepper and Tabasco sauce to taste

For marinade: Dice 1/2 of the vegetables and combine in a stainless bowl with the venison, spices, burgundy and brandy. Cover with plastic wrap directly on top of marinade, producing an airtight seal. Leave marinade in refrigerator for at least 2 days. **For soup:** After the meat is marinated, place the contents of the stainless bowl into a stockpot. Add water and bring to a boil. Reduce heat to medium then strain to produce a venison stock. Debone the venison ribs and finely chop the meat. Place the remaining 1/2 of the carrots, celery and onion in a food processor. Add venison and chopped vegetables to the stock and bring to a boil. In separate saucepan, heat oil. Add the flour and mix well to produce a fine blond roux. Add the roux to the boiling stock, mixing well with a wire whisk. Add salt. Add pepper and Tabasco sauce to taste.

Mr. Philippe Parola

One Step Further

Venison Parola

Save over 6.5gm fat and 60 calories per serving by omitting the oil-based roux and using 1/2 cup fat-free roux, found in the "Something Extra" section. Add 1/2 cup cold water to the roux flour, stir into paste and add to the boiling stock.

	Cal	Fat(g)	% Fat Cal	Sat Fat(g)	Chol(mg)	Sod(mg)
Per Serving	273	8.9	29	2.5	58	232

Grilled Fillet of Fresh Fish *in a Tomato Basil Coulis*
Yield: 4 servings

1 tablespoon light olive oil
2 tablespoons fresh lemon juice
1 tablespoon fresh thyme leaves
1/4 teaspoon salt
Pepper as desired
Four 6-ounce firm fleshed fish fillets

Mix together olive oil, lemon juice and seasonings. Lay fish on a baking pan and rub with mixture on both sides. Light barbecue grill and let burn until the fire is good and hot. Place fish on grill and cook for about 3 minutes on first side. Turn each piece gently and cook for 5 to 7 minutes on the second side. Remove from grill and keep warm.

Tomato basil coulis
2 very ripe medium tomatoes
1 teaspoon olive oil
1 clove garlic, minced
1/4 cup chopped onion
1 tablespoon chopped fresh basil
1/4 teaspoon salt
White pepper to taste

Coarsely chop the two tomatoes and set aside. Place a heavy bottom sauce pot over medium heat, sauté garlic and onion in olive oil until translucent. Add chopped tomatoes and cook until very soft. Add fresh basil and salt and pepper. Puree this mixture in a blender or food processor. Strain sauce equally onto 4 plates. Set warm fish in sauce and garnish with basil sprigs.

Chef Leon Lemoine
Country Club of Louisiana

	Cal	Fat(g)	% Fat Cal	Sat Fat(g)	Chol(mg)	Sod(mg)
Per Serving	328	13.8	39	3	71	345

Nutrition Note

Grilled Fillet of Fresh Fish
Analysis was based on using fresh tuna. Other firm fish, such as amberjack, can also be used.

Crawfish Cakes *with Lemon Butter Sauce*
Yield: 6 servings

1/4 cup chopped white onions
1/4 cup chopped celery
1/4 cup chopped green bell pepper
1 large clove of garlic, finely chopped
Pinch of thyme
3/4 cup defatted chicken or seafood broth, less salt, divided
1 pound fresh crawfish tails, lightly rinsed
2 tablespoons chopped green onions
Pinch of cayenne pepper
Dash of Worcesteshire sauce
1/4 cup grated Romano cheese
2 cups coarsely ground fresh bread crumbs
1 large egg, lightly beaten
1/4 teaspoon salt
Freshly ground black pepper to taste

Sauce
3 fresh lemons, peeled
1/2 teaspoon sugar
1/4 cup tub margarine
1/2 cup defatted chicken or seafood stock, less salt

To make cakes, sauté onions, celery, bell peppers, garlic and thyme in 1/2 the broth until onion is transparent. Reserve 12 crawfish tails for garnish. Add the remaining crawfish, green onions, cayenne pepper and Worcestershire sauce. Simmer 10 minutes, occasionally tossing very gently. Remove from heat and gently mix in cheese, bread crumbs, egg, salt, pepper and enough of the remaining broth to stick together. Pat gently into 12 round cakes 1/2 inch thick. Spray lightly with vegetable oil cooking spray and bake at 400 degrees for about 3 to 4 minutes. Once golden brown, turn and cook other side until brown. To make sauce, squeeze juice from lemons and mash the pulp in a 2-quart saucepan. Heat juice and pulp to a boil. Add sugar. Add the margarine and broth little by little, whisking after each addition until sauce boils again. When all margarine and broth has been added,

Nutrition Note

Crawfish Cakes with Lemon Butter Sauce

This has only 1/9 of the fat and even less of the saturated fat of the original. The substitution of broth and change of cooking techniques made these savings possible.

remove from heat, strain and keep at room temperature until time to serve. Garnish each with 1 whole boiled crawfish and sprinkle cakes with chopped parsley.

Palace Cafe
New Orleans

	Cal	Fat(g)	% Fat Cal	Sat Fat(g)	Chol(mg)	Sod(mg)
Per Serving	216	8.9	37	2.4	111	485

Spinach Dip
Yield: 12 servings

2 tablespoons tub margarine
1 medium yellow onion, finely diced
3 jalapeño peppers, seeded, rinsed and finely diced
2 tablespoons finely diced fresh garlic
Three 10-ounce boxes frozen spinach, thawed, squeezed
1/2 teaspoon cayenne pepper
1/2 teaspoon ground white pepper
3/4 teaspoon ground nutmeg
1/4 teaspoon salt
2 tablespoons anisette
8 ounces evaporated skim milk
8 ounces light sour cream
1/2 cup nonfat plain yogurt

Melt margarine in large nonstick skillet. Add onions, jalapeños and garlic. Sauté until soft and translucent. Puree spinach in food processor. Add to skillet and stir. Add seasonings and spice. Stir to mix thoroughly. Add anisette and evaporated milk. Mix thoroughly. Taste and correct seasonings. Should be a little spicy or peppery, but not overpowering. Remove from heat and stir in sour cream and yogurt. Taste again for seasonings. Consistency should be somewhat firm and spreadable, but not runny. If too loose, adjust with more sour cream or a light sprinkling of bread crumbs. If too tight, loosen with milk. This dip also makes a good stuffing or filler.

Larry Maciasz
Maci's Place

	Cal	Fat(g)	% Fat Cal	Sat Fat(g)	Chol(mg)	Sod(mg)
Per Serving	98	4.2	38	1.9	9	192

Roasted Tomato Garlic Pizza *with Pesto*
Yield: 12 slices

4 medium tomatoes
1 tablespoon olive oil plus 1 teaspoon
Cracked black pepper
4 tablespoons fresh minced basil, divided
1 whole clove garlic
Chicken Broth
3 tablespoons light pesto
1/2 cup grated Romano cheese
Prebaked pizza dough

Prepare pizza dough (see below). Spray baking pan well with vegetable oil cooking spray, preferably olive oil flavor. Slice tomatoes thick and lay flat in baking pan. Brush with 1 tablespoon olive oil. Sprinkle with cracked black pepper and 2 tablespoons of fresh basil. Lightly spray tomatoes with vegetable oil cooking spray and then cover pan with foil. Cut the clove of garlic across the top to expose all pods. Place in a custard cup. Brush with remaining teaspoon of olive oil and rub into pods. Cover with chicken broth and sprinkle with cracked black pepper. Cover with foil. Bake tomato and garlic in a preheated 225-degree oven for 1 hour. Lighly brush prebaked pizza dough with olive oil. Then spread on pesto and arrange tomatoes on top. Squeeze out garlic and arrange on top of tomatoes. Sprinkle with remaining basil and Romano cheese. Bake at 475 degrees on bottom rack for 5 minutes. Move to center rack and bake for 20 to 30 minutes longer.

Pizza Dough
1 tablespoon sugar
1 cup warm water (110 to 115 degrees F)
1 envelope active dry yeast
3 cups flour
1 teaspoon salt
1 tablespoon olive oil

In a small bowl, stir together sugar, water and yeast. Set aside. Combine flour, salt, and olive oil. Add yeast mixture and blend. Knead 15 minutes. Place in a bowl, well sprayed with vegetable spray. Let rise until doubled in size (about 45 minutes). Punch down and press into a 15- to

Nutrition Note

Roasted Tomato Garlic Pizza with Pesto

Use light pesto recipe in "Something Extra" section. May replace pecans with same quantity of pine nuts.

16-inch round pan. Prick dough with fork all over. Place on bottom rack of preheated 475-degree oven for 4 minutes.

Pam Hubbell

	Cal	Fat(g)	% Fat Cal	Sat Fat(g)	Chol(mg)	Sod(mg)
Per Serving	181	5.1	25	1.4	6	274

Louisiana Crawfish Marinara
Yield: 8 servings

2 1/2 tablespoons oil
2 tablespoons flour
1 cup chopped onions
1/2 cup chopped celery
1/2 cup chopped bell pepper
2 cups marinara sauce
3 cups hot water, divided
Salt and cayenne pepper to taste
1/2 cup chopped green onions, separate tops
2 pounds crawfish tails or shrimp
3 cups cooked tri-color shells

In heavy skillet, place oil over medium heat. Add flour and stir until golden brown. Add all seasonings except green onion tops. Sauté until done, approximately 5 minutes. Add marinara sauce. When well mixed add 2 1/2 cups of water a little at a time until all is used. Season to taste with pepper. Add green onion tops. Cook on simmer approximately 1 hour. Meanwhile, lightly rinse and drain crawfish tails. Heat the remaining 1/2 cup water in a heavy iron pot. Add crawfish tails and steam about 5 to 8 minutes, stirring occasionally. Add to sauce approximately 15 minutes prior to serving. Serve on tri-color shells.

Bruce Cain, Executive Chef CEC

	Cal	Fat(g)	% Fat Cal	Sat Fat(g)	Chol(mg)	Sod(mg)
Per Serving	270	7.7	26	1.1	155	466

Nutrition Nibble

Crawfish fat is generally found in the crawfish heads and in bags of peeled crawfish tails. This yellowish fat is high in saturated fat and should be rinsed from the crawfish tails and heads before using.

243

Southwest Tomato Soup *with Smoked Shrimp*
Mousse and Mardi Gras Relish
Yield: 10 servings

Two 14.5-ounce cans defatted chicken broth, less salt
4 1/3 cups water
4 cups diced tomatoes
2 red onions, 1/2-inch julienne strips
1 jumbo carrot, 1/2-inch julienne strips
2 cups sliced mushrooms
Dash cayenne pepper
1/2 teaspoon white pepper
1 teaspoon Tabasco sauce
1/2 teaspoon cumin
1/4 cup cornstarch
1/4 cup cold water

Heat stock and water in large stockpot. Add tomatoes, red onions, carrots and mushrooms. Add seasonings. Bring to a boil. Combine 1/4 cup water and cornstarch in separate bowl; then add it to soup to thicken. Remove from heat. Garnish each bowl with a dollop of smoked shrimp mousse and Mardi Gras relish.

Smoked Shrimp Mousse
1 pound 70-90 count shrimp, peeled and deveined
1 tablespoon corn oil
2 tablespoons minced cilantro
1 cup diced tomato
1/2 cup light cream cheese
3 tablespoons light sour cream
1 teaspoon garlic
1/8 teaspoon or less salt
Dash white pepper

Smoke shrimp by brushing with 1 tablespoon oil and topping with cilantro and diced tomatoes and marinating 4 hours. Smoke over hickory chips for 10 to 15 minutes. Puree smoked shrimp. Add cream cheese and sour cream. Season to taste. Place in a container, cover with plastic and chill.

One Step Further

Southwest Tomato Soup with Smoked Shrimp Mousse and Mardi Gras Relish

Save close to 2gm fat per serving by replacing the light cream cheese with 1/2 cup 1% low fat cottage cheese. Press out the liquid, then cream the cottage cheese and add light sour cream. Yogurt cheese with 1 to 2 teaspoons of lemon juice would save even more fat! See "Something Extra" section.

Mardi Gras Relish

1/2 cup roasted corn
1 roasted red pepper
1 1/2 cups firm cooked black beans
1 red onion, diced
1 tablespoon fresh chopped garlic
1 green bell pepper, diced
1 jumbo carrot, diced
1 tomato, peeled and diced
1/4 cup finely chopped parsley
1/4 cup finely chopped cilantro
1 tablespoon olive oil
3 tablespoons defatted chicken broth, less salt
2 tablespoons red wine vinegar
Pepper to taste

Roast corn and red pepper in oven for 15 minutes at 350 degrees. Place red pepper in plastic bag. Seal. Set aside to cool. Once cooled, peel, seed and dice. Add pepper to mixing bowl along with the other ingredients. Season to taste. Allow to stand 1 hour. Serve chilled.

Sous Chef Gary Schenk, Juban's Restaurant

	Cal	Fat(g)	% Fat Cal	Sat Fat(g)	Chol(mg)	Sod(mg)
Per Serving	222	7	27	2.4	80	476

Mary Ann Dressing
Yield: 40 servings of 2 tablespoons each

3 cups nonfat plain yogurt
1/2 cup low fat mayonnaise
1 cup pure honey
1/4 cup dijon mustard
1/4 cup dry mustard
4 tablespoons rice vinegar

Whisk ingredients together. Chill. Wonderful on grilled shrimp, chicken, tuna salad.

Brian Blackledge, Café Americain

	Cal	Fat(g)	% Fat Cal	Sat Fat(g)	Chol(mg)	Sod(mg)
Per Serving	48	1.1	20	0.2	<1	70

Pepper Crusted Red Snapper
Yield: 6 servings

1 egg white
1/2 cup low fat milk
2 tablespoons black peppercorns
2 tablespoons cornstarch
1/2 cup flour
1/2 small red onion
3/4 teaspoon kosher salt
Six 6-ounce red snapper fillets
1 tablespoon olive oil

Mix egg and milk in separate bowl. To make pepper crust, in another bowl add the rest of the ingredients, except the olive oil and fish. Prepare the fennel sauce below and set aside. Put the skin side only of each fillet in the egg wash, then pat the skin side only in the pepper crust mixture. Be sure to only coat the skin side of the fish. In a nonstick sauté pan, heat 1 tablespoon of olive oil. Place the fish skin side down in the sauté pan, reduce the heat to medium and cover the pan with a lid. *Do not turn the fish over.* The cover will steam the fish. Let cook for 2 to 3 minutes, depending on the thickness of the fish, or until done.

Fennel sauce
1 1/2 teaspoons olive oil
1/4 cup diced fennel bulb
1/8 cup diced red onion
1/8 cup diced celery
1/8 cup diced carrots
2 cups red wine fennel fumet
1/8 cup diced concasse tomatoes
1/8 bunch tarragon, diced
1 tablespoon margarine
Pepper to taste
1/4 teaspoon salt

Begin with the fumet below. While the fumet is simmering, prepare the fennel sauce by heating the olive oil in a non-stick skillet and sauté all vegetables, except tarragon and tomato. Add fumet. Add tomato and tarragon. Whisk in the margarine and add pepper to taste, and salt if needed.

Fumet
1 cup red wine
1 pound fish bones
1 small onion
3 ribs celery
3 tomatoes
1 bulb fennel
3 cups water

In a small pot add all of the ingredients except the water. On low heat, reduce wine by 1/2. Add the water and let simmer for 30 minutes. Put the fennel sauce on a plate and place the fish on the plate. Garnish with braised fennel.

Commander's Palace
New Orleans

	Cal	Fat(g)	% Fat Cal	Sat Fat(g)	Chol(mg)	Sod(mg)
Per Serving	347	8.5	22	1.6	67	529

Maison Lacour Lo-Cal Salad Dressing
Yield: 8 servings

1/4 cup sugar
1/4 teaspoon black pepper
1/16 teaspoon cayenne pepper
1/4 cup water
1/2 cup champagne vinegar

Mix all ingredients until sugar is completely dissolved. The dressing must be allowed to age at least 72 hours before using. Try with various fresh herbs and seasoned vinegars.

John and Jacqueline Geraud
Maison Lacour

	Cal	Fat(g)	% Fat Cal	Sat Fat(g)	Chol(mg)	Sod(mg)
Per Serving	25	trace	0	–	0	<1

Amaretto Oranges
Yield: 12 servings

12 fresh oranges
6 cups sorbet
1/3 cup amaretto
6 oatmeal cookies, chopped
8 egg whites
1/4 teaspoon salt
2/3 cup sugar
12 maraschino cherries

Cut top 1/4 off orange. Remove the meat from the orange leaving outer shell intact. Combine amaretto, sorbet, chopped meat of oranges and cookies, then pack into the hollowed oranges. Freeze until firm. Whip egg whites and salt until soft peaks start. Slowly add sugar as you continue whipping until mixture becomes stiff. Remove oranges from the freezer. Top with meringue. Bake at 375 degrees until brown. Garnish with maraschino cherries.

Miriam Juban
Juban's Restaurant

	Cal	Fat(g)	% Fat Cal	Sat Fat(g)	Chol(mg)	Sod(mg)
Per Serving	278	1.6	5	0.3	0	110

Puree of Green Vegetable Soup
Yield: 12 servings

1/2 gallon water
6 medium-sized potatoes, peeled and cubed
16 ounces broccoli heads, cut in pieces
1 medium-sized leek, thinly sliced
1 head of boston lettuce, shredded
2 teaspoons chicken base
1 pinch powdered thyme
4 teaspoons margarine
Salt and pepper to taste
4 ounces leaf spinach

Pour water in a large, thick-bottomed cooking pot. Add potatoes, bring to a boil and cook 20 minutes. Add all other ingredients, except spinach. Boil for 10 minutes. At the last 2 minutes add the spinach and stir. Remove from

Nutrition Note

Amaretto Oranges
To trim off sugar and almost 90 calories per serving, use a sugar-free sorbet. May also use a sugar-free, fat-free frozen "ice cream."

One Step Further

Puree of Green Vegetable Soup
Use salt-free chicken base or 2 cubes reduced salt chicken bouillon to lower the sodium content further.

the fire. Cool the soup for 2 hours and place in refrigerator. Leave in the refrigerator for 3 to 4 hours. Before serving, put soup in the blender and blend at high speed until smooth. Correct the seasoning.

Charles Brandt
Chalet Brandt Restaurant

	Cal	Fat(g)	% Fat Cal	Sat Fat(g)	Chol(mg)	Sod(mg)
Per Serving	98	1.6	14	0.3	0	235

If served as cold soup, garnish with a teaspoon of plain yogurt.

Charles Brandt

Heart Healthy Trout Verdé
Yield: 4 servings

1/2 cup chopped parsley
1 teaspoon oregano
1/2 teaspoon chopped garlic
6 tablespoons lemon juice
6 tablespoons water
3 tablespoons olive oil
1/4 teaspoon salt
Four 6-ounce trout fillets
2 teaspoons low sodium seasoning
1 teaspoon paprika
Parsley sprig
1 1/4 pounds boiled new potatoes
2 lemons

Mix parsley, oregano, garlic, lemon juice, water, olive oil and salt and set aside. Dip trout fillets in water and sprinkle seasoning and paprika over fillets. Broil in oven for about 10 minutes at 350 degrees. Place 1 fillet on each platter, pour 1/4 of the Verdé Sauce mixture on each. Add 5 ounces of boiled new potatoes to each platter and garnish with lemon wedges and parsley sprigs.

Ralph & Kacoo's
The Seafood Restaurant

	Cal	Fat(g)	% Fat Cal	Sat Fat(g)	Chol(mg)	Sod(mg)
Per Serving	400	16.6	37	3.2	142	353

One Step Further

Heart Healthy Trout Verdé
Reduce olive oil to 2 tablespoons and save an additional 3.5gm fat per serving. Omit salt for 133mg sodium per serving savings. Still a lot of great taste.

Banana Chutney
Yield: 8 servings

2/3 cup granulated sugar
1/2 cup rice wine vinegar
3 tablespoons apple juice
1/4 cup diced yellow onion
1 teaspoon chopped garlic
3/4 teaspoon salt
1/2 teaspoon ground ginger
1 tablespoon curry powder
1 bay leaf
1/4 cup diced red bell pepper
1/4 cup diced green bell pepper
1/4 cup chopped scallions
1 pound chopped ripe banana (1 1/2 pounds before
    peeling)

Melt sugar. Add vinegar and dissolve sugar. Add apple
juice, onions, garlic, and dry spices. Cook for 2 minutes
then add peppers, scallions and cook for 1 minute.
Remove from heat. Add bananas and let cool. Serve with
grilled chicken or pork.

Kevin Graham
The Windsor Court

	Cal	Fat(g)	% Fat Cal	Sat Fat(g)	Chol(mg)	Sod(mg)
Per Serving	123	0.4	3	trace	0	202

Nutrition Note

Banana Chutney
The original was
already free of added
fat, but high in sugar,
thus we cut the sugar
by 1/3 and added
apple juice.

**Grilled Chicken
Breast with
Roasted Red
Pepper Puree**
Combine herbs, black
and white pepper and
salt. Divide olive oil
and seasonings evenly
among the chicken
breasts and rub into the
flesh.

Grilled Chicken Breast *with Roasted Red Pepper Puree*
Yield: 4 servings

2 red bell peppers
2 ounces defatted chicken broth, less salt
4 skinless, boneless chicken breast halves
1 tablespoon olive oil
2 teaspoons fresh thyme, minced (1 teaspoon dry)
1 teaspoon fresh rosemary (1/2 teaspoon dry)
1 teaspoon cracked black pepper
1/4 teaspoon salt
White pepper to taste

Place 2 red bell peppers over flame of a gas stove or grill
and allow skin to blister and turn black. Plunge peppers

into ice water and cool for 5 minutes. Cut in half and discard stems and seeds. Place roasted peppers and chicken broth into a food processor and puree. Set aside. Season chicken breasts with olive oil, herbs, cracked pepper and salt. Grill over a hot charcoal fire for approximately 5 minutes per side. Warm pepper puree in a small saucepan. Divide sauce evenly among 4 plates. Place 1 grilled chicken breast on each plate and serve.

Chef Leon Lemoine
Country Club of Louisiana

	Cal	Fat(g)	% Fat Cal	Sat Fat(g)	Chol(mg)	Sod(mg)
Per Serving	197	6.7	31	1.4	74	238

Chicken Pollo de Enzo
Yield: 4 servings

2 tablespoons lemon juice
3 tablespoons white wine, divided
1 tablespoon extra virgin olive oil
2 tablespoons finely chopped garlic
Four 4.5-ounce skinless, boneless chicken breast halves
1/2 cup chopped fresh basil
1/4 cup chopped parsley
1 large tomato
1/4 teaspoon salt
Pepper to taste
Pinch fresh red pepper

Make marinade of lemon juice, 1 tablespoon white wine, olive oil and garlic. Pound chicken breasts with meat tenderizer. Pour marinade over chicken and set in refrigerator for 1/2 hour. Puree together remaining ingredients to make "Samarillo sauce." Simmer about 5 minutes in saucepan on top of stove. Grill chicken on open grill, slow cooking the chicken on low flame. Baste chicken with marinade while on grill. When chicken is cooked, cover with Samarillo sauce. Serve with your favorite vegetable and pasta for a light and healthy meal.

Chef Vincenzo J. Signorelli, Jr.

	Cal	Fat(g)	% Fat Cal	Sat Fat(g)	Chol(mg)	Sod(mg)
Per Serving	220	6.8	28	1.4	73	204

Nutrition Nibble

Marinades should not be used to baste meat at the end of grilling or roasting unless the marinade is first brought to a boil. Raw meat, fish and poultry harbor bacteria which will be transferred to the marinade liquid. Thus, the marinade is unsafe unless first boiled on the stovetop or in the microwave.

Seafood Sauce Piquante
Yield: 14 servings

1/3 cup oil
1/2 cup flour
1 cup chopped onions
1 cup chopped celery
1 cup chopped bell pepper
2 tablespoons diced garlic
One 8-ounce can tomato sauce
1 cup diced tomatoes
1 tablespoon diced jalapeños
2 whole bay leaves
1/2 teaspoon thyme
1/2 teaspoon basil
1 1/2 quarts fish stock
1 pound 21-25 count shrimp, peeled and deveined
1 pint select oysters in liquid
1 pound redfish, cubed
1 cup chopped green onions
1 cup chopped parsley
1/4 teaspoon salt
Cracked black pepper to taste
1 pound jumbo lump crabmeat
4 cups cooked rice

In a 1-gallon heavy bottom sauce pot, heat oil over medium heat. Using a wire whisk, add flour, stirring constantly until dark brown roux is achieved. Add onions, celery, bell pepper and garlic and sauté until vegetables are wilted, approximately 3 to 5 minutes. Add tomato sauce, diced tomatoes, and jalapeños, blending well into roux mixture. Add bay leaves, thyme, and basil. Slowly add fish stock stirring constantly until all is incorporated. Bring to a low boil, reduce to simmer and cook 30 minutes. Add additional fish stock if necessary to retain volume. Add shrimp, oysters in liquid, fish and continue to cook 5 to 10 additional minutes. Add green onions and parsley. Season to taste using salt and cracked black pepper. When shrimp are pink and curled, carefully fold in lump crabmeat. Adjust seasonings if necessary. Serve over rice.

Chef John Folse

One Step Further

Seafood Sauce Piquante

Save close to 100mg sodium or better per serving when using no-salt-added tomato sauce. Use our fat-free roux recipe in the "Something Extra" section and save 45 calories and over 5gm more fat per serving.

	Cal	Fat(g)	% Fat Cal	Sat Fat(g)	Chol(mg)	Sod(mg)
Per Serving	273	8.3	28	1.4	125	319

Cajun Catfish Pasta

Yield: 4 servings

2 tablespoons olive oil
1 pound catfish fillets, 1-inch cubes
1/2 cup flour
1/4-1/3 cup defatted seafood stock OR chicken broth, less
    salt
1/2 cup diced yellow squash
1/2 cup diced zucchini squash
1/2 cup mushrooms
2 tablespoons diced yellow bell pepper
2 tablespoons diced green bell pepper
2 tablespoons diced red bell pepper
2 tablespoons lemon juice
3 cups evaporated skim milk
1 cup marinara sauce
1/2 cup chopped green onions
1/4 teaspoon salt
2 cups tri-color rotini

In a nonstick skillet or heavy pan, heat olive oil over medium high heat. Lightly dust catfish in unseasoned flour. Sauté catfish in olive oil until slightly brown, about 3 minutes on each side. Remove catfish and drain on paper towels. Wipe skillet clean. Add 1/4 cup chicken broth or seafood stock and all the vegetables; heat and sauté vegetables 3 to 5 minutes. Add lemon juice and reduce to 1/2 volume. Add evaporated skim milk, marinara sauce and green onions and bring to a boil. Reduce to simmer and cook until sauce is well thickened. Season to taste with salt and pepper. Add rotini and toss well.

Bruce Cain, Executive Chef CEC

	Cal	Fat(g)	% Fat Cal	Sat Fat(g)	Chol(mg)	Sod(mg)
Per Serving	**503**	**12.3**	**19**	**2.4**	**73**	**723**

If you can eat it, Louisiana has a festival in its honor. Jambalaya, Crawfish, Catfish, Boudin, Andouille, Gumbo, Alligator, Crab, Shrimp, Pecans, Yams, Okra, Poke Salad, even the simple Tomato. Each festival offers up a cornucopia of delectable dishes crafted from the honoree. And each is a part of what makes food in Louisiana so much fun.

Catfish Pecan

Yield: 6 servings

Six 5- to 7-ounce catfish fillets
1 cup roasted pecans, divided
1 cup bread crumbs
3 egg whites
1/2 cup skim milk
1 cup flour
1 teaspoon pepper
1 teaspoon seafood seasoning

Meunière Sauce
2 cups fish stock
1 teaspoon Worcestershire sauce
Juice of 1/2 lemon
Dash of Tabasco sauce
2 tablespoons evaporated skim milk
2 tablespoons margarine

Trim all fat from catfish. Separate out 6 pecans; coarsely chop and reserve for garnish. Puree remaining pecans and bread crumbs in a food processor. Make egg wash with egg whites and milk. In a separate bowl, season flour with pepper. Season catfish with seafood seasoning; dredge in seasoned flour. Next, put in egg wash, then dredge in bread with pecans. Spray cookie sheet with vegetable oil cooking spray. Place fillets on sheet and spray again lightly. Cook in oven at 450 degrees for 5 to 8 minutes, until fish flakes and is done. **Meunière sauce:** Reduce fish stock, Worcestershire sauce, lemon juice and Tabasco sauce by 1/2. Add milk and reduce for 1 or 2 minutes. Remove from heat and whip in margarine. Serve over cooked fish and sprinkle with reserved pecans.

Palace Cafe
New Orleans

	Cal	Fat(g)	% Fat Cal	Sat Fat(g)	Chol(mg)	Sod(mg)
Per Serving	**491**	**23.6**	**43**	**3.6**	**87**	**735**

One Step Further

Catfish Pecan
This has only 1/2 the calories and sodium and only 1/3 the fat of the original. To cut sodium by over 200mg more, omit the seafood seasoning and use your favorite salt-free seasoning blend.

254

Something
Extra

1990s

1992

- Arts in Education
- Family Literacy Project
- Girl Talk/Teen Talk
- Glasgow Middle School Adoption
- Growing Pains
- High School Quiz Bowl
- Middle School Quiz Bowl
- Parker House Pals
- Art Carte
- Food Bank Saturday Workers
- LASC Science Station
- River Road Ramblers
- Volunteer Connectors

1994

- 20,000 copies, RRRIII published

Jogging, exercising and "eating right" were all in vogue. Responding to these trends, the Junior League of Baton Rouge completed one of its most recent projects, *River Road Recipes III: A Healthy Collection.* Not only will this cookbook be a source for delicious, healthier eating, it will also raise funds for Junior League projects aimed at ultimately benefiting our community.

Yogurt Cheese

Yield: 1 cup, 16 servings of 1 tablespoon each

2 cups nonfat yogurt

Read the yogurt's list of ingredients and use one that does not contain gelatin or carrageenan. These are stabilizers that will not allow the yogurt to separate well, as is needed in this recipe. Place the yogurt into a large piece of cheese-cloth and tie at the top. Hang this over a bowl to catch the liquid (whey) that drains out. (May also drain in a cheese-cloth- or coffee filter-lined colander over a bowl.) Refrigerate for 8 to 24 hours. Remove from cloth once it reaches the degree of thickness you desire. Less time for a thick sour cream texture or longer for a cream cheese thick-ness. It should drain to almost half the original amount. Store in the refrigerator in a covered container for 10 to 15 days. If you use this in a cooked recipe (as cheese cake) blend in 1 tablespoon of cornstarch or flour per one cup of yogurt cheese before cooking. If cornstarch or flour is not used the mixture will separate when heated. Add herbs, spices and/or fresh cracked pepper to produce a tasty spread for crackers or a vegetable dip or a topping for baked potatoes.

	Calories	Fat(g)
Yogurt cheese, 1 tablespoon	15	0
Cream cheese, 1 tablespoon	50	5
Light cream cheese, 1 tablespoon	30	2.5
Mayonnaise, 1 tablespoon	99	11
Light mayonnaise, 1 tablespoon	40	4
Sour cream, 1 tablespoon	31	3
Light sour cream, 1 tablespoon	20	1.5

You can lighten some of our recipes further by trying yogurt cheese as a substitute for cream cheese, mayonnaise, ricotta cheese, or sour cream. This will save calories and fat, while adding calcium.

Bagel Chips
Yield: 3 dozen (18 servings of 2 slices broken into chips)

6 bagels (at least day old)
Nonstick butter-flavored cooking spray

Optional:
Salt
No-salt-added herb blends
Minced onions
Minced garlic
Sesame seeds

Slice bagels as thin as possible, approximately 6 slices per bagel. Place slices on ungreased cookie sheet. Spray moderately with cooking spray. Add salt, onion, garlic, etc., if desired. Bake at 350 degrees for 12 to 15 minutes. **Variations:** Make pita chips or taco chips in the same way. Using flour tortillas, corn tortillas or pita bread, cut across the circle into pie shapes. Spray with nonstick cooking spray and continue as above.

Beth Arceneaux Hanks

	Cal	Fat(g)	% Fat Cal	Sat Fat(g)	Chol(mg)	Sod(mg)
Per Serving	59	1	15	trace	3	66

Orange Sauce for Fruit
Yield: 8 servings, 2 tablespoons each

3/4 cup orange juice
1 tablespoon shredded orange peel
2 tablespoons sugar
2 tablespoons orange or cherry flavored liqueur

Stir all ingredients together until the sugar is dissolved. Pour over desired fruit.

Mrs. Wray E. Robinson

	Cal	Fat	% Fat Cal	Sat Fat	Chol	Sod
Per Serving	31	0	0	0	0	trace
25% of calories from alcohol, 1.1gm per serving						

Nutrition Note

Bagel Chips

Nutritional content will of course vary with toppings you choose to add. To keep sodium content close to nutrition information provided, choose no-salt-added seasoning blends, herb blends, onion and/or garlic. Over spraying the bagels with cooking spray will increase fat content.

Orange Sauce for Fruit

Try without the sugar and save 10 calories per serving. If desired, 2 to 3 packages of sugar substitute may be used instead. This sauce adds flavor while helping keep cut fruit from turning brown.

Piña Colada Sauce
Yield: 20 servings of 2 tablespoons each

16 ounces light ricotta cheese
One 6-ounce can piña colada mix, thawed

Blend ricotta cheese in your food processor with 2 ounces of piña colada until smooth. Gradually add piña colada mix until you reach the desired consistency. It may not take all of the piña colada mix.

Mrs. Wray E. Robinson

	Cal	Fat(g)	% Fat Cal	Sat Fat(g)	Chol(mg)	Sod(mg)
Per Serving	49	1.5	28	1.2	3	22

Pecan Pesto
Yield: 2 cups

2 cups fresh basil leaves, washed and dried
6 garlic cloves
1/3 cup shelled pecans, lightly toasted
2 tablespoons olive oil
2/3 cup defatted chicken broth, less salt
1/2 cup fresh grated Parmesan cheese
2 tablespoons grated Romano cheese
1/4 teaspoon salt
1/4 teaspoon pepper

Combine the basil, garlic and pecans in the bowl of a food processor; coarsely chop. With motor still running, add the combined oil and broth in a slow, steady stream. Shut the motor off and add the cheeses, salt and pepper. Process briefly to combine. This can be stored in the freezer, or refrigerated with a thin film of oil on top in a tightly covered jar. Excellent over cooked pasta, broiled fish or steamed vegetables.

Margo Bouanchaud
Unique Cuisine

	Cal	Fat(g)	% Fat Cal	Sat Fat(g)	Chol(mg)	Sod(mg)
Per Serving	58	4.5	69	1.1	4	128

Nutrition Note

Pecan Pesto
Still proportionally high in fat, but less than 1/3 the fat and calories of the original. Use in small to moderate quantities to season. Also good without pecans saving 1.5gm fat per serving.

One Step Further

Piña Colada Sauce
For even lower fat results (<1gm per serving), use 2 cups or 16 ounces of yogurt "cheese," found in the "Something Extra" section.

Pickled Pineapple

Yield: 1 quart, 16 servings of 1/4 cup each

Two 20-ounce cans unsweetened pineapple chunks
3/4 cup plus 2 tablespoons reserved pineapple juice
1/2 cup sugar
2/3 cup white vinegar
10 whole cloves
1 cinnamon stick, broken
6 whole allspice
Pinch salt

Drain pineapple chunks and reserve juice. Place chunks in either a 1-quart jar, 2 pint jars or 4 half-pint jars. Place reserved juice and all other ingredients in a small saucepan over medium heat. Cook for 15 minutes. Pour over pineapple. When cool, cover and refrigerate at least 3 days before serving. Keeps refrigerated for 2 months.

Kay Ewing's Everyday Gourmet Cooking School

	Cal	Fat(g)	% Fat Cal	Sat Fat(g)	Chol(mg)	Sod(mg)
Per Serving	66	trace	1	0	0	18

Blueberry Spice Sauce

Yield: 10 servings of 1/4 cup each

2 cups fresh blueberries (1 pint), divided
1/4 cup sugar
1/4 cup apple cider vinegar
2 tablespoons fresh lemon juice
2 teaspoons grated lemon peel
1/2 teaspoon ground cinnamon
1/4 teaspoon ground cloves
1/4 teaspoon ground nutmeg

Combine 1 cup crushed blueberries with remaining 7 ingredients. Heat in a medium saucepan to boiling. Reduce heat and simmer 5 minutes. Add remaining 1 cup whole blueberries and cook 2 to 5 minutes. Cool slightly and serve over vanilla yogurt, angel food cake, waffles or granola.

Shug Lockett (Mrs. Walker)

	Cal	Fat	% Fat Cal	Sat Fat	Chol	Sod
Per Serving	37	0.1	2	trace	0	2

Creveling Hot Fudge "Pudge" Sauce

Yield: 24 servings of 1 tablespoon each

1/3 cup cocoa powder
1/2 cup sugar
2/3 cup evaporated skim milk
1/2 cup light corn syrup
2 tablespoons tub margarine
1 teaspoon vanilla extract

Mix cocoa and sugar. Gradually add milk and corn syrup, stirring to make a paste. Cook in a heavy pot until mixture boils. Boil 1 minute. Stir in the margarine and vanilla. Store in the refrigerator. Is great over ice cream, warmed first in the microwave! **Variations:** For a thicker chocolate dip, add 1 1/2 tablespoons of cornstarch. Stir this into the cocoa and sugar mixture. Once mixture boils, simmer for 2 to 4 minutes, stirring frequently. Also good with 1 tablespoon of cointreau or kahlua in place of vanilla. This dip is great served with fresh strawberries, pineapple, kiwi and angel food cake squares.

Maretta Creveling

	Cal	Fat(g)	% Fat Cal	Sat Fat(g)	Chol(mg)	Sod(mg)
Per Serving	50	0.9	18	0.2	trace	21

Basic Gravy

Yield: 1 cup, 16 servings of 1 tablespoon each

2 tablespoons fat-free roux/browned flour
1 cup liquid (defatted meat drippings or broth)

Blend 1/4 cup of the chilled liquid into the flour to make a smooth paste. Heat the remaining liquid and stir in the flour solution until well blended. Simmer until heated through and thickened, stirring constantly. Season. May add wine, skim milk or other liquids to change flavor. Try various spices, herbs and seasonings. For a thicker gravy, add more flour.

	Cal	Fat(g)	% Fat Cal	Sat Fat(g)	Chol(mg)	Sod(mg)
Per Serving	5	.07	13	trace	71	35

Nutrition Note

Basic Gravy
This analysis is based on the use of 1 cup of less-salt canned chicken broth. Analysis will vary with liquid used.

No Fat Chocolate Sauce
Yield: 15 servings of 1 tablespoon each

3/4 cup granulated sugar
1/3 cup cocoa powder
4 teaspoons cornstarch
2/3 cup evaporated skim milk
1 teaspoon butter substitute granules
1 teaspoon vanilla extract

In small saucepan stir together sugar, cocoa, and cornstarch. Add skim milk. Cook and stir until thick and mixture bubbles. Stir 2 minutes on low. Add butter substitute granules. Stir well and remove from heat. Add vanilla. Good topping for fresh fruit, especially on fresh pineapple.

Mrs. Frank Bacot, Jr.

	Cal	Fat(g)	% Fat Cal	Sat Fat(g)	Chol(mg)	Sod(mg)
Per Serving	58	.3	5	trace	<1	18

Light Pie Crust
Yield: One 9-inch pie, 10 servings

1 cup plus 2 tablespoons all-purpose flour
1/4 teaspoon sugar
1/8 teaspoon salt
3 tablespoons cold skim milk
1/4 cup vegetable oil

Mix dry ingredients together. Pour the cold milk and oil into 1 measuring cup. Do not blend. Pour this all at once into the dry ingredients. Stir with a fork until well mixed. Form into a small ball. Roll out between two 12-inch squares of waxed paper until the pastry is thin and reaches the edge of the paper. Peel off one sheet of wax paper. With wax paper up, place into a pie plate and carefully peel off the paper and gently fit pastry into pie plate. Do not stretch. Trim edges and flute. Fill and bake following your recipe or, for a no-bake pie, prick and bake.

Linda Powell Vannoy

Nutrition Note

Light Pie Crust

While this crust is still moderately high in fat, it has 10% less fat calories. The real savings is that it has less than 1/2 the saturated fat of a typical store brand or homemade crust.

	Cal	Fat(g)	% Fat Cal	Sat Fat(g)	Chol(mg)	Sod(mg)
Per Serving	101	5.6	50	0.7	trace	29

Grand Marnier Cream Sauce

Yield: 14 servings of 2 tablespoons each

2 tablespoons Grand Marnier
1 1/2 cups nonfat vanilla yogurt
1/2 cup powdered sugar
1/4 cup evaporated skim milk

Blend the Grand Marnier, yogurt and powdered sugar together. Add milk a little at a time until you reach the consistency desired. Serve with fresh fruit as a dip or over fruit as a sauce. May substitute amaretto for Grand Marnier. To make even thicker, you may use 2 1/2 cups of yogurt cheese. (See "Something Extra" section.)

Jean Comeaux

	Cal	Fat(g)	% Fat Cal	Sat Fat(g)	Chol(mg)	Sod(mg)
Per Serving	43	trace	0	trace	<1	17

Saucy Cranberries

Yield: 12 servings of 1/4 cup each

One 12-ounce bag fresh cranberries
1 medium orange
1 Granny Smith apple
2/3 cup sugar
1/2 cup apple juice
1 small cinnamon stick
Dash nutmeg

Rinse cranberries and remove any stems. Place in a medium-size saucepan. Reserve zest from the orange. Peel, seed and remove membrane from orange. Chop pulp and add to cranberries, along with zest. Peel and core the apple. Dice and add to saucepan. Stir in sugar, apple juice, cinnamon and nutmeg. Bring to a boil over medium high heat. Lower heat and simmer about 40 minutes, stirring occasionally. Remove cinnamon stick and cool. Store refrigerated in a covered jar.

Kay Ewing's Everyday Cooking School

	Cal	Fat(g)	% Fat Cal	Sat Fat(g)	Chol(mg)	Sod(mg)
Per Serving	70	.01	1	trace	0	1

Nutrition Note

Grand Marnier Cream Sauce
This version has less than 1/2 the calories, 6.7gm less fat, and 21mg less cholesterol than the original!

Avocado-Tomatillo Relish

1 avocado, diced into 1/2-inch cubes
2 tablespoons diced tomatillo
1 tablespoon diced red bell pepper
1 tablespoon diced green bell pepper
1/2 teaspoon minced jalapeño pepper
1 tablespoon chopped scallions
2 tablespoons defatted chicken broth, less salt OR
    2 tablespoons white wine
2 teaspoons olive oil
1 tablespoon lime juice
1/4 teaspoon salt

Combine all ingredients in a bowl and season with lime juice and salt. Chill until ready to serve.

Joan W. Chastain

	Cal	Fat(g)	% Fat Cal	Sat Fat(g)	Chol(mg)	Sod(mg)
Per Serving	44	4	80	0.6	trace	82

Garlic Jelly

Yield: Six 8-ounce jars, 1 teaspoon per serving

2 whole heads of garlic, finely chopped
3/4 cup minced fresh parsley OR 1/4 cup dried
2 cups white wine vinegar
2 cups apple juice
1 teaspoon salt
1 package pectin for reduced sugar recipes
4 cups sugar, divided

Mix all ingredients except pectin and sugar in a pot. In a separate bowl, mix 1/4 cup of the sugar with pectin. Stir into the juice mixture. Bring to a rolling boil, stirring constantly. Quickly stir in remaining sugar. Return to a full boil and boil for 1 minute, continuing to stir. Spoon into clean jelly jars and seal with tops. Cool. Keep refrigerated until used.

Joanne Martin Roberts

Nutrition Note

Garlic Jelly

This recipe has 1/3 less sugar than the original.

	Cal	Fat(g)	% Fat Cal	Sat Fat(g)	Chol(mg)	Sod(mg)
Per Serving	71	trace	0	-	0	47

Herb Oils

Yield: 2 1/2 cups, 2 tablespoons per serving

2 1/2 cups virgin olive oil
12 or 14 leaves of fresh basil
Zest of lemon, orange or lime
Garlic, optional

Put basil leaves, zest and garlic in olive oil. Leave in a warm place for 2 to 4 days. Strain the oil into a fresh bottle and store in a cool place. You may put a few fresh basil leaves in the strained oil for eye appeal. **Variations:** Rosemary — 2 short sprigs of rosemary in sunflower or olive oil. Use on endive or bean salads. Dill — Add 4 to 6 sprigs of fresh dill to grapeseed or sunflower oil. This is excellent on green salads and with hot or cold potatoes.

Shirley King Thompson

Basic Vegetable or Corn Oil

	Cal	Fat(g)	% Fat Cal	Sat Fat(g)	Chol(mg)	Sod(mg)
Per Serving	120	13.6	100	1.7	0	trace

Olive Oil

	Cal	Fat(g)	% Fat Cal	Sat Fat(g)	Chol(mg)	Sod(mg)
Per Serving	120	13.6	100	1.9	0	trace

Sunflower Oil

	Cal	Fat(g)	% Fat Cal	Sat Fat(g)	Chol(mg)	Sod(mg)
Per Serving	120	13.6	100	1.4	0	trace

Grapeseed Oil

	Cal	Fat(g)	% Fat Cal	Sat Fat(g)	Chol(mg)	Sod(mg)
Per Serving	120	13.6	100	1.3	0	trace

Seasoned Bread Crumbs

Yield: 1 cup

1 cup plain bread crumbs
1 teaspoon basil
1 teaspoon marjoram
1 teaspoon oregano
1/2 teaspoon light Creole seasoning

Mix all ingredients and store in a covered container.

Linda Powell Vannoy

	Cal	Fat	% Fat Cal	Sat Fat	Chol	Sod
Per Serving	100	1.3	12	0.3	0	211

Nutrition Notes

Herb Oils

These flavored or herb oils have essentially the same amount of fat and roughly the same amount of calories as the oils they are made from. The advantage in using these oils is that they lend more flavor when using less in a lightened recipe.

Seasoned Bread Crumbs

This can be prepared quickly and easily and has only 1/3 of the sodium found in most ready-made seasoned bread crumbs. Save even more sodium when you prepare your own bread crumbs from day-old bread.

265

"First you make a Roux!" How very often we have all heard "good French cooks" begin to share a recipe with just those words! And the roux is certainly the foundation of many sauces and gravies.

Fat-Free or Oil-Free Roux
Yield: 2 portions of 1/2 cup each

1 cup all-purpose white or whole wheat flour

Spread flour about 1 inch thick across the bottom of an iron pot, baking pan or cookie sheet. Bake at 400 degrees for 1 to 1 1/2 hours. Stir occasionally, being sure to stir in the flour from along the edges and corners. Cook until light brown or darker. When water is added, it will darken even more. Remove the amount of flour your recipe calls for to make a roux. Store the rest in zippered plastic bags for future recipes. To the portion using, slowly stir in an equal amount of cold water and form a smooth paste. Stir this paste gradually into the simmering stock, soup, gumbo, etc. Cook for at least 20 minutes, stirring occasionally.

	Cal	Fat(g)	% Fat Cal	Sat Fat(g)	Chol(mg)	Sod(mg)
Per 1/2 cup	228	0.6	2	trace	0	1

Basic Traditional Roux
Yield: 2 portions of 1/2 cup each

1 cup butter, shortening or bacon drippings
1 cup flour

Melt the butter, shortening or bacon drippings in thick pot or skillet. Add the flour and stir constantly until *dark* brown, being careful not to burn. If there is the slightest indication of over-browning, dispose of the roux and start over. Even a slightly burned sauce will ruin a savory dish. To this basic roux, add seasoning and stock to make various sauces and gravies.

River Road Recipes

	Cal	Fat(g)	% Fat Cal	Sat Fat(g)	Chol(mg)	Sod(mg)
Per 1/2 cup	1191	110	82	14	0	1

Sweet and Sour Hot Mustard

Yield: 24 servings of 1 tablespoon each

2/3 cup dry mustard
2/3 cup brown sugar
1/8 teaspoon salt
1/3 cup white vinegar
1/3 cup defatted chicken broth, less salt

Mix all ingredients together until smooth. Refrigerate several hours in a covered container before serving.

Sharon Randall Lanius

	Cal	Fat	% Fat Cal	Sat Fat	Chol	Sod
Per Serving	37	1	24	trace	trace	22

Pearl Onion Glacee

Yield: 4 servings

18 small pearl onions, peeled (approx. 8 oz.)
1 teaspoon tub margarine
1 teaspoon olive oil
1/2 cup chicken broth, divided
1/4 teaspoon salt
1/2 teaspoon pepper
2 bay leaves
2 tablespoons white vermouth
2 tablespoons chopped parsley

Cut a cross in root of each onion to prevent center from falling out. Brown onions in margarine, oil, and 1 tablespoon chicken broth; season with salt and pepper. Put in baking dish and stir in the remaining chicken broth, bay leaves and vermouth. Cover and cook at 350 degrees for 1 hour, turning every 20 minutes. Garnish with parsley. Great over steaks!

Cindy Stewart

	Cal	Fat(g)	% Fat Cal	Sat Fat(g)	Chol(mg)	Sod(mg)
Per Serving	49	2.1	36	0.4	1	228

Nutrition Note

Sweet and Sour Hot Mustard

This mustard sauce is comparable in fat content to most mustards, yet has only a fraction of the sodium content and is packed with flavor.

One Step Further

Pearl Onion Glacee

If you omit salt, you save over 130mg sodium per serving.

Raspberry Vinegar

Yield: 1 quart bottle, 2 tablespoons per serving

1 pound crushed raspberries (fresh or frozen)
1 quart white vinegar (5% acidity or higher)

Combine the raspberries and vinegar in a glass or plastic container. Let sit in a cool, dark place for 3 to 4 weeks. Strain through cheesecloth into a bottle. Will keep for 18 months. Also makes a great marinade for pork or chicken.

Josephine Gomez

Herb Vinegar

Yield: 1 bottle, 2 tablespoons per serving

White wine vinegar
Slender strips of red, green and yellow bell pepper
Red or green hot pepper
Fresh red and/or green basil
Stems of dill, rosemary and lemon thyme
Bay leaf
2 or 3 cloves garlic, peeled
1 tablespoon red wine

Heat vinegar. Strip peppers and add one of each color (depending on size of bottle), whole hot pepper, herbs and garlic. Pour hot vinegar into bottle over selected herbs and peppers, adding wine last. I always put bottle in a pan of hot water so that the hot vinegar will not crack the bottle. Cork immediately. This process can be repeated depending on the number of bottles you wish to fill. Let sit for a couple of days. The flavor improves with age. I make many varieties of vinegars from the fresh herbs which I grow. I am constantly looking for unusual bottles for which the cork stoppers can be bought at hardware stores. Just take the bottle along to make sure the cork fits well. The size of the bottle determines the amount of ingredients you use.

Shirley King Thompson

Nutrition Note

**Raspberry Vinegar
Herb Vinegar
Herbed Vinegars**

Flavored or "herbed vinegars" have very little calorie content and are essentially fat free, yet full of flavor. These can enhance your favorite marinade and salad dressings and thus help you cut back on salt and oil. Nutrient content will vary only slightly with herbs and fruits chosen and quantity used, so only 1 nutrient breakdown is provided for all 3.

Herbed Vinegars

Yield: 1 bottle, 2 tablespoons per serving

White wine, cider, white or red wine vinegar
Assorted fresh herbs: dill, lemon basil, lemon balm, basil,
        chives, rosemary, tarragon, savory, mint, bay, fennel,
        thyme, etc.
Peeled garlic cloves
Lemon slices
Black, white and green peppercorns

For each bottle of vinegar, wash and dry 1/2 to 1 cup fresh herbs. Loosely fill a glass jar. To enhance flavors, add garlic cloves, lemon slices, and peppercorns as desired. Warm but do not boil vinegar and pour over herbs in bottle. Use white vinegars for delicate herbs; darker vinegar for stronger flavored herbs. Let vinegar sit for 4 to 6 weeks. If desired, strain through a coffee filter, then put 1 sprig herb in bottle as decoration and refill bottle. Experiment with different combinations: lemon basil or balm with 2 slices lemon in white vinegar; basil and oregano with garlic and peppercorns in cider vinegar. Use in marinades and salad dressings. Basil vinegar sprinkled over sliced tomatoes and feta cheese makes a delightful salad with no need for salt.

Ashley Hamilton Higginbotham

Raspberry, Herb and Herbed Vinegars

	Cal	Fat(g)	% Fat Cal	Sat Fat(g)	Chol(mg)	Sod(mg)
Per Serving	5	0	-	0	0	1

Creme de Menthe Sauce

Yield: 1 cup, 8 servings of 2 tablespoons each

1 cup powdered sugar
3 or 4 tablespoons creme de menthe

Sift sugar to remove any lumps. Gradually add creme de menthe until desired consistency.

Mrs. Wray E. Robinson

	Cal	Fat	% Fat Cal	Sat Fat	Chol	Sod
Per Serving	75	trace	0	0	0	trace

20% of calories from alcohol, 2.1gm per serving

Nutrition Note

Creme de Menthe Sauce
This sauce is essentially fat free and sodium free, but of course high in sugar. An alcohol-free sauce which saves over 20 calories per serving can be achieved using a mint extract and water.

Garlic and Parsley Vinaigrette
Yield: 16 servings of 1 tablespoon each

1/3 cup olive oil
1/2 cup defatted chicken broth, less salt
4 tablespoons white wine vinegar
4 teaspoons fresh lemon juice
1 tablespoon fresh minced garlic
1 teaspoon pepper
1/2 teaspoon dry mustard
3 tablespoons finely minced fresh parsley

Combine all ingredients, mixing with a whisk for 1 minute. Let stand 1 hour at room temperature. Toss with greens. Reshake before each use. Store in refrigerator, but bring to almost room temperature before serving.

Jane Vance Smith

	Cal	Fat(g)	% Fat Cal	Sat Fat(g)	Chol(mg)	Sod(mg)
Per Serving	42	4.5	95	0.6	trace	14

Honey Dijon Vinaigrette
Yield: 12 servings of 1 tablespoon each

3 tablespoons defatted chicken broth, less salt
2 tablespoons olive oil
3 tablespoons red wine vinegar
3 tablespoons dijon mustard
1 1/2 tablespoons honey
1/2 teaspoon dried thyme
1 1/2 teaspoons reduced sodium soy sauce
1/4 teaspoon black pepper

In a bowl whisk together broth, oil, vinegar, mustard and honey until combined. Add thyme and soy sauce whisking again until blended. Add pepper to taste.

Mrs. Shepard F. Perrin, III

	Cal	Fat(g)	% Fat Cal	Sat Fat(g)	Chol(mg)	Sod(mg)
Per Serving	34	2.5	65	0.3	trace	121

Nutrition Note

Garlic and Parsley Vinaigrette
This has less than 1/2 the fat and calories of the original! You can add your favorite minced herbs/spices. Try fresh basil or Italian seasoning blend.

Honey Dijon Vinaigrette
This dressing has less than 1/2 the fat and saturated fat content of the original! To trim the sodium by over 150mg per serving, omit the mustard and add mustard powder to taste and 2 tablespoons wine.

Orange Vinaigrette

Yield: 1 quart, 32 servings of 2 tablespoons

1 cup red wine vinegar
3/4 teaspoon black pepper
3/4 teaspoon salt
2 teaspoons chopped garlic
1 tablespoon dried tarragon
1/2 teaspoon dried basil
1 tablespoon Worcestershire sauce
2 tablespoons dijon mustard
Juice of 1 lemon
1/2 cup olive oil
1 cup orange juice
1 cup water

Mix all ingredients and store in the refrigerator.

Genie Harrison

	Cal	Fat(g)	% Fat Cal	Sat Fat(g)	Chol(mg)	Sod(mg)
Per Serving	36	3.4	80	.05	0	77

Mustard and Apple Cider Vinegar Dressing

Yield: 1 cup, 16 servings of 1 tablespoon each

2 tablespoons reduced calorie mayonnaise
6 tablespoons mustard, preferably with rough grain
1 package artificial sweetener
2 tablespoons apple cider vinegar
4 tablespoons lemon juice
2 tablespoons nonfat yogurt
1/8 teaspoon basil

Mix all ingredients well and refrigerate.

Shug Lockett (Mrs. Walker)

	Cal	Fat(g)	% Fat Cal	Sat Fat(g)	Chol(mg)	Sod(mg)
Per Serving	13	0.9	58	0.3	trace	92

One Step Further

Orange Vinaigrette
Trim the fat content in half by replacing 1/4 cup of the oil with defatted chicken broth. Save sodium by omitting the salt (close to 50mg of sodium savings per serving) or reducing the amount.

Mustard and Apple Cider Vinegar Dressing
To save over 75mg sodium per serving, omit the mustard and add 3 tablespoons of wine, 2 1/2 tablespoons of dry mustard powder and 2 tablespoons of water.

Sid's Dressing *with a Punch*
Yield: 8 servings

3 ounces vinegar (balsamic works best)
2 ounces water
1 teaspoon coarse ground black pepper
1 teaspoon caraway seeds
1 teaspoon chopped chives
1 tablespoon Creole mustard
1 package artificial sweetener
1/2 teaspoon celery seed
1 teaspoon horseradish

Mix above ingredients together. Serve over lettuce or thinly sliced cabbage. Low sodium and low fat—rich in flavor!

Sid Blitzer

	Cal	Fat(g)	% Fat Cal	Sat Fat(g)	Chol(mg)	Sod(mg)
Per Serving	8	0.2	24	trace	0	45

Sweet Onion, Corn and Tomato Salsa
Yield: 6 servings

1 1/2 cup chopped tomatoes, with juice
1/4 cup chopped sweet onion
2 ears cooked corn, scraped
1 tablespoon wine vinegar
1 tablespoon olive oil
1 tablespoon fresh basil
1 tablespoon chopped fresh parsley
1/4 teaspoon dried thyme
1/4 teaspoon salt
Pepper to taste

Combine all ingredients in a bowl by gently tossing. Prepare at least 1 hour ahead, drain and serve. Will keep nicely until the next day.

Melanie Hansbrough

	Cal	Fat(g)	% Fat Cal	Sat Fat(g)	Chol(mg)	Sod(mg)
Per Serving	60	2.0	30	0.4	0	85

Benefits of "Light" Cooking

The primary goal in lightening the recipes featured in *River Road Recipes III: A Healthy Collection* was to reduce the fat content of the original recipes. Cutting back on fat calories, especially saturated fat, can help reduce the risk of heart disease and cancer.

An added benefit to trimming fat is the significant overall reduction of calories. Other pluses are general weight loss and the possibility of lowering blood cholesterol levels.

A common problem with trying to reduce fat intake is that many people return to old eating habits after dieting, and find that their blood cholesterol has risen again, and/or they have regained weight. Routinely using lower fat recipes and techniques can help decrease health risks and maintain a more desirable weight. It is most helpful when those recipes are delicious, as well.

The goals strived for in these lightened recipes follow the American Heart Association (AHA) guidelines listed here:

  30% or less of calories from fat

  10% or less saturated fat calories

  300 milligrams(mg) or less cholesterol daily

  3,000 milligrams(mg) or less sodium daily

Some individuals on medically prescribed diets may need stricter goals and should consult their physician and a registered dietitian/nutritionist on how these recipes can fit specific needs. Use the nutritional information provided with each recipe to choose accordingly. Note the "One Step Further" comments on many of the recipes. If you need to restrict further, or are already accustomed to lower fat or lower sodium foods, you will find these tips helpful.

Some of our lightened recipes may still have moderately high fat or sodium content. All recipes either meet or exceed the goals outlined or are greatly reduced when compared to the original recipe. Higher fat or higher sodium dishes can be combined with dishes of lower content to achieve a meal that meets the overall goals.

Louisiana Banquet

Andalusion Salad
(45%)
Page 79

Crawfish Etouffée over Rice
(21%)
Page 180

Spinach Madeline
(39%)
Page 114

Poached Bosc Pears
(3%)
Page 219

Pralines de Louisiane
(44%)
Page 220

Total Cal = 861
Total Fat = 21.7g
Total Sat Fat = 4.5g
23% Cal from Fat
165mg Chol

The % under each menu item refers to percentage of calories from fat. Note how items of higher and lower fat content are blended in one meal to meet <30% of the calories from fat.

The original versions of these recipes would have yielded a total of: 1480 Cal, 83g Fat, 21g Sat Fat, 306mg Chol and 50% of the calories from fat.

How to "Lighten" Your Favorite Foods

by Linda P. Vannoy, M.S., L.D.N., R.D.

The key to successfully changing your eating patterns is start gradually. Routinely finding lighter ways to enjoy y favorite foods will increase your chances of sticking to y health goals. Start by first cutting one-fourth, then one-third, th one-half the fat, salt or sugar asked for in a recipe.

The following tips are offered to help you in lightening y own favorite recipes. As your taste adjusts to lower fat foo you may want to experiment in lightening some of our reci even further!

Know your sources of fat and use less of them:

Use vegetable oils and soft margarines low in saturated Some good choices include canola, safflower, sunflower, cc olive and soybean oils. Use sparingly.

Avoid margarines with hydrogenated oils listed first in ingredients list on the side of the package.

Avoid vegetable shortening, lard and animal fats.

Avoid coconut and palm oils. These are very high in saturo fat which raises blood cholesterol levels.

Although stick margarine has essentially the same num of fat grams and calories as butter, butter has more than th times the saturated fat content. Margarine is cholesterol f butter has more than 30 milligrams per tablespoon.

Limit dairy fat found in creams, cheeses and whole m Dairy fat is highly saturated fat. Use the alternative skim or fat products.

Use leaner cuts of meat and those with less marbled fat. T all visible fat.

Use well-trimmed ground round or sirloin instead of gro beef.

Remove the skin and underlying fat from all poultry game.

Some easy tips on basic food preparation include:

Bake, broil, roast or grill whenever possible. Use a meat rack to allow fat to drip away.

Use nonstick skillets and pans to help cut back the fat called for in a recipe.

Sauté foods with very little oil or margarine or try vegetable or chicken broth, wine or juices.

Chill broths, soups, gumbos and skim off the fat that rises to the top.

Prepare more fruits, vegetables, breads, cereals and starch. Serve smaller meat portions, with a goal of keeping to 3-ounce cooked portions.

Enhance the flavors in your recipe with these tips:

Use more spices and herbs—greater quantities of those already in the recipe and perhaps some additional ones.

When available, fresh herbs instead of dried herbs can often improve or enhance the flavor of a dish.

Flavors can be enhanced with defatted broths, wine, lemon juice and other fruit juices.

Try flavorful oils to help you use less. Smaller amounts of olive oil often enhance certain dishes more than a basic oil. Try some of the flavored oils found in the "Something Extra" section.

Use interesting vinegars appropriate to the dish or salad dressing. Some flavorful choices include cider vinegar, balsamic vinegar and rice vinegar, along with the herb-flavored vinegars found in "Something Extra."

Use fewer cheeses and use the lowfat alternatives. Use those richest in flavor, such as freshly grated Parmesan and Romano, or sharp reduced fat cheddar.

Roast nuts to achieve more flavor from smaller portions.

Trim Fat, Trim Calorie Alternatives

Instead of:	Use:	Fat(g) Savings	Sat Fat(g) Savings	Calorie Savings
Butter or shortening, 1/2 cup	Margarine, 1/2 cup	0*	39	0
	Tub margarine, 1/2 cup	22	42	180
	Oil, 1/3 cup	19	47	164
	Reduced fat margarine, 1/2 cup	43	48	400
Oil, 1/2 cup	Half called for in recipe (1/4 cup)	54	7	482
	Sautéing in Broth	108	13.6	952
	Baking: 1/4 cup oil + 1/4 cup applesauce	54	7	455
Whole milk, 1 cup	Skim milk, 1 cup	7.7	4.8	64
Whipping cream, 1 cup	Evaporated skim milk, 1 cup	74	46	503
Half-and-Half, 1 cup	Evaporated skim milk, 1 cup	27.3	17	116
Buttermilk, 1 cup, 1%	Skim milk, 15 tbsp + 1 tbsp vinegar	1.7	1	17
Cream cheese, 8oz.	Light cream cheese 8oz	40	25	320
	4oz light cream cheese + 4oz light ricotta creamed	57	36	465
	Nonfat yogurt cheese, 1 cup✓	80	50	559
Sour cream, 1 cup	Reduced fat sour cream, 1 cup	20	12	175
	1% cottage cheese + 1 tsp lemon juice blended, 1 cup	46	28.5	328
	Nonfat yogurt, 1 cup	48	30	373
Mayonnaise, 1 cup	Light mayonnaise, 1 cup	112	9.6	942
	1/2 cup light mayonnaise + 1/2 cup nonfat yogurt	144	17.6	1202
	Nonfat plain yogurt	176	25.6	1582
Chocolate, unsweetened baking square (1oz)	3 tbsp cocoa powder + 2 tbsp water + 2 tsp sugar	11	6.4	57
Chocolate, semi-sweet baking square (1oz)	3 tbsp cocoa powder + 2 tbsp water + 2 tsp sugar	6.6	5	28

✓ = Recipe included in book

* Margarine has similar calorie and fat quantity as butter but butter has 3 times the saturated fat and 245mg cholesterol; margarine has no cholesterol.

Instead of:	Use:	Fat(g) Savings	Sat Fat(g) Savings	Calorie Savings
Coconut, 1/4 cup	Coconut extract, 1 tsp	8.3	7.3	101
Pecans and other nuts, 1/2 cup	Toasted pecans, etc. 1/4 cup	18	1.5	180
Egg, 1 large	2 egg whites or 1/4 cup whites or	5	1.6	41•
	1/4 cup egg substitute	3	1	22•
Bacon, 3 strips	Canadian bacon, 1oz	8	2.8	76
	Extra lean ham 1oz (5% fat)	8	2	74
Cheddar cheese, 1oz	Reduced fat cheddar cheese, 1oz	4.4	3	35
Chicken breast half, roasted with skin	Chicken breast half, roasted without skin	4.6	1.3	51
Ground beef, 3oz	Trimmed round, ground 3oz	12.7	5.2	70
Cream of Mushroom soup, 1 can	Reduced fat and salt cream of mushroom soup	17.7	3	150
Traditional Roux 2 tbsp flour 2 tbsp oil	Reduced oil roux 2 tbsp flour 1 tbsp oil (stir constantly)	13.6	1.7	120
	Fat Free Roux 2 tbsp browned flour ✓	27.3	3.5	241

Cutting Back Sugar Content in Recipes

Sugar substitutes are available to replace some or all sugar in recipes. Successful substitutions will vary with foods being prepared and substitutes used. Read the directions for substituting on each package.

Some of the other means of reducing sugar in recipes are listed below.

Instead of:	Use:	Calorie Savings
Sugar, 1 cup	Use 1/4 less sugar than recipe calls for, 3/4 cup here	540
	Applesauce, unsweetened 1 cup	615
	Fruit juice concentrate, frozen apple 1/2 cup	487

✓ = Recipe included in book

• Savings of 213 mg of cholesterol as well.

Saving Salt and Sodium Tips

Instead of:	Use:	Sodium(mg) Savings
Mustard, prepared yellow, 1 tbsp	1 tsp mustard powder 1 tsp wine or vinegar 2 tsp water	194
Salt, 1 tsp	Herb and spice blends with no salt added to taste	2130
	Citrus juices and zest (lemon, lime, orange, etc.) enhance flavor without sodium	2130
Soy sauce, 1 tbsp	Reduced sodium soy sauce, 1 tbsp	501
	Worcestershire sauce, 1 tbsp	970
Broth, canned concentrate chicken, 1 cup	Reduced sodium chicken broth, canned concentrate, (1 cup)	351
Cream of mushroom soup, 1 can (10.75oz)	Cream of mushroom less salt and low fat soup, 1 can	1227
Tomato sauce, canned 1 cup	low sodium or no-salt-added tomato sauce, 1 cup	1417
	Tomato paste, no-salt-added 1/2 cup plus 1/2 cup water	1390
Tomatoes, canned 1 cup	No-salt-added canned tomatoes, 1 cup	359
	Fresh tomatoes, 1 1/3 cup chopped and simmered 10 min.	

Index

→ Notes

➡ **Notes**

RIVER ROAD RECIPES – The Junior League of Baton Rouge

Please send me _____ copies of *River Road Recipes* @ $12.95 each _____
Please send me _____ copies of *River Road Recipes II: A Second Helping* @ $12.95 each _____
Please send me _____ copies of *River Road Recipes III: A Healthy Collection* @ $17.95 each _____
Shipping per book @ $1.75 each _____
Louisiana residents add 8% sales tax _____
Total Enclosed _____

☐ Check or Money Order enclosed made payable to River Road Recipes, Inc.
5280 Corporate Blvd., Baton Rouge, LA 70808-2503

SHIP TO:

Name _____

Street Address _____

City & State _____ Zip _____

Daytime Phone Number ( ) _____

....

RIVER ROAD RECIPES – The Junior League of Baton Rouge

Please send me _____ copies of *River Road Recipes* @ $12.95 each _____
Please send me _____ copies of *River Road Recipes II: A Second Helping* @ $12.95 each _____
Please send me _____ copies of *River Road Recipes III: A Healthy Collection* @ $17.95 each _____
Shipping per book @ $1.75 each _____
Louisiana residents add 8% sales tax _____
Total Enclosed _____

☐ Check or Money Order enclosed made payable to River Road Recipes, Inc.
5280 Corporate Blvd., Baton Rouge, LA 70808-2503

SHIP TO:

Name _____

Street Address

City & State _____ Zip _____

Daytime Phone Number ( ) _____

....

RIVER ROAD RECIPES – The Junior League of Baton Rouge

Please send me _____ copies of *River Road Recipes* @ $12.95 each _____
Please send me _____ copies of *River Road Recipes II: A Second Helping* @ $12.95 each _____
Please send me _____ copies of *River Road Recipes III: A Healthy Collection* @ $17.95 each _____
Shipping per book @ $1.75 each _____
Louisiana residents add 8% sales tax _____
Total Enclosed _____

☐ Check or Money Order enclosed made payable to River Road Recipes, Inc.
5280 Corporate Blvd., Baton Rouge, LA 70808-2503

SHIP TO:

Name _____

Street Address _____

City & State _____ Zip _____

Daytime Phone Number ( ) _____

(OVER)

Name and addresses of bookstores, gift shops, etc. in your area would be appreciated.

_____
_____
_____
_____
_____
_____
_____
_____
_____
_____

Name and addresses of bookstores, gift shops, etc. in your area would be appreciated.

_____
_____
_____
_____
_____
_____
_____
_____
_____
_____

Name and addresses of bookstores, gift shops, etc. in your area would be appreciated.

_____
_____
_____
_____
_____
_____
_____
_____
_____